Male bias in the
development process

Male bias in the development process

Edited by
Diane Elson

Manchester University Press
Manchester and New York

Distributed exclusively in the USA and Canada by *St. Martin's Press*

Copyright © Manchester University Press 1991

Whilst copyright in the volume as a whole is vested in Manchester
University Press, copyright in individual chapters belongs to their
respective authors, and no chapter may be reproduced wholly or in
part without express permission in writing of both author and publisher.

Published by Manchester University Press
Oxford Road, Manchester M13 9PL, UK
and Room 400, 175 Fifth Avenue,
New York, NY 10010, USA

Distributed exclusively in the USA and Canada
by St. Martin's Press, Inc.,
175 Fifth Avenue, New York, NY 10010, USA

British Library cataloguing in publication data
Male bias in the development process. — (Contemporary issues
  in development studies).
  1. Developing countries. Sex roles. Social aspects
  I. Elson, Diane, *1946* –   II. Series
  305.3091724

Library of Congress cataloging in publication data
Male bias in the development process / edited by Diane Elson.
     p. cm.
  Includes index.
  ISBN 0-7190-2555-9
  1. Sexual division of labor—Developing countries.   2. Sex role in
the work environment—Developing countries.   3. Sex discrimination
in employment—Developing countries.   4. Sex discrimination against
woman—Developing countries.   I. Elson. Diane.
HD6060.65.D44M35   1990
306.3'615'091726—dc20   90–6460

ISBN 0 7190 2555 9 *hardback*

Phototypeset in Great Britain
by Megaron, Cardiff, Wales

Printed in Great Britain
by Billings of Worcester

Contents

Notes on contributors

Delia Davin is a Senior Lecturer in East Asian Studies at the University of Leeds. She lived in China for some years and is still a frequent visitor. She has written extensively about women, the family, and population policy in China. Her publications include: *Womanwork: Women and the Party in Revolutionary China* (1976); *China's One Child Family Policy* (edited with Elisabeth Croll and Penny Kane, 1985), and *Chinese Lives: An Oral History of Contemporary China* (Penguin, 1989).

Carolyne Dennis is a Lecturer at the Development and Project Planning Centre, University of Bradford. Previously she taught for many years at Obafemi Awolowo University in Nigeria, and has recently worked in Kenya, India and Zimbabwe. Her publications include *Women, Recession and Adjustment in the Third World* (co-edited with Haleh Afshar).

Diane Elson is a Lecturer in the Department of Economics, University of Manchester. She has written widely on gender and development, and on women's employment and the internationalisation of capital; and has acted as consultant to the Commonwealth Secretariat, FAO and ILO. Her previous books include *Women's Employment and Multinationals in Europe* (co-edited with Ruth Pearson).

Susie Jacobs is a Senior Lecturer in Sociology at St Mary's College of Higher Education, London. She has published contributions on gender relations in Zimbabwe in several journals and books, of which the latest is *Southern African Women* (edited by D. Gaitskill, M. Vaughan, and E. Unterhalter).

Ruth Pearson is a Lecturer in Economics at the School of Development Studies, University of East Anglia. She has written widely on women's employment issues in the Third World and the UK. Her current research is on the internationalisation of services, including a study of women's employment in data processing in the Caribbean. Her previous books included *Women's Employment and Multinationals in Europe* (co-edited with Diane Elson).

Alison MacEwen Scott is a Lecturer in the Department of Sociology, University of Essex. She has carried out research in Argentina, Venezuela and Peru on urban and gender issues; and recently she has become involved in research on women and employment in Britain. She has contributed to various books including Stichter and Parpart (eds.), *Women, Employment and the Family in the International Division of Labour* (1990), and was editor of *Rethinking Petty Commodity Production*, a special issue of *Social Analysis* (1986). She is shortly to publish *Gender, Class and Underdevelopment: an analysis based on Peru* (Routledge and Kegan Paul) and is editing a volume on gender and the labour market based on British material for Oxford University Press.

1 *Diane Elson*

Male bias in the development process: an overview

This is not another book about women in development. Books about women in development have been a necessary stage in making gender relations visible in the development process, but posing the issue in terms of women in development has several limitations. It facilitates the view that 'women', as a general category, can be added to an existing approach to analysis and policy, and that this will be sufficient to change development outcomes so as to improve women's position. It facilitates the view that 'women's issues' can be tackled in isolation from women's relation to men. It may even give rise to the feeling that the problem is women rather than the disadvantages women face; and that women are unreasonably asking for special treatment rather than for redress for injustices and for removal of distortions which limit their capacities. It tends to encourage the treatment of women as a homogeneous group with the same interests and viewpoint everywhere. It is necessary to move on from 'women in development' to approaches that emphasise gender relations.

Gender relations are the socially determined relations that differentiate male and female situations. People are born biologically female or male, but have to acquire a gender identity. Gender relations refer to the gender dimension of the social relations structuring the lives of individual men and women, such as the gender division of labour and the gender division of access to and control over resources. An emphasis on gender highlights the fact that work is gendered; that some tasks are seen as 'women's work', to do which is demeaning for men; while other tasks are 'men's work', to do which unsexes women. An emphasis on gender relations encourages a questioning of the supposed unity of the household and facilitates the posing of questions about the relative power of women and men.

There is a wealth of evidence demonstrating the differences in power between women and men throughout the world. It is not that women are powerless victims or that no women are in positions of power over men, but rather that, relatively speaking, women are less powerful than men of similar economic and social position. A graphic example is the risk of sexual violence faced by any woman who finds herself alone in a public place at night. The rich woman whose car has broken down is in the same position as the poor woman waiting for a bus. They are both at risk because they are breaking a gender norm, the norm that 'respectable' women should not be alone at night in public places. In breaking this norm they can be perceived as legitimate targets, as 'asking for it'. Men too may risk violence on the streets, but mugging has a quite different significance from rape.

A gender approach has greater flexibility than a women-in-development approach. For instance, an emphasis on gender relations tends to permit greater awareness of the different ways that different women experience gender. Though rich and poor women both face a common danger of rape if they are alone in a public place after dark, poor women have more of an interest in improvements in public transport than do rich women.

The asymmetry between male and female gender can be expressed in terms of the language of gender subordination: the idea that women as a gender are subordinate to men as a gender. But this language focuses on structures rather than agents. It can obscure individual responsibility and suggest the presence of immovable social forces in whose operation we can only acquiesce. It can even be used to justify the denial of equal opportunities to women, as in the case of Equal Opportunity Commission *v*. Sears, Roebuck & Co. in the USA (Kessler-Harris, 1987).[1] Women active in grass-roots feminist activities, such as Women's Aid and Rape Crisis Centres, have suggested to me that it is also a language which is too academic, too sanitised, too polite. It is time to stop talking about gender subordination and start talking about male bias.

Male bias

Talk of bias can be simply emotive, so it is certainly necessary to think carefully about criteria for use of the term. There are some precedents for using it in examining development issues, most notably the term 'urban bias' (Lipton, 1977). Whatever reservations one has about the explanatory power of 'urban bias', there is no doubt that it served to mobilise analysis and policy to address the important question of rural-urban inequality. An essential contribution to its mobilising ability was the way it combined the flavour of condemnation of the word 'bias' with appeals to objective criteria and empirical evidence. It is in the same spirit that I shall use the term 'male bias'.

By *male* bias I mean a bias that operates in favour of men as a gender, and against women as a gender, not that all men are biased against women. Some men have contributed substantially to the diagnosis and understanding of male bias and have campaigned to overcome it. Some women show little understanding of the operation of male bias and do much to perpetuate it. To emphasise this point, in what follows I shall draw on the work of a male economist, A. K. Sen, who has provided some useful conceptual tools for the elucidation of male bias. Nevertheless, on the whole women are more likely to recognise the significance of male bias, and to wish to combat it, than are men. But this is a matter of differences in the experience of women and men, not of differences in some essential femininity or masculinity.

What is bias? It is asymmetry that is ill-founded or unjustified. There is no problem in demonstrating gender asymmetry in the outcomes of development processes, in the lived experience of women and men throughout the world; the arguments are about the extent to which such asymmetry is ill-founded and unjustified. No attempt will be made here to review the enormous literature depicting gender asymmetry in developing countries. A useful overview of the literature and summary of key features of gender relations in the major regions of the Third World is provided by Brydon and Chant (1989). Compilations of statistical evidence can be found in United Nations publications, from organisations like the International Labour Office (ILO/INSTRAW, 1985) and the Department of International Economic and Social Affairs (UN, 1986). But there remains a question of interpretation. How far do the asymmetries represent male bias, and how far difference and complementarity?

Male bias in development outcomes

The first point that must be tackled is the issue of the bench-
mark against which bias in development outcomes is to be judged.
What counts as lack of bias? Equal treatment of equals? But equal
in what respects? Different people in different situations have
different needs and different talents. Removing bias does not
mean complete standardisation and removal of all differences. One
approach to defining bias is in terms of differences which are not
the result of differences in endowments and preferences. This is
the procedure favoured by neo-classical economists setting up
models of the labour market and the household (for example,
Becker, 1981). Such models tends to downplay the prevalence of
bias through using oversimple, uncritical notions of endowments
and preferences.

Aptitudes that are often ascribed to endowments, such as
women's supposedly 'nimble fingers', may be due to the upbringing
women have received at home and at school, which trains them in
sewing and in repetitive sorting tasks (like tidying up and separating
grains of rice from stones and husks), and emphasises the virtues of
patience and endurance of routine (Elson and Pearson, 1981). It is
virtually impossible to separate out endowments from acquired
characteristics for a wide range of attributes (Block and Dworkin
(eds), 1977). Levels of nutrition before birth can have an impact on
subsequent achievements. Characteristics that are unproblematic-
ally genetic endowments, such as eye colour, are those which are
least interesting from the point of view of explaining social
outcomes. Part of the problem of male bias is that it tends to hamper
women from acquiring those characteristics which are well-
rewarded in the market; and that it tends to hamper social scientists
from understanding the limitations of notions of male and female
endowments of aptitudes or talents.

If innate aptitudes cannot be taken for granted, neither can well-
defined individual preferences. Sen argues that family identity may
exert such a strong influence on the perceptions of rural Indian
women that they find it unintelligible to think in terms of their own
preferences and welfare. Instead, they think in terms of the welfare
of their families (Sen, 1987). This is a theme which has also run
through much feminist literature on women's consciousness in
developed countries. Part of the problem of male bias is that it tends

to hamper women from forming well-defined notions of what they want; women submerge their own interests beneath those of men and children.

Instead of judging bias against endowments and preferences, it may be judged against rights and capabilities (Se, 1984, ch. 13). Equal rights have been a rallying cry for many women's movements, and in many countries women have won a substantial measure of legal equality. But even in countries where equal rights for women are enshrined in the constitution, women find enormous difficulties in exercising those rights. Key rights for poor rural women, such as rights to land, have no practical purchase because land rights are vested in household heads: that is, in men, unless there are no adult males in the household (Jiggins, 1988). Key rights for poor urban women, such as equal pay, have no purchase because women are concentrated in the informal sector where legislation does not reach, or in female ghettos in the formal sector where there is no male standard with which to establish equality (Joekes, 1987). Moreover, entitlement systems, governing who can have use of what, which regulate market transactions, typically do not regulate intra-household resource distribution (Sen, 1987). Thus, an emphasis on rights has to be supplemented by an emphasis on socially conferred capabilities – what are women in practice able to do? Are they able to be well-nourished; to enjoy good health and long lives; to read and write; to participate freely in the public sphere; to have some time to themselves; to enjoy dignity and self-esteem? How does women's enjoyment of these capabilities compare with that of men? Do women face constraints which are not faced by men? In so far as women enjoy fewer and more circumscribed capabilities than do men, then there is male bias in development outcomes. Constraints on women operate to men's advantage in the short run, as in bargaining within the household (discussed below). Male bias exists even if women do not manifest any lesser satisfaction with their lot in life than do men. As Sen points out:

There is much evidence in history that acute inequalities often survive precisely by making allies out of the deprived. The underdog comes to accept the legitimacy of the unequal order and becomes an implicit accomplice. It can be a serious error to take the absence of protests and questioning of inequality as evidence of the absence of that inequality. (Sen, 1987, p. 3)

Sen's argument has force with respect to any kind of inequality, and in emphasising male bias I do not intend to imply that it is the only important form of bias. Class bias, regional bias, urban bias, racial and ethnic bias, are all important; and the different kinds of bias are imbricated with one another, forming differentiable but not separated aspects of a whole lived situation for any individual. Thus all women do not face the same kind and same degree of male bias; and they may enjoy the fruits of other kinds of bias, or share the deprivations, with men in the same class, region, ethnic group.

What perhaps is unique about male bias is that those who are disadvantaged by it live daily in intimate personal relationships with those who are advantaged by it. The relationship between women and men living together in households has been usefully depicted by Sen (1985, 1987) in terms of co-operative conflicts. Women and men gain from co-operating with one another in joint living arrangements in so far as this increases the capabilities of the household as a whole; but the division of the fruits of co-operation is a source of conflict. Women are at a disadvantage in bargaining over the division of the fruits of co-operation because their fall-back position tends to be worse. That is, if no bargain is struck, and women are on their own, without husband, father, brother or other male relative to co-operate with, they tend to be worse off, in terms of capabilities, than if they agree to strike a bargain and enter into some kind of co-operation with men. The evidence of the poverty of female-headed households is overwhelming testimony to the weakness of women's fall-back position. However, co-operative conflicts between people of different genders are more than simple bargaining problems because of the gender differentiation in the specification of preferences discussed earlier. As a result of an upbringing shaped by male bias, women tend not to have such sharp perceptions as men of their own interests, needs, rights or deserts. And this perpetuates male bias, because the co-operative arrangement arrived at is likely to be less favourable to those individuals with less well-defined perceptions of their own interests.

Male bias is contradictory in that while it preserves the subordination of women as a gender to men, it also has costs for society considered as a whole. For instance, male bias distorts resource allocation by denying women adequate access to productive inputs. This lowers women's productivity and reduces total output in comparison with what could be achieved if resource allocation were

free of gender distortion (Palmer, 1988). Thus male bias is a barrier
to the achievement of development objectives such as growth of
output. So why don't more men show eagerness to overcome male
bias? Perhaps it is because the disadvantages of relinquishing male
power are more immediately apparent, while the distribution of the
gains is uncertain and the transition period may be painful. If
women's productivity is enhanced because male bias in resource
allocation is reduced, total output may rise, but so may women's
bargaining power. The total size of the cake may increase, but men's
share of it may fall.

The proximate causes of male bias in development outcomes

The proximate causes of male bias in development outcomes can be
analysed in terms of male bias in everyday attitudes and actions, in
theoretical reasoning, and in public policy. The underlying
supports of male bias are to be found in the particular ways in which
getting a living is integrated with raising children.

Male bias in everyday attitudes and actions may be the result of
prejudice and discrimination at the conscious level, but this is not
necessarily the case. Bias may be deeply embedded in unconscious
perceptions and habits, the result of oversight, faulty assumptions, a
failure to ask questions. For instance, women's contribution to
family income tends to be overlooked because much of it is unpaid
or takes the form of repetitive services rather than products that can
be massed together in an unmistakable sign of contribution made.
As a result, women tend to be regarded as less deserving than men
when it comes to intra-household distribution (Sen, 1987). Such
unconscious bias is not unreachable and unchangeable. People can
be brought to recognise it through education, consciousness-raising
groups, politicisation, social change. Domitila Barrios de
Chungara, a women's leader and miner's wife in a tin-mining
community in Bolivia, explains how she went about doing this:

> But in spite of everything we do, there's still the idea that women don't
> work, because they don't contribute economically to the home, that only
> the husband works because he gets a wage. We've often come across that
> difficulty.
> One day I got the idea of making a chart. We put as an example the price
> of washing clothes per dozen pieces and we figured out how many dozens of
> items we washed a month. Then the cook's wage, the babysitter's, the
> servant's. We figured out everything that we miners' wives do every day.

Adding it all up, the wage needed to pay us for what we do in the home, compared to the wages of a cook, a washerwoman, a babysitter, a servant, was much higher than what the men earned in the mine for a month. So that way we made our companeros [husbands] understand that we really work, and even more than they do in a certain sense. (Johnson and Bernstein (eds), 1982, p. 235)

However, conscious and unconscious male bias in thought and action is frequently buttressed by economic and social structures which make such practices seem rational, even to those who are disadvantaged by them. Thus it can seem entirely rational for mothers to allocate more food to sons than to daughters when food is short, in circumstances where sons are more valuable, socially and materially, than daughters; and where future survival of the household depends crucially on survival of sons to adulthood, then it can seem entirely rational to prioritise their needs and neglect those of daughters. Such behaviour is acclaimed by neo-classical economists as evidence that their harmonious 'joint utility' models of the household are correct (Rosenzweig, 1986), though it can equally well be explained in terms of a co-operative conflicts model (Folbre, 1986). But the important point is that although actions that perpetuate male bias are rational from the point of view of a highly constrained individual, they do not testify to the overall rationality, much less desirability, of the social system. Rather, they suggest that the constraints on individuals need to be changed through some collective process. In the absence of such a process, individual women will certainly find it rational to do things that perpetuate male bias. This has been recognised by careful thinkers about individual choice and well-being, such as Sen, who points out that:

Deprived groups may be habituated to inequality, may be unaware of possibilities of social change, may be hopeless about upliftment of objective circumstances of misery, may be resigned to one's fate, and may be willing to accept the legitimacy of the established order. The tendency to take pleasure in small mercies would make good sense given these perceptions, and cutting desires to shape (in line with perceived feasibility) can help to save one from serious disappointment and frustration. (Sen, 1987, p. 9)

Male bias in theoretical reasoning may often not be so immediately apparent because the reasoning is presented in terms which appear to be gender neutral. Rather than talking about women and men, and sons and daughters, use is made of abstract concepts like the economy, the formal sector, the informal sector, the labour force, the household. Or the argument is conducted in terms of socio-economic categories which, on the face of it, include both women and men, such as 'farmer', and 'worker'. It is only on closer analysis that it becomes apparent that these supposedly neutral terms are in fact imbued with male bias, presenting a view of the world that both obscures and legitimates ill-founded gender asymmetry, in which to be male is normal, but to be female is deviant. This is more immediately apparent in analysis conducted in terms of socio-economic groups, where we soon read of 'farmers and their wives' and 'workers and their wives' but never of 'farmers and their husbands' and 'workers and their husbands', despite the fact that large numbers of women are farmers or wage-earners in their own right.

Let us examine this more closely using the example of the category 'farmer'. Though this appears to be a gender-neutral category, it is used in a way that implies farmers are men; this suggests that major decision-making and farm management is undertaken by men, while women serve as unpaid family labour, helping their husbands. While this may be true of some areas, and some types of farming, we have enough case study data to know that it is certainly not universally true. Many countries in sub-Saharan Africa have large numbers of women who farm in their own right, either because of a high incidence of female-headed households in rural areas (as in Botswana, Lesotho, Sierra Leone and Zambia, for instance), or because there is a traditional demarcation of crops into 'men's crops' and 'women's crops' (as in Cameroon, Ghana and Malawi) (FAO, 1986). Outside Africa, women are more likely to be managing post-harvest activities, such as processing, storage and marketing, than managing production of staple crops; or managing livestock-related activities or horticulture. But whatever the differences in the particular activities undertaken, the point remains that many women in agriculture do undertake management responsibilities.

The picture of farmers as men disadvantages women farmers and hinders attempts to improve agricultural productivity. When there is an implicit assumption that farmers are men, it is not surprising if new agricultural technology and inputs flow mainly to men – and there is a wealth of evidence that this is what has happened in developing countries over the last three decades. Despite the attempts of concerned researchers to make rural women 'visible' to policy-makers in the 1970s, most rural projects up to the early '80s still addressed women through welfare and home economics programmes for farmers' wives. Governments still fail to collect comprehensive, reliable and unbiased statistics on the contribution women make to agricultural production (Safilios-Rothschild, 1987). But we know from village-level studies that when resources are redirected to women there are increases in agricultural productivity and efficiency (Jiggins, 1987; Staudt, 1987).

To see the male bias in analysis which is conducted in terms of abstract categories, we have to examine the implicit assumptions structuring the definition and use of the abstract categories. Is there a hidden assumption about the homogeneity of sectors of the economy regardless of gender? For instance, is it assumed that surplus labour can be withdrawn from agricultural production because those left behind will be able to make up any shortfall, without considering the division of agricultural tasks into 'men's tasks' and 'women's tasks'? This does seem to the implicit assumption in many dual-sector models of development – including Sen's (Sen, 1966). Ignoring the gender division of labour may result in failure to consider the overloading of women and reduction in agricultural productivity that male migration from the rural sector may induce. Is there a hidden assumption about the costs of reproduction of labour power and who bears them? Most models of the economy treat labour, like land, as an unproduced factor of production. In effect, there is an implicit assumption that the necessary inputs of time and effort required to ensure its continuing supply will be forthcoming even though these inputs are unpaid. These inputs are, of course, disproportionately supplied by women in their roles as wives, mother and daughters, ministering to the needs of other family members. Time budget studies from around the world show that these activities are undertaken by most women in addition to activities that are counted as 'economic' (Goldschmidt-Clermont, 1987). Women have far less leisure than men because of this 'double day'. Ignoring women's unpaid domestic work obscures both the burdens women bear and the constraints this work places upon women's capacity to respond to opportunities for paid work. There is no intrinsic reason why the work of caring for others should not be shared equally between women and men. But a reduction in this asymmetry is unlikely while male bias continues to deny the economic contribution such work makes.

Is there a hidden assumption about the benevolence of the ties that bind households together? The household is in some sense a social unit, but can we assume it is a unity? The models of the household constructed by neo-classical economists do assume unity, implying, for instance, that the welfare of household members can be judged on the basis of aggregate household income, and that extra income accruing to one household member will 'trickle down' to others. But a growing volume of case-study evidence supports alternative models, such as Sen's co-operative conflict model. They suggest a picture of a home divided over income and expenditure decisions (Dwyer and Bruce (eds), 1988). Households are in some sense pooling and sharing organisations but to imply that this pooling and sharing is unproblematic is to reveal male bias. There is considerable evidence to suggest that while women typically pool and share their income, especially with their children, men are more inclined to reserve part of their income for discretionary personal spending (*ibid.*). Uncritical theorisation of existing forms of family life is a barrier to securing real reciprocity. Overcoming male bias does not mean the disintegration of pooling and sharing of resources between women and men. Rather, it means more extensive pooling and sharing and a disintegration of unjust gender asymmetries in family relationships.

When supposed gender neutrality masks male bias, this serves to obscure the distribution of costs and benefits of development processes between men and women. It also serves to obscure the barriers that gender asymmetries constitute to the successful realisation of many development policy objectives. To overcome such bias, it is not enough to affix 'women' as an afterthought. For that tends to obscure the differences between different groups of women, and to perpetuate the gender blindness of analytical concepts. What is needed is a gender-aware conceptualisation in the first place. Otherwise, male bias will remain even though 'women' are present.

Male bias in development policy is encouraged by male bias in everyday attitudes and practices and by male bias in analysis, reinforced by male bias in politics. Until the late 1970s women were largely invisible to policy-makers, whose perspective might be summed up in the old Russian proverb: 'I thought I saw two people coming down the road, but it was only a man and his wife'. Women were treated merely as dependents of men. Development objectives were disaggregated on a household basis and it was assumed that resources targeted to men would equally benefit dependent women and children. For a variety of reasons, including the advocacy of 'women in development' experts, and the breakdown of family support systems leading to increases in the numbers of female-headed households in dire poverty, by the end of the '70s women had become visible to policy-makers – but as recipients of welfare benefits rather than as producers and agents of development. There was a proliferation of special women's projects, many of which failed to become self-supporting because of lack of gender awareness in their design, perpetuating the idea of women as a drain on the public purse (Buvinic, 1986).

In the 1980s more attention has been paid to women as agents of development, but as agents of social development whose caring and nurturing could substitute for expenditure on health, education and social services (Antrobus, 1988; Dwyer and Bruce (eds), 1988). Moreover, there remains the problem of male bias in the policy process itself. With few exceptions, women's interests are marginalised in the formulation and implementation of economic policy (Moser, 1989). Women's voices play little part. At the grass-roots level, there are frequently factors that inhibit women from speaking out in public meetings. A study of women and village government in ten villages in Tanzania in 1981 found that village officials gave the following reasons for women's low attendance at village meetings: women are still too shy to attend public meetings; women are too busy at home to come; it is not the woman's job to roam and survey the village and attend things like meetings – it is her job to watch the house; women can't speak Kiswahili; women are uneducated; women don't understand the discussions; it's difficult for a woman to get a pass from the house to come; only one person from a household need come, so it is always the man; women don't need to come because we ask the men to tell them what we have discussed; women are not used to sitting together with men; there are still some men here who don't like to see women in meetings (Wiley, 1985, p. 170).

In the corridors of power there are relatively few women. The experience of women's bureaux and ministries of women's affairs is particularly discouraging, as they tend to be underresourced, overstretched and cut off from the economic policy-making process (Gordon, 1984). Development objectives are defined in practice in ways that are more beneficial to men than to women. Thus in practice it is not more food output *per se* that tends to be sought, but more of the kind of food output which is produced under the direction and control of men (for examples, see Mblinyi, 1988); not more private trading *per se* but more of the kind of private trading undertaken by men – large scale and capital intensive – rather than the kind of trading undertaken by women – localised and with a quick turnover (for an example from Ghana, see Loxley, 1988).

That is not to claim that male policy-makers deliberately define objectives in terms that benefit men more than women, but rather that they tend to see as in the general interest policies that in practice are male-biased, and to perceive policies that reduce gender asymmetry as female-biased.

The underlying supports of male bias

I have discussed the proximate causes of male-biased development outcomes in terms of male bias in everyday attitudes and decisions, in theoretical analysis, and in the process of defining and implementing public policy. Underlying these individual and collective acts are structural factors that circumscribe and shape them. The key structural factor is not the way in which getting a living is organised, nor the way that raising children is organised, but the way these two processes are interrelated.

The crucial question is how children, and those people engaged in raising children, get their living. Do they have an entitlement to the necessary resources in their own right? Or are they dependent on other family members to secure access to the required resources? It would be possible for children and those engaged in caring for them to have an adequate independent entitlement through independent access to a basic minimum income paid to all members of society regardless of the work they do;[2] or through independent access to adequate earning opportunities coupled with adequate child care facilities. But this would require the integration of getting a living and raising children not being confined to the family; it would require integration through social provision and the mediation of organisations in the public sphere; it would require access to a basic minimum income as of right, to be independent of family circumstances. Such an entitlement is extremely rare. In practice, most children and those caring for them are either dependent on other family members for access to income or resources, or, when there is no one to depend on, they suffer poverty and deprivation because of difficulties in combining child care and income-generating activities. Relief may be available through charities or state welfare schemes but this relief is generally not an absolute entitlement and creates a new form of dependence. The opportunity to earn an income through selling labour or products in the market may seem to offer independence to women. But in practice this independence is open only to a small minority. For the market does not provide adequate and affordable child care facilities for most women, and does not guarantee them an adequate income. On the whole, markets tend to lead to the concentration of income in the hands of those who start off with most resources. Unless markets are socially regulated they offer only the semblance of independence for women, and not the reality (Elson, 1989). The lack of an independent and secure entitlement creates a bias operating against those people who have the task of child care and weakens their bargaining position in the co-operative conflicts of the family.

The desire for an independent entitlement is not confined to well-educated feminists. A study of ten villages in Tanzania in the early 1980s reports the following comments as typical of those made by village women about their situation:

'Now we are sitting in meetings, but my husband can still beat me if I complain. We are still dependent on men.'
'Women are still the same because the money belongs to the husband still.'
'A man can still refuse you anything because he owns all the things.'
'Our main problem here is that the men are drinking our money and we have no way to get more.'
'In my opinion it would be better if the Council gave every woman one acre for herself.' (Wiley, 1985, p. 171).

The lack of an independent entitlement for children and those who care for them tells against women. It gets women 'locked in' to child care. There are some phases of raising children which physically have to be undertaken by women – pregnancy, childbirth, breast-feeding – but the rest could be undertaken by men too. However, if lack of an independent entitlement forces women into dependence for these phases of child-rearing, phases which are particularly difficult to combine with income-earning, then women are likely to get locked in to all the other phases. Dependence and its associated lack of bargaining power at one stage are transmitted to later stages. The winners of a co-operative conflict in one round have enhanced bargaining power for the future. The transmission can also work intergenerationally, perpetuating asymmetry over time (Sen, 1987). It is biology that creates the initial link between women and children; but it is the socially determined lack of entitlement that turns this link into the underpinning of male bias.

Overcoming male bias is not simply a matter of persuasion, argument and changes in viewpoint in everyday attitudes, in theoretical reasoning and in the policy process. It also requires changes in the deep structures of economic and social life, and collective action not simply individual action. It requires profound changes in the way that raising children and getting a living are integrated, so as to make maternity economically autonomous. Marriage clearly cannot do this; and existing forms of market opportunity and state provision have not done it either. The question of how to make progress on this issue is among those addressed in the final chapter of this book.

Testing male bias

The material in this book has been organised so as to exemplify and provide tests of the arguments about male bias put forward so far; and also to test male bias as a living practice, in the sense of probing its variety, its limits, its changes. Several of the chapters discuss what might be thought to be 'hard cases' for the position advanced in this chapter: situations where male bias seems rational and is reinforced by women; situations in which women feel their position is improving; situations in which women have a large measure of economic and social independence; situations in which women's employment opportunities are rapidly expanding. Several seek to identify explicitly the operation of male bias in theory and policy, and show how eliminating male bias could lead to better theory and better policy. Between them they provide examples of the operation of male bias at all the levels we have identified: in rural and urban settings; in agriculture, industry and services; in self-employment and wage-employment; at the micro-level and the macro-level; in Africa, Asia and Latin America. They discuss both the structures that perpetuate male bias and the processes that change its form, and intensify it or diminish it.

In chapter 2, Delia Davin examines gender relations in the Chinese peasant household of the 1980s. She describes how decades of legislation, propaganda and education have failed to eradicate one of the most open forms of male bias in everyday attitudes: a marked preference for sons, on the part of women as well as of men. This preference is reflected in capabilities: girls suffer more malnutrition than boys, and boys have higher survival chances. Davin shows how this is not, as is often claimed in China, the result of lingering feudal attitudes. Rather, it is because sons remain indispensable to the economic well-being of peasant families. The reforms in the organisation of the rural economy in the 1980s reinforced this indispensability; and the one child per family population policy turned the birth of a girl from a disappointment to a near-disaster. This case provides an illustration of how male bias in everyday attitudes and practices may be rational for individuals who are highly constrained in the choices open to them. Peasant men and women need sons to look after them in their old age, so long as there is virilocal marriage and a tradition that a married daughter does not contribute to the support of her ageing parents. Production systems that put a premium on the amount of labour available to a household can only reinforce son-preference.

However, Davin's study also shows how the degree and intensity of male bias in everyday attitudes and practices changes as parameters constraining individual choice change. There was a lessening of the degree and intensity of male bias when agriculture was organised through the commune system, for the commune system did more to make women's work socially visible and enabled them to escape to some extent from the confines of the home and to work with people from outside their families. The new household responsibility system tends to push women back into the family, working under the direction of the male family head.[3] It diminishes the role of communal support systems and reinforces the family as the basic unit of agricultural production. The impact of the one-child family policy in this context has lead to a resurgence of violence against women: forced abortions, beatings of women who have given birth to daughters, female infanticide.

By focusing on how systemic changes affect the degree of male bias, Davin's study enables us not merely to see how male bias may be rendered rational at the micro-level, but also to take a critical approach to that rationality and see how it might be modified by appropriate systemic changes. The one-child family policy also shows how even in the context of the household responsibility system of production, what is rational for one individual may be self-defeating at the societal level. If son-preference were fully satisfied, there would be a shortage of daughters-in-law.

The systemic changes in this particular case were a direct result of government decisions, and throw some light on the operation of male bias in development policy. Davin shows how the objectives of policy in the 1980s were expressed in terms of more output and fewer births. The gender implications were simply not considered. If they had been, this might have led to recognition of the fact that the household responsibility system and the one child per family policy pull in opposite directions – the former creating an incentive for bigger families, the latter for smaller families. Though the new inheritance law may appear to confer new property rights on peasant women, Davin shows how the household responsibility system will tend to undermine the actual exercise of those rights. In contrast, some attention was paid to women's needs in the collectivisation of agriculture in the 1950s, and the services provided by communes made some attempt to meet them. The fact that the communes did not succeed in eradicating male bias altogether might perhaps be because women were still left dependent on male household heads. As Davin points out, women did not normally receive their earnings into their own hands; the income earned by all family members was usually paid to the male household head. Nevertheless, the commune system appears to have gone some way towards transforming the way that getting a living and raising children were integrated, making that integration a communal as well as a family affair.

The overall conclusion of chapter 2 is pessimistic: male bias has been intensified in rural China even though peasants may have better housing and more consumer goods. The main hope for a future reduction in male bias may be an erosion of virilocal marriage as more and more families have only daughters as a result of the one-child family policy.

Chapter 3 is more optimistic. Susie Jacobs discusses the case of rural Zimbabwean women, who feel their lives have improved as they have moved with their families to individual family resettlement areas. The women Jacobs interviewed felt that in the resettlement areas their workload was less, their role in household decision-making greater, and there was less male violence directed against them. It is certainly not the case that gender relations are inevitably either static or deteriorating. Cases where male bias is diminishing to some extent are particularly important for the clues they give about how it might be overcome. But such cases are also useful for revealing the limits to improvements, and the extent to which the underpinnings of male bias persist.

Jacobs sets her contemporary case study in historical context, outlining gender relations in pre-colonial and colonial times and showing how the codification of customary procedures reduced women's rights. She traces the appropriation of land by the white settlers and confinement of African farmers to the Reserves, now known as the Communal Areas. She describes the 'feminisation' of the agricultural workload in the Communal Areas as men migrated to the settler areas for work, arguing that nevertheless men in Zimbabwe retained rights to make major decisions about agricultural production. Post-independence, there have been a variety of land resettlement schemes, and Jacobs' study looks at the type that creates individual family farms. There is clear male bias in the policy on the allocation of land rights: women are normally unable to hold land in their own right in the scheme unless they are divorced or widowed. They depend on their husbands allocating them a small plot on which to grow subsistence crops. Prior to resettlement, between twenty and twenty-five per cent of families in Jacobs' sample had been split by male migration for wage work; but men who have been granted land rights in the scheme are not allowed to migrate and must cultivate the land themselves.

Whereas the renewed emphasis on the household as a unit of production in China has helped to intensify male bias at the level of everyday attitudes and practices, this was not the case in Zimbabwe, where Jacobs found a reduction in male bias at that level. The clue to the difference would seem to lie in the fact that in China the renewed emphasis on the household was accompanied by a dismantling of communal structures, whereas in Zimbabwe it was accompanied by a strengthening of communal structures. Resettlement means living in villages in closer proximity to other households than in the Communal Areas, under the watchful eye of a Resettlement Officer. Jacobs concludes that perhaps the most important factor in more men becoming what their wives saw as 'good husbands' was the scrutiny of behaviour by Resettlement

Officers, though the absence of beer halls in the resettlement areas also helped.

But as Jacobs shows, the improvement in men's treatment of women did not signify any undermining of the ultimate supports of male bias. Women were still dependent on men for access to the resources required to make a living and raise children, and could easily lose this access through divorce. The women she interviewed wanted independent incomes and sexual autonomy, not just 'good husbands'.

Women in West Africa are often thought of as already having independence; women traders in particular are frequently held up as exemplars of autonomy. It is perfectly true that these women are not constrained by the social pressures that confine women to the household in many developing countries. But as Carolyne Dennis shows in chapter 4, such women face constraints outside the home to their pursuit of independent careers, and these constraints are growing over time. Dennis discusses the case of Yoruba women in Nigeria, who are customarily expected to earn an income of their own, and typically aspire to do this through self-employment in trade or small urban businesses, in a context in which the informal sector is viewed as an arena for advancement not as a site of super-exploitation. There is in this case no male bias in everyday attitudes against such aspirations. But women's ability to fulfil them depends partly on their access to capital, to other inputs and to markets; and partly on the structure of the informal sector in which they must compete with many other aspirants. Dennis shows how most women are increasingly confined to small-scale low-return activities in an increasingly polarised informal sector.

There are two main ways for most women to amass the resources required for self-employment: they can acquire them from their husbands or from employment in the urban formal sector, in manufacturing or government services. These access channels are structured by class. Wives of wealthy and well-connected husbands can acquire resources easily and exercise what is expressively known as 'bottom power', and is derivative of their husband's power. Such women, through their husbands, can obtain lucrative contracts to supply the public sector with imported goods. They loom large in the contemporary mythology of Nigeria, but the majority of women in the informal sector are confined to petty trade or petty production. For women whose husbands are unable to provide them with start-up capital, and who lack educational qualifications, entry even into low-return independent careers is problematic. Such women often hope that wage employment in the industrial sector, which does not require such high educational qualifications as the public sector services, will provide them with a springboard to self-employment. This is a common hope among Nigerian industrial workers, both male and female. But as Dennis show, male bias in the organisation of the industrial labour process tends to mean that the chances of doing this are remote for female industrial workers.

The kind of jobs that women do in the industrial sector are unlikely to provide them with opportunities to acquire the skills, contacts and savings needed for successful self-employment, whereas those that men do hold out some possibilities for advancement. This is illustrated with the case of a textile factory, in which women are shown to be confined to dead-end low-paid jobs, while men are better paid and may advance to the position of mechanic or electrician, accumulating the skills, contacts and savings that enable them to set up their own businesses.

Thus even when there is no overt prejudice against women earning their own incomes, and when the aspiration to an independent career is quite legitimate, less obvious forms of male bias deny women the resources required to be truly independent. The availability of income-earning opportunities through the market is not enough when the distribution of capital and education is biased against women, and when women are directed to dead-end 'women's jobs'. The strengthening of market forces, as is happening under Nigeria's structural adjustment programme, is, Dennis suggests, tending to limit further the possibilities of an independent career for most urban women.

Chapter 5 also deals with opportunities for women in the urban labour market, drawing on a detailed empirical study of Lima, Peru. In this chapter, Alison MacEwen Scott not only shows how male bias operates in the workings of the urban labour market, but also how bias enters into the conceptualisation of urban labour markets because of a failure to consider the gender differentiation of work and conditions of work. As both Dennis and MacEwen Scott point out, the concept of the informal sector is notoriously ambiguous. In West Africa, it is widely seen as offering the prospect of individual advancement. But as MacEwen Scott points out, much theoretical writing about the informal sector in Latin America and Asia associates it with low-paid, low-skilled casual work, in contrast to the formal sector which is seen as a source of high-paid, high-skilled stable employment protected by trade unions and government legislation. MacEwen Scott argues that this conceptualisation ignores gender as an axis of segmentation. Illustrating her argument with detailed evidence from Lima, she suggests that in manual occupations, female employment, whether in the formal or informal sector, tends to have the characteristics that theorists have associated with the informal sector; and that male employment, whether in the formal or informal sector, tends to have the characteristics associated with the formal sector.

This chapter provides a good illustration of the difference between a 'women in development' approach that seeks to make women visible, and a gender-aware approach that seeks to make gender relations visible and to show how a gender-blind approach leads to biased theory. It indicates how studies which concentrated only on showing that there were a lot of women in the informal sector who had been overlooked, missed the key point that the whole conceptualisation of the urban labour market in developing countries was faulty because it ignored segmentation by gender. It is not that the informal sector is 'female' in the sense of being predominantly composed of women; indeed, as in the case of Lima, the informal sector may be predominantly composed of men. The important point is that gender differentiation cuts across the informal/formal distinction. The quality of employment depends on whether it is 'women's work' or 'men's work', not just on whether it is in the formal or informal sector.

MacEwen Scott pinpoints the opportunity for career progression as a key factor differentiating the occupations in which women in Lima were concentrated from those in which men were concentrated. Almost all women's occupations were classified as unskilled, and were either in the formal sector (for example, textile workers) or, more usually, in the informal sector (for example, domestic servants, street pedlars). Many men's occupations were skilled and could be carried on as wage employment in large enterprises or as self-employment (for example, carpenters, electricians, bricklayers, mechanics, shoe-makers). Men could learn a trade in the formal sector and move to artisanal work in the informal sector, in both cases enjoying high wages and job security as compared to women in both sectors. The only comparable occupation for women was dressmaking. These findings are complementary with those of Dennis for Nigeria, where women's career progression was also limited by dead-end jobs with few transferable skills.

Why did women in Lima not enjoy the same artisanal opportunities as men? Women apparently did take part in production in family businesses, such as making shoes or running garages. But this was not publicly recognised, and women could not set up in these trades on their own. MacEwen Scott's research suggests male bias in everyday attitudes and practices played a large part. Women were excluded from exercising authority in the public sphere, and thus restricted in their capacity to manage large amounts of capital or control workshops staffed by men. Male bias in the policy process also played a role: male artisanal trades were defended in negotiations with municipal authorities by urban guilds, from which women were excluded. The importance of the exclusion of women in the informal sector from the policy process has been emphasised by Ela Bhatt, who initiated the Self-Employed Women's Association in India as a way of trying to overcome this particular form of male bias (Bhatt, 1989).

In Lima, few working-class women had formal sector jobs, and in Nigeria, women factory workers were very much a minority. In neither case was there a rapid expansion of modern, industrial employment for women. Such an expansion, in some views, is a potent force for improving the status of women and dissolving 'traditional' forms of male bias. Chapter 6 by Ruth Pearson throws light on this issue through an examination of the case of Mexico's border industries, in which women form the majority of the work-force and in which women's employment grew rapidly from the mid-1970s. Pearson explores both male bias in the evaluation of this phenomenon and in the constitution of the gender division of labour in the new industries.

A particularly obvious form of male bias was evident in popular views that the border industrialisation programme had failed because it had created too many jobs for women and not enough for men. More subtle forms of male bias can be found in research evaluating the programme, bias arising from simply adding-on 'women' as an empirical category without rethinking conceptual-isations – for instance, research on whether the border industries increased the problem of female unemployment, displayed male bias stemming from a failure to re-conceptualise 'economically active' and related concepts to take account of the gender differentiation of work experience.

In judging the benefits of such employment for women, researchers have tended to treat women as a homogeneous category. Pearson demonstrates the importance of a gender relations approach which does not lump all women together but instead disaggregates and compares the experience of different categories of women, working in different circumstances. The electronics factories offered better wages and working conditions than the garment factories and were able to select younger workers with higher educational qualifications and fewer domestic commitments. Electronic firms preferred workers with no children to detract from their productivity, flexibility and availability for shift work. Such attempts to escape sharing the costs of the reproduction of the next generation of workers are a covert form of male bias. More overt forms of male bias also appear to play a role in their selection procedures: a pretty face is also reckoned to be a useful attribute.

The most sobering part of Pearson's analysis concerns the gender composition of the work-force in the border industries in the 1980s. During this period there has been a sectoral diversification, with the growth of metal products, furniture and wood products and transport equipment; and an occupational diversification with the growth of technical, administrative and managerial employment. This all sounds very positive when set alongside the widespread concern that export processing zones offer only unskilled jobs in low-tech assembly processes. Yet that diversification does not seem to be benefiting women. The proportion of women in the border industry work-force has been falling just when the quality of jobs on offer has been showing some improvement. The main reason, according to Pearson, is that the new occupations and sectors are 'men's work'. In a growing and diversifying industrial complex, male bias still operates to place severe constraints on the gains that women may make. Pearson concludes that any assumption that the border industries provide an avenue of incorporation of women into the industrial labour force on anything more than a short-term, low-paid, risky basis has been shown to be false.

The reallocation of women to export-oriented industries like those of the Mexican border is a feature of the process of structural adjustment programmes in many developing countries. Such programmes, which are promoted by the World Bank and the International Monetary Fund, are examined by Diane Elson in chapter 7. Elson focuses her attention on the conceptual framework that underpins structural adjustment programmes, arguing that although this framework is couched in gender-neutral terms, it is nevertheless imbued with male bias; this male bias at the conceptual level predisposes such programmes to male bias in operation and outcome. Three types of male bias are identified: (1) concerning the sexual division of labour; (2) concerning the unpaid domestic work necessary for producing and maintaining human resources; (3) concerning the workings of the household. The source of this bias is traced to a hidden set of assumptions about the allocation and reproduction of human resources, which are treated in the conceptual framework as if they were like natural resources.

Elson shows how the biases she identifies prevent the adjustment process from working in the way macro-economic theory typically suggests that it should. For instance, an important aspect of structural adjustment programmes in sub-Saharan Africa is encouraging farmers to produce more crops for the market by raising the prices paid to them. But this encouragement is unlikely to reach women for the work they do on crops marketed by their husbands. For in this case, payment goes to their husbands and there is plenty of evidence to suggest that the benefits to women are far from certain. Men tend to keep a high proportion of their income for their own use, and women much prefer to put their efforts into work that produces an income that they themselves control. Thus the agricultural supply response to higher crop prices may be held back by the gender division of labour and income.

To the extent that structural adjustment programmes do succeed in their objective of improving the balance of payments and promoting growth, this is at the expense of women bearing the hidden costs of adjustment. For instance, cuts in public expenditure, which are a usual feature of such programmes, put more burdens on women. Thus cuts in funding of health services mean that women have to spend more time on family health care. Cuts in food subsidies mean that women have to spend more time on cooking, as cheaper foods tend to take longer to prepare.

Divisions within the family hamper women from reallocating resources in the most effective way for maintaining the well-being of their families. Rises in the prices of basic necessities are a feature of structural adjustment programmes; but women are hampered in reallocating more family expenditure to food, clothing and fuel, and away from luxuries like tobacco, alcohol and entertainment, because of incomplete pooling and sharing of household income. There is abundant evidence that women tend to spend more of income accruing to them on family needs than do men.

The conceptual framework underpinning structural adjustment programmes in effect relies on the availability of unlimited supplies of female labour.[4] But male bias prevents this being immediately apparent to the designers of such programmes. Unfortunately, women's labour is not infinitely elastic. It cannot stretch to cover all the deficiencies left by reduced public expenditure. It cannot absorb all the shocks of adjustment. When the limit is reached, economic adjustment fails; and human resources disintegrate.

Overcoming male bias in structural adjustment programmes requires a gender-aware reconceptualisation of economic processes. But it also requires the redirection of resources. The question is how far are those with economic and political power prepared to channel resources directly to women, rather than relying on resources channelled to men to trickle down to women and children? How far are those with economic and political power prepared to adjust the structure of gender relations? The question of action for change is taken up in by Elson in the final chapter. There are no magic instant recipes for success. Unlike the heroes of adventure stories who could with one bound be free, winning freedom for women is a long and roundabout task. Women have to act simultaneously within and against the societies in which they live (Kessler-Harris, 1987, p. 59).

Chapter 8 offers a brief discussion of strategies for contesting male bias in everyday attitudes and practices, in theoretical reasoning, and in the policy process. The ways in which the underlying supports of male bias might be weakened through new ways of integrating getting a living and raising children are also considered. Possible and appropriate strategies will differ across time and place and for different groups of women in different social and political situation. But there are some common themes, in particular the importance of women getting together and acting publicly.

It is not enough to rely on the development process itself to diminish male bias. The development process acts in multifarious ways on male bias: reinforcing some forms of the subordination of women, decomposing other forms, and recomposing yet new forms (Elson and Pearson, 1981). Women's lives may improve or worsen in complex and contradictory ways. The extension of the market brings new opportunities, but also new risks. As Judith Bruce concludes, 'Few who have studied women's position would conclude that fundamental change for women . . . can be based solely on increasing their individual earning power. Feminist theorists have identified collective action as a primary step for women in achieving personal power and status in the public domain' (Bruce, 1989, p. 987).

Such collective action is stressed by the 'empowerment' approach to gender and development (Moser, 1989). This approach arises out of the feminist writings and grass-roots organisational experience of Third World women, and has begun to raise the question of alternative forms of development rather than integrating women into existing patterns of development (DAWN, 1985). In that direction, through women's collective action and through attempts to reconceptualise development in a gender-aware way, would seem to lie the best prospects for overcoming male bias.

Notes

1 Sears, Roebuck & Co. argued that they were not guilty of discrimination against women. Rather, the gender structure of society meant that women did not offer themselves for certain types of job.

2 Such an entitlement differs from most existing welfare state provisions by being unconditional and paid to individuals. For more discussion of this issue, see the *Bulletin* of the Basic Income Research Group.

3 There are few female-headed households, not even *de facto* ones, in China as compared to sub-Saharan Africa and Latin America.

4 I am grateful to Mark Figueroa for pointing out the similarity to perhaps the most famous macro-economic development model of all – Lewis's 'Economic development with unlimited supplies of labour' (Lewis, 1954).

References

Antrobus, P. (1988), 'Consequences and responses to social and economic deterioration: the experience of the English-speaking Caribbean', Workshop on Economic Crisis, Household Strategies, and Women's Work, Cornell University.

Becker, G. (1981), *A Treatise on the Family*, Harvard University Press, Cambridge, Mass.

Bhatt, E. (1989), 'Toward empowerment', *World Development*, vol. 17, no. 7.

Block, N., and Dworkin, G. (eds), (1977), *The IQ Controversy*, Quartet Books, London.

Bruce, J. (1989), 'Homes divided', *World Development*, vol. 17, no. 7.

Brydon, L., and Chant, S. (1989), *Women in the Third World*, Edward Elgar, Aldershot.

Buvinic, M. (1986), 'Projects for women in the Third World: explaining their misbehaviour', *World Development*, vol. 14, no. 5.

DAWN (Development Alternatives with Women for a New Era) (1985), *Development, Crisis, and Alternative Visions: Third World Women's Perspectives*, DAWN, Delhi.

Dwyer, D., and Bruce, J. (eds) (1988), *A Home Divided: Women and Income in the Third World*, Stanford University Press, Stanford.

Elson, D., and Pearson, R. (1981), ' "Nimble fingers make cheap workers": an analysis of women's employment in Third World export manufacturing', *Feminist Review*, no. 7.

Elson, D. (1989), 'The impact of structural adjustment on women: concepts and issues', in B. Onimode (ed.), *The IMF, the World Bank and the African Debt*, vol. 2: *The Social and Political Impact*, Zed Books, London.

Folbre, N. (1986), 'Cleaning house: new perspectives on households and economic development', *Journal of Development Economics*, vol. 22.

FAO, (1986), *Report of the Workshop on Improving Statistics on Women in Agriculture*, 21–23 October, Rome.

Goldschmidt-Clermont, L. (1987), *Economic Evaluations of Unpaid Household Work: Africa, Asia, Latin America and Oceania*, International Labour Office, Geneva.

Gordon, S. (1984), *Ladies in Limbo*, Commonwealth Secretariat, London.

ILO/INSTRAW (1985), *Women in Economic Activity: A Global Statistical Survey (1950–2000)*, International Labour Office, Geneva.

Jiggins, J. (1987), *Gender-Related Impacts and the Work of the International Agricultural Research Centers*, CGIAR Study Paper No. 17, World Bank, Washington DC.

——(1988), 'Women and land in sub-Saharan Africa', Rural Employment Policies Branch, Employment and Development Department, International Labour Office, Geneva.

Joekes, S. (1987), *Women in the World Economy: an Instraw Study*, Oxford University Press, New York.

Johnson, H., and Bernstein, H. (eds) (1982), *Third World Lives of Struggle*, Heinemann, London.

Kessler-Harris, A. (1987), 'Equal Opportunity Commission *v.* Sears, Roebuck & Co.: a personal account', *Feminist Review*, no. 25.

Lewis, A. (1954), 'Economic development with unlimited supplies of labour', *Manchester School*, vol. 22.

Lipton, M. (1977), *Why Poor People Stay Poor – Urban Bias in World Development*, Temple Smith, London.

Loxley, J. (1988), *Ghana: Economic Crisis and the Long Road to Recovery*, North-South Institute, Ottawa.

Mbilinyi, M. (1988), 'Agribusiness and women peasants in Tanzania', *Development and Change*, vol. 19, pp. 549–83.

Moser, C. (1989), 'Gender planning in the Third World: meeting practical and strategic gender needs', *World Development*, vol. 19, no. 11.

Palmer, I. (1988), *Gender Issues in Structural Adjustment of Sub-Saharan African Agriculture and Some Demographic Implications*, Population and Labour Policies Programme, Working Paper No. 166, International Labour Organisation, Geneva.

Rosenzweig, M. (1986), 'Program interventions, intra-household distribution and the welfare of individuals: modelling household behaviour', *World Development*, vol. 14, no. 2.

Safilios-Rothschild, C. (1987), 'Women in Agriculture: the need for sex-segregated data', in Ministry of Agriculture and Fisheries of the Netherlands, *Operational Strategies for Reaching Women in Agriculture*, The Hague.

Sen, A. K. (1966), 'Peasants and dualism with or without surplus labour', *Journal of Political Economy*, vol. 74, pp. 425–50.

——(1984), *Resources, Values, and Development*, Blackwell, Oxford.

——(1985), *Women, Technology, and Sexual Divisions*, UNCTAD and INSTRAW, Geneva.

——(1987), 'Gender and co-operative conflicts', [mimeo.], World Institute of Development Economics Research, Helsinki.

Staudt, K. (1987), 'Uncaptured or unmotivated? Women and the food crisis in Africa', *Rural Sociology*, vol. 52, no. 1.

UN (1986), *World Survey on the Role of Women in Development*, Department of International Economic and Social Affairs, New York.

Wiley, L. (1985), 'Tanzania: the Arusha Planning and Village Development Project', in C. Overholt, M. Anderson, K. Cloud, and J. Austin (eds), *Gender Roles in Development Projects*, Kumarian Press, West Hartford.

Women, work and property in the Chinese peasant household of the 1980s

In China today, the persistent inequality of men and women in the countryside and the unchanging peasant preference for sons are often attributed to the lingering influence of feudal ideas. The explanation is comforting, for it implies that surviving gender inequalities have no rational basis and may in time be expected to die away. In this chapter I argue that the inequality of women is rooted in family structures, and that as these structures have been reinforced by recent economic policy, it is unrealistic to think that such inequality will be eliminated in the near future.

Since the establishment of the People's Republic in 1949, there has been a concerted effort through legislation, propaganda and education to reform the family, to strengthen women's position within it, and to make it possible for women to play an equal role in society. In the cities, the waged economy, employment for women, educational opportunities and greater geographical and occupational mobility have partially undermined the old power of the patriarchal family. In the countryside, practices such as footbinding, child-betrothal, forced marriage and the open sale of girls and women mostly came to an end in 1949 or earlier, but the peasant family has in a sense been strengthened by purging it of the worst abuses with which it was formerly associated (Stacey, 1983). The household is still normally headed by a man (Parish and White, 1978, p. 153), and women and young people occupy a clearly subordinate place within it. In the villages today, both men and women will often assert that men are superior to women. Perhaps it is good that people feel free to come out with what they really think, rather than with what they know they are supposed to think, but it says little for the effects of decades of propaganda for equality that they still think this way. A strong preference for sons persists and is reflected in the superior survival chances of male infants (Aird, 1983, pp. 618–19; Davin, 1987, p. 117). Female children suffer more malnutrition than their brothers (Xin Tiyu, 1987); fewer of them attend school and they leave earlier (Wolf, 1984, pp. 124–6). There are few women cadres in the countryside, and women are severely underrepresented on the elected bodies which now run village affairs and in the skilled jobs that attract the best remuneration.

These are but a few indicators of the way in which women continue to be disadvantaged in the Chinese countryside. It is a discouraging situation. In those developing countries where women's issues have been ignored or given low priority for years, it comes as no surprise when women as a group benefit little from development. In China, where women have been on the agenda throughout the period of the People's Republic, and where they were explicitly included in policies for land reform and for collectivisation (Davin, 1976), peasant women appear to have gained less than might have been expected. It is important to try to discover why this should be so and to use this understanding to consider the prospects for the future now that collectivisation has been abandoned, and the countryside is undergoing a profound social and economic reorganisation.

Women under collectivisation.

When agriculture was collectivised in China, one of the claims made for the new form of organisation was that it would liberate women. Nurseries, canteens and sewing stations were to relieve them of heavy home responsibilities, while as members of production teams in their own right, they would earn work-point income as men did. Work in the collective fields would take them out of the house and into contact with non-family members. Economic independence conferred by their earnings would allow them to play an equal role with men in the affairs of the family, the village and the collective, and to take up the civil and political rights already granted to them in law.

In the event, things turned out rather differently. Canteens were uneconomic and poorly managed. They were never popular with the peasants, and most closed within a year or two. Rural nurseries had only a little more success; the few full-time ones that survive today are in areas where the demand for women's labour is strong. Temporary ones open elsewhere if there is a demand in the busy agricultural seasons, but the majority of young peasant children are cared for by their mothers or grandmothers. The family solution is usually cheaper and is also felt to be more reliable: a particularly important point as small families raise the level of anxiety about the health and safety of each child.

Under the commune, large numbers of women were members of production teams and the proportion of agricultural work done by women rose in the 1950s and '60s, although in most cases men continued to do more. This reflected the fact that women were still heavily burdened with domestic work and child care. Often, collectivisation shifted these tasks from the younger to the older women, who might otherwise have been allowed to start taking life a little easier. Women also did much of the work on private plots, the strips on which families were allowed to grow vegetables for their own consumption and sometimes for the market.

Thus even in this period, much of the work which women did was still in the private sphere: invisible and unmeasured. However, when they worked for the collective, whether in the fields or in sideline production, their work was recorded in terms of work points. At the end of the season, when collective income was distributed, the amount received by each household depended on the number of work points earned by each of its members. A clear sexual division of labour existed, 'women's jobs' being in general the least well-paid. Even when women did the same jobs as men, their work points were frequently lower, despite campaigns and protests. Nor did women normally receive their earnings into their own hands; the income of all the members of the family was usually paid over to the household head. Nonetheless, despite these drawbacks, the collective system did involve the public measuring of each individual's contribution to household income, and thus made a part of women's work more visible than it had been before.

A real gain for women in the period of collectivisation was that they were no longer so restricted to the home. As children, many girls attended school, at least for a time; and later, when they worked in the fields, they did so with people from other families. Even attendance at meetings after the working day, although resented by women who had work waiting for them at home, did familiarise them with issues concerning the village, the commune or even the nation, and with the cadres who spoke on such occasions. Most rural cadres were male, but a women's affairs cadre was supposed to sit on the commune management committee and, at a lower level, on the committees of the brigade and the production team. Occasionally, women held other official posts, and they tended to be better represented, although still in a minority, as medical workers, teachers and accountants. These developments at least produced more acceptance of the idea of women in public roles.

The marriage law of 1950 had been expected to play an important part in the liberation of women (Meijer, 1971). It defined marriage as an agreement freely entered into by two parties, forbade interference by outsiders, and established the right of divorce by consent or at the wish of one spouse if all attempts at mediation failed. By requiring the registration of marriage and divorce, the new law established the interest of the state in what had traditionally been regarded as a family matter. Despite the central message of the law that marriage was to be based on free choice, parents continued to play a major role in the arrangement of their children's marriages. A sort of compromise was reached in which the young people were usually permitted to meet before the match was finalised and might even exercise a veto. In most cases, however, the parents took the first steps, and even when this was not so, their role was paramount in the negotiations over the complex financial arrangements associated with marriage (Croll, 1981).

At times, and especially during the Cultural Revolution, the political climate forced peasant families to be discreet over the bride-price and the wedding gifts, and to moderate the extravagance of wedding feasts. But custom continued to reflect the rural reality that marriage had significant economic implications for both the households involved. The bride's natal family required compensation for the labour power it was losing; indeed, ironically, as the woman's earning power increased, so did bride-price (Parish and White, 1978, pp. 186–7). Moreover, the new couple needed a room, furniture and bedding. As their earnings had always gone into a common household budget, they could not hope to make such purchases without the co-operation of the older generation.

Some of the most vivid material on the countryside under collectivisation comes from the recollections of former Red Guards who, from 1969 on, were sent to 'learn from the peasants and reform themselves through labour'. Most of these record the shock young city people felt at the work peasant women had to do, at their unequal earnings, and at general attitudes to women in the countryside. Liang Heng, a young man exiled from Changsha, wrote of his peasant hostess:

Guo Lucky Wealth's wife's hands were busy from the moment she woke up to the moment she went to bed. It was through living with her that I learnt to have compassion for peasant women. Not only did she have to work with the men in the fields (and for fewer work points), but she was also responsible for the hundreds of household tasks: hauling water from the pond, washing vegetables for pig and human food, feeding the fire with brushwood, cooking, scrubbing clothing, repairing the grass roof when it leaked, spinning thread for cotton for mending, and cleaning the kitchen so that not even a fly could feed itself in it. Although she was still young, her hands were rough and cracked like old boards (Liang and Shapiro, 1983, p. 193).

Sometimes the indignation of these sent-down youth had an influence on young village women, who began to object to a system which paid them less than the worst workers among the men, no matter how much better they themselves worked (Chan, 1984, p. 93).

Other sent-down youth were shocked to discover that wife-beating was still accepted as normal in the villages (Zhang and Sang, 1985). A few city girls themselves suffered sexual harassment and even rape. Liang Heng tells of a city girl who was raped and who then felt she had no choice but to marry the boy. His family thus gained a bride without having to pay bride-price which in that area would have cost them about 1,000 yuan (about £200). Incidents of this sort were disillusioning as well as traumatic. A woman who suffered a sexual attack by a village cadre in Guangdong Province then had to fight off advances from other men who assumed that she was easy game (Frolic, 1980, pp. 52–3). She commented that the experience had made her aware how little the status of women had changed in that village, despite twenty years of Party propaganda. 'Top cadres could easily abuse their power and most people didn't care or were afraid to say anything . . . Forced sexual relations were not uncommon, and even rape was seen as part of the male-female relationship.'

On their own, without families to protect them, these young women were no doubt more vulnerable than village women, and even among them these terrible experiences were exceptional. But the tone of all the reports from former sent-down youths indicates the contrast between the city attitudes to women to which these young people were accustomed, and what they found in the countryside. Over a decade has now passed since most of them returned to the towns. Since Mao's death in 1976, and the introduction of economic reforms from 1978, momentous changes have occurred. What have they meant for women?

The rural reforms

By the end of the 1970s there was considerable concern in the Chinese leadership about what was felt to be too slow a rate of economic growth, with agriculture being seen as a serious bottleneck. In absolute terms, good increases in output had been achieved, but improvements in per capita yields were modest because of a near doubling of the population since 1949. The advocates of economic reform argued that faster growth in agricultural output was a prerequisite for China's modernisation and that it could only be achieved by giving the peasants greater material incentives. They condemned the collective system for 'allowing everybody to eat out of the same big pot' regardless of their contribution to production. New organisational forms known as household responsibility systems or contract systems were introduced to the countryside, slowly and on a limited scale at first, but generally and rapidly later.

Land is now contracted out to individual peasant households which take entrepreneurial responsibility for its cultivation. In return, the household undertakes to deliver a set quota of produce with the surplus being its own to consume or sell. At first, contracts for what is called responsibility land were for quite short periods, but in 1984 the Central Committee authorised contracts of fifteen years or more, in order to encourage peasants to invest in the land's long-term fertility rather than exhausting it by snatching a quick yield. Technically this land does not belong to the peasants who till it, and they cannot buy or sell it. This will be hard to uphold, and it seems that some market in responsibility land is already developing.

Responsibility systems extend to many forms of economic activity. Non-agricultural sideline production is also contracted out, as are the transport and repair enterprises which were formerly run by the collective. Even under the collective system, most peasant families engaged in some sort of sideline production – a vague term which included, for example, pigs, chickens, vegetables and tobacco raised on private plots, as well as silk cocoons and handicraft items. Other sidelines involved harvesting the bounty of nature: brushwood, medicinal herbs, bird dung for use as fertiliser, besoms for brooms and so on.

Official attitudes to private income-generating activity was at best ambivalent. At the height of the Cultural Revolution it was often suppressed. Even without outright suppression, the low prices offered by state purchasing agencies provided little incentive, while prohibitions on private trading made it difficult for the peasants to market their products in any other way. Since the late 1970s, official attitudes have changed completely. Peasants can now raise loans to set themselves up as sideline producers; raw materials and advice are more easily obtainable; the State offers higher prices than before, and there are flourishing private markets. By 1982, thirty-eight per cent of rural household income was generated by this sector. (State Statistical Bureau, 1983).

Family planning policy

At the very time that responsibility for production was being turned over to the individual peasant household, the Chinese government attempted to intervene on a level unprecedented anywhere in the world in the very private area of family planning. Concern about population growth was apparent in the early sixties and was heightened by the sample census of 1964. In the 1970s, couples were strongly encouraged to limit their families to two; contraception and abortion were widely available and the acceptance of sterilisation after two children was rewarded. The realisation in the late 1970s that sixty-five per cent of the population was under thirty years of age, and that in the 1980s ten million women annually would marry and become potential child-bearers, caused great alarm. Demographers forecast that if families averaged three children each, the population would double yet again within forty-five years. Drastic action was undertaken. Couples were asked to limit their families to a single child. Not only were incentives offered to persuade them to comply, quite harsh penalties were visited on those who refused (Croll, Davin and Kane, 1985).

It was always recognised that this programme would be difficult to implement in the countryside where children, and especially male children, are essential to the maintenance and continuation of the household economy. From the beginning, the exemptions from the policy were more generous for the rural areas, and it now seems to be accepted that many peasant families will have two children, especially if the first-born is female. Nevertheless, China's population policy remains the strictest in the world.

These two policies – the devolution of responsibility for production to the peasant household, and the attempt to intervene in its power of decision over reproduction – have reshaped the whole of rural society over the past decade; but it is with their specific effects on women that the rest of this chapter will be concerned.

Women's work under the responsibility system

As a result of the household responsibility system, women are now likely to work as part of the family labour force rather than in a larger group. They will usually be directed by the male family head – their fathers, fathers-in-law or husbands. Whether they work on the family responsibility land or in household sidelines, they are less likely to be in continuous contact with people outside the immediate family circle. Deprived of leisure by the heavy burden of domestic work, they have always had less chance than men to make friends at other times. This is particularly unfortunate for young married women. Rural brides usually move in from some distance away and are thus strangers in their husbands' villages. It is hard for these young women to stand up for themselves in family conflicts and the lack of friends outside the family makes it harder still. Women's contact with cadres has also been reduced. Cadres no longer supervise all productive work as they did under collectivisation, and there are fewer meetings. The cadres of the new administrative units, the village group and the village committee, have less need to be in contact with the individual villagers on a day-to-day basis; they will often deal with the household heads as representatives of the whole household. In the past when family disputes arose, women sometimes found it difficult to appeal to local cadres who, given the patrilocal marriage system, were often relatives, or at least friends of the husband and his family. The difficulty will be compounded if women do not know the cadres well.

In families mainly engaged in farming, the sexual division of labour will relegate women to the care of the vegetable plots, of pigs,

chickens and other stock kept close to the house – jobs which are comparatively easily combined with domestic responsibilities and child care.

In such a vast country there are naturally considerable local variations in the sexual division of labour. Even before 1949 women did more farm work where men worked away, for example in fishing villages, or in areas of Guangdong province with heavy male emigration. Since 1949 the growth of cities and the development of rural industry has drawn many peasants into the non-agricultural work force. Where non-agricultural employment is in transport, lumber or other areas reserved predominantly for men, women may take most of the responsibility for farming. This situation is found quite often in the environs of the great cities. In the past, peasants were virtually tied to the soil, they could not move to the cities without urban residence papers which were practically unobtainable, nor could they move at will to another commune. Permanent city residence is still denied to peasants, but since the introduction of the economic reforms, peasants who come into the cities for temporary periods of work or to trade are less likely to be summarily rounded up and sent away.

The diversification of the rural economy has made much more non-agricultural employment available in the countryside itself. When this attracts large numbers of male peasants from the land, women replace them in the fields and presumably experience more autonomy in their work. But it is worth recalling that they take over only when farm work has become less desirable to men than some better-remunerated alternative.

In other places, the sexual division of labour draws *women* into non-agricultural tasks. Many domestic sidelines are ones in which women's traditional skills are utilised. Women are involved in sewing, knitting, weaving, embroidery and basket-making, to name but a few crafts through which they now produce for the market. Such employment is depicted as especially appropriate for women; and many probably do prefer it to farm work, for it is cleaner, lighter and easier to fit in with domestic responsibilities.

Some women have met with enormous success, much vaunted in the press, by producing luxury products such as mink pelts, cultured pearls and angora wool, though the inevitable failures in these enterprises are given less publicity. In any case, these eye-catching examples are not typical. Most sideline production is

labour-intensive, dull, repetitive, undercapitalised and poorly remunerated. Women take it up with enthusiasm only because they lack better opportunities.

Peasant women are also sometimes employed in small factories and workshops which may be private or co-operative ventures or may be managed by the township or the county. These are usually mechanised to some degree, although, in certain cases, for example in carpet manufacture, there may be deliberate retention of hand methods because of the superior prices the products will then command. Work in these enterprises is usually no less dull and repetitive than work in domestic sidelines, and safety precautions may be inadequate. However, unlike most work available to peasants, jobs in rural industry mean a regular monthly wage, set hours and frequently some modest fringe benefits. Understandably, they are much sought-after – an indication of their popularity is that such jobs have been used as a reward for mothers promising to have only one child.

Although in some villages men have a near-monopoly on jobs in rural industries, in others, women share them or even predominate in them. This is particularly likely to be the case in enterprises producing textiles or clothes, for reasons obviously connected with traditional notions of women's work. (It is a cause for concern that in such enterprises, supervisors, designers and other senior staff are overwhelmingly male.) In all, half of the sixty-four million employees of rural enterprises are female (Li Ning, 1987, pp. 24–5). Sometimes the workforce is predominantly female even where the work is quite different from anything normally done by women. All the workers sharpening blades in a metal-working shop in Longbow village, Shaanxi Province, filmed by Carma Hinton, were female. Asked about this, the manager explained that young men had been tried in the job but they did not have the patience for such dull work (Hinton, 1984).

For women, the way in which work is remunerated is very significant. Traditionally, the Chinese peasant household holds property in common and shares a budget. All income is pooled, and budgeting is in the charge of the family head, normally the senior male, although day-to-day affairs may be taken care of by the senior female. When cash income comes from the sale of a crop or of sideline produce which is the result of pooled family labour, this tradition is likely to be strictly adhered to, and the contribution of

the woman, or indeed of any individual, becomes invisible. When, on the other hand, cash is raised from the sale of items produced by women alone, their contribution is harder to ignore and they may even get some spending money, especially if they market the goods themselves. They will benefit even if the work is done under a household contract, but their hands may be further strengthened if they hold the contracts as individuals. Women who are actually in waged employment are in a particularly strong position. Custom may require that they pool their wage with the rest of the family income, but everyone is at least aware that they earned it.

The effects of responsibility systems and contracts on women will vary considerably according to individual circumstances. When women work for a wage in a non-family enterprise they may be little affected, while if they themselves are contract-holders and their enterprise does well, they may benefit. Generally speaking though, because the household responsibility system has restored the peasant family – an institution within which women are still very much disadvantaged – as the basic unit of agricultural production, the reforms seem likely to reinforce many aspects of sexual inequality. One of the mechanisms through which this continues is the transmission of property.

Property and the peasant household

In traditional society, Chinese women were almost entirely without property rights. There was in fact little individual property. Land, houses, stock, equipment and tools belonged to the family (Shiga, 1969). Women had the right to use these things like other members of the household, but they could not inherit them. The property of their natal family would be shared among their brothers, while that of the family they married into also passed along the male line. If widows inherited at all, it was as representatives of their infant sons, for whom they might keep property in trust. Family property passed from one generation to another through inheritance or family division. Family division took place when the members of a household composed of ageing parents, their adult sons and daughters-in-law and grandchildren, agreed to start to live as separate units, each with its own stove and its own budget. Usually one of the sons would remain with the parents while each of the others formed a separate household with his share of the property.

Sometimes this process took place on the death of the oldest member of the household, in which case it tended to become blurred with inheritance. More often, it was precipitated by the growing complexity of the household as sons married and had their own children. A woman's dowry, in theory at least, remained apart from family property and belonged to the woman and her husband alone. Jewellery and clothing belonged to her personally, but these were the only individual property rights she enjoyed.

Concern was shown for women's property rights even in the earliest Chinese soviets – the first areas to be administered by the Chinese Communist Party (Davin, forthcoming). All communist land laws from the 1920s to the 50s stipulated that women should have their own share of land (Davin, 1976, ch. 1). Later, with collectivisation, land ownership ceased to be an issue. Inheritance has been the subject of less legislation in communist history, although in the 1940s, the laws of the communist-administered areas of both Shaan-Gan-Ning and Jin-Cha-Ji guaranteed women's inheritance rights. There was no inheritance law in the People's Republic prior to 1985, but some court decisions upheld the right of women to inherit. The marriage laws gave husband and wife equal rights in the possession and management of property and the right to inherit from each other. They also stipulated that children and parents had the right to inherit from each other regardless of sex. In practice, rural women continued to suffer discrimination in regard both to property and inheritance. In the 1950s in particular, women who attempted to exercise their right to divorce and tried to leave, taking with them the share of land they had received in land reform, suffered violence on an enormous scale. According to official figures, tens of thousands were murdered by husbands or in-laws (Davin, 1976, p. 87). The Party was unable to protect them adequately, because women's rights had not won solid enough support either among peasants as a class, or among peasant cadres.

After the collectivisation of land, less was at stake, but women still lost out whenever they moved from one household to another: on marriage, divorce or remarriage after widowhood. In any of these cases, they left a household to which they had contributed through their labour, helping it to accumulate household goods, housing and savings; yet on leaving it they took none of this with them. First-time brides were, of course, provided with a dowry by their father's household, but as we have seen, it was not their private property. On divorce or remarriage, women left their in-laws' homes with nothing but their own clothing and jewellery.

When a family division took place, or when an old man died, if married daughters' rights received any acknowledgement at all it was usually so that they could be asked to waive them in favour of their brothers. Only women without brothers seem to have done better at inheriting patrimony. The courts found in their favour against the weaker claims of their male cousins on the father's side (Davin, forthcoming).

The new importance of property and inheritance

Collectivisation effectively limited what could be privately owned to housing, tools, some stock and household goods. The major means of production belonged to the collective. Since the introduction of responsibility systems, this has changed completely. Peasants not only own more quilts, watches, thermos flasks and bicycles than ever before, but in the wealthier areas they have items undreamed of twenty years ago: transistor radios, televisions, rice-cookers and even fridges or washing-machines. There has been an unprecedented boom in the construction of privately-owned housing in the countryside. Finally, and this is the greatest change of all, the reform of the economic system has brought about the private ownership of quite significant means of production. The peasant household may own small plant and machinery, commercial vehicles for transporting goods and people, sewing-machines, knitting-machines, and equipment for other crafts and trades. In agriculture, tractors, electric pumps and other agricultural machinery, tools, draught animals and other livestock are all now privately owned. Even shares in private enterprises may form a part of individual or family property.

Contracts may also be considered among the assets of an individual or a household. In agriculture, contracts like leases give use-rights to the land, in exchange for which the cultivator hands over a part of the crop, while contracts for non-agricultural production in effect guarantee a market in advance, thus removing some of the small entrepreneur's risk. The contract is usually signed by a household head acting on behalf of other members, although individuals or groups of individuals may also undertake contracts. Contracts are not defined as property and the law does not include them in the definition of heritable estate, although it permits them to be passed on in certain circumstances (*Inheritance Law*, 1985). It seems probable that in farming at least, the interests of stability and continuity will be best assured by allowing contracts for responsibility land to pass from one generation to another like other household property. The sale and purchase of contracts is prohibited, but there is evidence that a market in them is developing (Myers, 1985, p. 20).

The new leadership in China regards the proper protection of property rights as essential to its strategy for promoting modernisation. It has firmly dissociated itself from the attacks on property that took place during the Cultural Revolution. The 1982 Constitution included a guarantee of the right of citizens to own and inherit property, while an inheritance law, the first in the history of the People's Republic of China, came into force in October 1985 (*Inheritance Law*, 1985).

At first sight the new law appears to give strong support to women's inheritance. Article nine prohibits discrimination between the sexes in the right to inherit. Spouses, sons and daughters and parents all share the status of heirs of the first order. Brothers and sisters and paternal and maternal grandparents are heirs of the second order. The heritable estate is divided equally among the heirs of the first order. Second-order heirs cannot inherit unless there is no first-order heir. The property of married people is held to be conjugal. When one spouse dies, if the property is then divided for inheritance purposes, one-half is retained by the survivor as individual property while the other is divided among the first-order heirs, including, of course, the widow or widower.

The Inheritance Law implicitly deals with individual property rights. However, as we have seen, by custom most property is regarded as belonging collectively to the family. This poses obvious problems with which the law deals only cursorily in Article twenty-six: 'if the heritable estate forms part of family property, it must be separated out before the estate is divided.' In addition, the drafters of the law appear to have expected that the division of the estate might sometimes be delayed by agreement between the heirs.

Other problems, however, arise for which the law makes no clear provision. An obvious one is that the division of property between brothers who have remained in their parents' home or village and married-out daughters would involve the transfer of property from one household to another and, in all probability, from one village to another. As we have seen, this property might include the assets of a farm or business enterprise. Its transfer could threaten the stability or the viability of the business and of the household economy. It would thus incur the resentment and perhaps the outright opposition of the brothers and possibly also of the village cadres. The disruptive effects of such a transfer would then make it of concern to the state, which is so anxious to ensure stable economic growth in the countryside with the peasant household economy as its cornerstone. It seems unlikely that the transfer will often be allowed to occur. There is little evidence that married women often inherited from their parents in the countryside before 1985, and there are hints in the new law that will not change this (Meijer, 1976; Davin, forthcoming).

Under the 1985 law, heirs are permitted to give up their rights to an estate or to reach agreement through consultation on the timing of the division of the estate and the way it is to be divided. If they cannot agree, they may seek arbitration. These provisions would give legal respectability to a married woman's renunciation of her rights, or a significant share of them, in favour of her brothers. The brothers' rights are further strengthened by Article 13 which lays down that heirs who have lived with, or provided for the deceased person have the right to receive an extra share while heirs who have not, will receive a smaller share or nothing. As women normally marry out of the family and cannot easily provide for their parents, they are likely to be disadvantaged by this provision.

The principle of inheritance as a reward is taken even further in Article 31, which deals with care-legacy agreements. Under such an agreement a citizen may promise a legacy to another person in exchange for care in old age and responsibility for burial. Old people with sons are unlikely to need to make an arrangement of this kind; it is those who have only daughters and thus lack co-resident children who may resort to them, thereby possibly disinheriting their daughters. Finally, the law requires that the division of heritable property should be favourable to production and the needs of everyday life, another principle that could be used to argue against inheritance by daughters who have left their natal families.

Women may do rather better with their right to inherit within the families they join on marriage. While their husbands survive, they enjoy no right to inherit from their parents-in-law although they would benefit indirectly from their husbands' right to do so. However, under Article 12, widows (or widowers) who have made major contributions to the support of their parents-in-law join the ranks of their first-order heirs. Interestingly, the first draft of the law only granted them this status in the absence of blood relations who could be first-order heirs, but the article was revised after discussion in the National People's Congress (Zhang, 1985).

This measure, together with the right of the wife to half the conjugal property and to a share in her husband's estate, could amount to considerable safeguards for a widow. Furthermore, there is a good chance that they may be implemented, at least where the widow has been married some time and is expected to remain as a member of her dead husband's household. Although the law's insistence on the widow's rights in her own person is not consistent with Chinese custom, the practice it would produce is not so different from the past when she inherited property as a representative of her dead husband or held it on behalf of her infant sons.

The real conflict over a married woman's rights to the property of the family into which she married is likely to arise in cases of divorce or remarriage: both events which result in the woman leaving one household for another, and taking her property with her if the law is complied with. Before the 1985 Inheritance Law, women in these situations were usually unable to assert rights to property. It is not clear whether they will do better in future.

The right of a daughter to patrimony is potentially the most disruptive of a woman's property rights under the law, since its implementation would involve every peasant family. Divorce and remarriage are still comparatively rare events and fewer families are affected by them. It is therefore a reasonable assumption that any campaign for women's property rights is likely to concentrate on issues of remarriage and divorce. However, it is by no means clear that there will be a campaign. The Inheritance Law was drawn up primarily in order to promote a clear and stable system of property which it was felt would encourage effort and accumulation. At the same time, law functions as a showcase; women's property rights had to be enshrined in the law if China was to retain her socialist credentials. She is not thereby obliged to implement them, and is not likely to do so if they appear to pose a threat to the primary goal of economic stability.

Population policy: its special consequences for women

The strict family planning policy now in force in the Chinese countryside has various specific implications for women. Tension has always surrounded the birth of a child as the anxious family waits to discover its sex. In almost all cases sons were preferred, as Chinese parents needed boys to support them in old age and to continue the family line. In the past, the birth of a girl might be accepted or even welcomed in a family which had already had at least one boy. When the first-born was a girl, her arrival did not cause too much dismay; it at least demonstrated that her parents were fertile. However, women who had one daughter after another without a son suffered grievously from a sense of failure and from slights and ill-treatment by others.

Now that the one-child family policy is in force over most of China, such suffering is more general. In the countryside it is sometimes possible for couples to get permission to have a second child, but two is the absolute limit (Davin, 1985). Such couples have to forego the single-child family benefits. The birth of a daughter is now experienced as a tragedy since it faces the parents with the stark choice of doing without a son or paying a heavy price to defy the policy and try again. A moving account of the feelings of a woman who was willing to do this is contained in a recently published volume of oral histories (Zhang and Sang, 1986). Big Sister Zheng, a forty-six year-old peasant woman in Sichuan province, had given birth to a boy who died in infancy and then to seven daughters, one of whom also died. When she told her story in 1984, the eldest girl was already married and Big Sister Zheng had finally produced another son two years before. During her pregnancy, she had come under so much pressure from officials to abort that at one stage she hid with relatives in another village. She checked out the fine she would have to pay in advance. Fines are calculated on a sliding scale increasing with the parity of the child. In this case the birth counted as the seventh, as two of her children had already died, and her fine was 1300 yuan. She had had to borrow 900 yuan and it had taken two years to pay it back, but she thought it had been well worth all the cost.

It is clear that the mother is usually blamed and indeed may blame herself for the sex of the child. There have been many reports of women being badly treated or beaten by resentful in-laws after giving birth to a girl. The official women's organisation, the Women's Federation, has responded by producing posters condemning violence against women, publicising cases in which families have been punished for such outrages, and seeking out women who are suffering and helping them to reason with in-laws. It has also attempted to spread a scientific understanding of what determines the sex of the foetus and to convince parents that a daughter should be as much valued as a son. These efforts may be of some value, but they cannot change the basic situation: the lot of a woman who gives birth to a daughter will inevitably be hard as long as births are so severely restricted and sons remain indispensable to the well-being of the peasant family.

Condemnations of violence against women have frequently been accompanied by condemnations of female infanticide: another terrible practice whose incidence seems to have increased as a result of population policy. In China as elsewhere in the world, unwanted babies were in the past quite frequently abandoned, suffocated or drowned (Lee, 1981). Female infanticide was fiercely attacked after 1949 and seems, judging from the sex ratios of the newly-born, to have declined (Aird, 1983). It appears that when peasant parents could afford to bring up their baby girls, they were willing to do so. The one-child family policy faced them with a painful choice. The couple who brought up a girl would no longer have the chance to try again for a son. It was inevitable that this situation would lead to some incidence of female infanticide. Without more evidence, no estimate of its extent is possible.

The fact that female infanticide could occur on any scale in China in the 1980s produced real concern and probably contributed to the partial relaxation of the one-child policy in the countryside in the form of an acceptance that many peasant families whose first-born is female will have a second child. Such concessions ease the problem, but they do not solve it. The peasant family's preference for sons has been reinforced by the responsibility systems which make labour power the prime determinant of household income. As long as couples are limited to one or even two children, there will be many without sons. They face an insecure future in which as they age and their daughters marry out, household income will wane. All the members of such families will be affected, but the mothers who have 'failed' to bear a son and the daughters who have 'failed' to be born male will surely suffer most.

After the birth of their single child, women bear the brunt of efforts to prevent conception. IUDs are the most commonly-used contraceptives, with the pill trailing a long way behind and barrier methods occupying an almost insignificant place (Chen, 1985, pp. 139–42). Sterilisation is also an important method because it was accepted by large numbers of couples who completed their child-bearing in the 1970s. The one-child family campaign has increased resistance to sterilisation because couples who sign the one-child family pledge fear that something may happen to their only child and are resolved to preserve their ability to have another. Where sterilisation has been accepted, again the burden usually falls on the woman. Of all rural couples practising contraception, 26·4 per cent rely on tubectomies, whereas the figure for vasectomies is only 11·5 per cent.

Abortion is available on request in China and when actively sought by the women is usually performed early. Unfortunately, the present strictness of population policy has increased the incidence of late abortions. Although many terminations are the result of mistakes or contraceptive failures, others end pregnancies which have been deliberately entered into in defiance of birth planning. Some women are quickly persuaded to end such pregnancies, but others hold out for months. Some have succeeded in concealing their pregnancies into the third trimester, only to be discovered and persuaded to abort as late as the seventh or eighth month.

It would be wrong to present the struggle over the control of reproduction in China as a struggle for a woman's right to chose. It is the family not the individual which is the state's adversary in this matter. The intervention of the state has caused women to suffer, but its defeat would merely reinforce their subordination to the family. Moreover, the argument that strict population control is necessary to the well-being of the whole Chinese nation is not easily dismissed. It is the misfortune of women that it is their bodies and their reproductive power which have become the disputed territory in this battle between the state and the patriarchal family.

Conclusion

The new economic policies have been much vaunted both inside and outside China for their positive effects on output. Increased production has led to increased prosperity and consumption.

Though some of the reforms have given rise to their own problems, the evidence of higher incomes in the countryside is obvious in the form of new buildings, better clothing and more consumer durables. Obviously, women share the benefits of all this as members of their families and communities.

On the other hand, the new policies certainly have some negative implications for women. Nothing new has been done to tackle the roots of woman's subordination within the peasant family, but the power and authority of the family have been considerably expanded. Although the contract system has created a few independent women producers, most are now dependent for their access to land and other means of production on their membership of a family, and this membership in turn depends on their relationship to a man. They are more vulnerable in marriage than are men, for divorce would cut them off from their livelihood and from the accumulated fruits of their labour. The inheritance law, for all its condemnation of discrimination against women, seems unlikely to establish their property rights satisfactorily.

In making the control of labour power of such paramount importance to the peasant household the responsibility systems have intensified the entrenched peasant preference for sons, while population policy has made it both difficult and costly to have more than one or two children. The interaction of the policies has produced many families with one or two female children where mothers will feel great and lasting unhappiness at their failure to produce sons.

When Chinese agriculture was collectivised in the 1950s, women's issues were given real consideration and women's perceived needs influenced the services provided by the communes. The evolution of the rural reform policies provide a sharp contrast. Although there has been extensive debate about their political and economic implications, there was much less interest within China in their repercussions for relations within the family and between the sexes. Where such issues were finally taken up, it was mainly in connection with infanticide and violence against women after these phenomena had emerged as problems, and the action taken was not a radical attack on the fundamental causes of the problem.

The rural reforms have already brought great changes to the Chinese countryside, and the advent of much smaller families seems likely to keep up the momentum of that change. The effects will take time to work through. Couples who have to limit their families to one or two female children in the 1980s will be faced with the problem of support in their old age. It may be that some solutions will begin to erode customs which are basic to women's continuing subordination, such as virilocal marriage or the norm that the married daughter does not contribute to the support of her ageing parents. For the moment, however, it is hard to escape the conclusion that the rural reforms will actually make it more difficult for women to improve their position in rural society.

References

Aird, J. S. (1983), 'The preliminary results of China's 1982 census', *China Quarterly*, vol.96, pp. 613–41.

Chan, A., Madsen, R., and Unger, J. (1984), *Chen Village: The Recent History of a Peasant Community in Mao's China*, University of California Press, Berkeley.

Chen, P. (1985), 'Birth control methods and organisation in China', in E. Croll *et al.* (eds), *China's One-Child Family Policy, op. cit.*

Croll, E. (1981), *The Politics of Marriage in Contemporary China*, Cambridge University Press, Cambridge.

Croll, E., Davin, D., and Kane, P. (eds) (1985), *China's One-Child Family Policy*, Macmillan, London.

Davin, D. (1976), *Womanwork: Women and the Party in Revolutionary China*, Clarendon Press, Oxford.

——(1987), 'Gender and population in the People's Republic of China', in H. Afshar, (ed.), *Women, State and Ideology*, Macmillan, London.

——(forthcoming), 'China: the new Inheritance Law and the peasant household', *Journal of Communist Studies*.

Frolic, B. M. (1980), *Mao's People*, Harvard University Press, Cambridge, Mass.

Hinton, C. (1984), 'Small happiness: women of a Chinese village', [a documentary film].

Inheritance Law of the People's Republic of China (1985), in *Selected Major Laws of the PRC* (1986) [in Chinese], Shanghai People's Publishing House, Shanghai.

Lee, J. (1981), 'Female infanticide in China', in R. Guisso, and S. Johannsen (eds), *Women in China; Historical Reflections*, no. 8, Youngstown, New York.

Li Ning (1987), 'Rural women come into their own', *Beijing Review*, vol.30, no. 10.

Liang Heng and Shapiro, J. (1983), *Son of the Revolution*, Chatto & Windus, London.

Meijer, M. J. (1976), *Marriage Law and Policy in the Chinese People's Republic*, Hong Kong University Press, Hong Kong.

Myers, R. H. (1985), 'Price reforms and property rights in Communist China since 1978', *Issues and Studies*, vol. 21, no. 10.

Parish, W. L., and Whyte, M. K. (1978), *Village and Family in Contemporary China*, University of Chicago Press, Chicago.

Shiga, S. (1969), 'Family property and the Law of Inheritance in traditional China', in D. C. Buxbaum, (ed.), *Chinese Family Law and Social Change in Historical and Comparative Perspective*, University of Washington Press, Seattle.

Stacey, J. (1983), *Patriarchy and Socialist Revolution in China*, University of California Press, Berkeley.

State Statistical Bureau (1983), *Sample Survey of Peasant Household Incomes and Expenditures* [in Chinese], Chinese Statistical Publishing House, Beijing.

Wolf, M. (1985), *Revolution Postponed: Women in Contemporary China*, Stanford University Press, Stanford.

Xin Ti Yu [New Sports Magazine] (no. 2, 1987) 'The state of student health', quoted in *Beijing Review*, 27 April 1987.

Zhang Xinxin and Sang Ye (1985 and 1986), 'Whirlpool' and 'Planning her family', in *Chinese Lives* (a collection of oral histories first published in Chinese), pp. 74–80 and pp. 130–2. English edition edited by W. J. F. Jenner, and D. Davin, (1988), Macmillan, London.

Zhang Youyu (1985), 'The National People's Congress Law Committee's Report on the Draft Inheritance Law of the PRC', quoted by the Beijing Domestic Broadcasting Service (Daily Report, 16 April 1985).

Changing gender relations in Zimbabwe: the case of individual family resettlement areas

Questions of land – access to it, its productivity, how people are organised on it – are crucial in Zimbabwe. The liberation war was fought in the first instance for the regaining of the peasantry's 'lost lands' (Ranger, 1985), and land issues are among the most important concerns of current debates and of policy-making. The resettlement programme, which aims to redistribute land mainly to rural producers in the overcrowded and impoverished Communal Areas, has been one of the most significant reforms undertaken by the independent state. What is still sometimes forgotten, however, is that most of the producers on the land today are 'farmer-housewives' often attached to male migrant 'worker-peasants'.[1] That is, most of the Communal Area peasantry today, as in colonial times, is female.

This chapter examines the experiences of women in several resettlement schemes in northeastern Zimbabwe and argues that, although the resettlement programme has in many ways benefited women, resettlement policies also continue to keep women the dependents of men. This is the case particularly because women are not granted land use-rights in the same manner as are men, who are viewed as 'household heads'. Land resettlement has partially reversed the feminisation of agriculture which developed in the Communal Areas. As in other realms and in other societies, there is a bias against women because issues are not explicitly formulated in gender terms.

Rural women in contemporary Zimbabwe are still among the most disadvantaged and oppressed sectors of the population. It should not be assumed, however, that rural women constitute a uniform analytical category, since rural as well as urban women are divided by class. Recent legislative changes[2] have meant that black Zimbabwean women now have more rights before the law (Kazembe, 1986; Jacobs and Howard, 1987); however, they are still not the equals of men in legal terms. In effect, black women, virtually regardless of their class positions, remain disadvantaged.[3] This inequality is both a historical legacy and an aspect of contemporary society.

Women's position in pre-colonial society

It is exceedingly difficult to discuss the situation of women in pre-colonial Shona (and Ndebele) societies,[4] given the ways in which our knowledge is distorted by the colonial period. Although there is much debate, mostly concerning the exact status of Shona women before the colonial occupation, and especially about the extent of their inequality *vis-à-vis* men (Milroy, 1982 and 1983; May, 1983; Mpofu, 1983; Makamure, 1984), nevertheless some general observations can be made.

Pre-colonial Shona society was strongly male-dominated, so that the authority of fathers and husbands remained absolute, and women were largely excluded from political authority. This domination was enacted through a patrilineal kinship system in which male elders controlled access to the means of production and to the labour of junior men and of women.

The economy of the Shona peoples in the nineteenth century was based on subsistence production and on plentiful supplies of land, the household being the main unit of production and of consumption. The chief was caretaker and dispenser of land use-rights, since no land was 'owned' as such. In agriculture and in domestic work there was a strict gender division of labour. Men did participate in agricultural tasks, especially ploughing and harvesting, but women did the bulk of tedious agricultural labour. Each adult male as household head had use-rights to a given piece of land, which could be subdivided to women as wives or as inherited widows. Each wife had her own plot on the family fields, on part of which she could produce a crop for her own use: groundnuts, for instance, were traditionally a 'woman's' crop. Women had rights to dispose of any produce from 'their' plots, and they also had control over granaries of staple foods. However, a woman also had obligations to feed the man, her children and herself and had to work on the husband's fields (Bourdillon, 1982, p. 69). The agricultural sphere has been seen by some writers (Holleman, 1952, p. 206 and p. 208; May, 1983, pp. 26–7) as an important source of power and influence for Shona women.

However, this influence operated in a context in which women's economically-based sources of power and social esteem were limited. Men had authority over land use and could convert any surplus into livestock and eventually into more wives, since polygyny was permitted and common for men who could afford it. Women could own cattle, but had no right to husbands' herds. They did not gain social esteem from their labour in agriculture as such, nor could they control the surplus from family fields. Within the household economy, women had responsibility for meeting needs for food but men had (and still have) the power to allocate resources. Women were (and remain) likely to lose access to their plots if widowed or divorced.

Bride-wealth (*lobola*) payments were a crucial underpinning of women's social position.[5] Bride-wealth was and is the basis of marriage and of its dissolution. At marriage, women moved to their husbands' villages and so had no kinship bond uniting them, while village men belonged to one 'blood'. A woman acquired social status or esteem through hard work and through bearing children, particularly sons; a barren Shona wife could be divorced. But a wife had no permanent authority over her children; if divorced, she would lose access to them as soon as they were old enough to manage without her care. Men had exclusive sexual rights over wives, but women had no such rights over husbands, and a women was enjoined never to refuse her husband's sexual demands (Goldin and Gelfand, 1975, p. 176). However, a Shona women did have a range of rights and was not totally subordinate: for instance, in principle she had rights to dispose of income from her own crops and from activities such as beer-brewing, handicrafts or midwifery,[6] rights to a satisfactory sexual relationship (Holleman, 1952, p. 214) and to have children, and rights to refuse remarriage upon widowhood. With settler colonialism, these limited rights were eroded.

Settler colonialism

White settlers began to expropriate land belonging to black Zimbabweans in the 1890s. Colonial agricultural history has been extensively documented elsewhere (see, for instance: Yudelman, 1964; Arrighi, 1970 and 1973; Palmer and Parsons, 1971; Weinrich, 1975; Palmer, 1977; Bush and Cliffe, 1984). It suffices here to note that once hopes of a second 'Rand' or South African-type 'development' based mainly on mining precious metals had declined, attention was focused on the development of capitalist agriculture in the hands of a white bourgeoisie. Land expropriation was the main means of solving European settlers' needs for land and for cheap labour; by 1902, three-quarters of African land had been expropriated. The land division was legally enforced by the Land Apportionment Act of 1930, which established exclusive European rights over half the total land. Hut taxes and, later, a poll tax were imposed, so that African men were forced into wage employment in mines, agriculture and in European households. Women were not in general incorporated into the proletariat,[7] and so they, along with children, elderly men and young men unable to find employment, were left behind in barren reserves.

Colonialism affected black women as members of an oppressed people, but the effects on them were quite different from those on African men. In the reserves, the colonial administration attempted to consolidate the customary or tribal tenure system – for instance, by emphasising the role of chiefs *v.* headmen in land allocation and by allowing Africans to continue to marry under customary procedures. The system created was, of course, not the same as the tribal system had been, but rather, was a distortion of it.

Women's status in the tribal system was often misinterpreted and further reduced by the system of customary law enacted. However one views women's pre-colonial situation, it is certainly the case that with colonialism, women's customary rights were diminished and their position reduced to one of legal minority. The majority of African women became unable to make contracts, to represent themselves in court or to marry without the consent of a male guardian. Customary procedures were codified and deemed 'Customary Law', so that practices which had some degree of flexibility and which were subject to community (and elders') opinion became more rigidly imposed. It may be that codification reduced the leeway that some women were able to enjoy. Although some colonial officials attempted to protect the position of African women as they saw it – for instance, outlawing forced marriage and child betrothal – women's position deteriorated. This deterioration probably occurred as much because of changes in men's position with capitalist development as because of the creation of Customary Law itself. Younger men able to engage in wage labour and to earn cash to pay for their own bride-wealths were for the first time able partially to escape from constraints imposed by the community and by their lineage elders, whereas previously neither women nor younger men were able to act independently (Chigwedere, 1982, p. 36). In particular, this meant that it became much easier for men to divorce wives, and that a woman had little recourse to the protection of the man's family (Pankhurst, 1986a). Many women today have realistic fears of being arbitrarily divorced or expelled by their husbands.

The situation in which African women are effectively legal minors continues today, in spite of the passage of the Legal Age of Majority Act (LAMA) of 1983. This Act, which gives women and men the right to vote at age eighteen, has been subject to different interpretations both by sociologists and in the courts (Kazembe, 1986, p. 390; Jacobs and Howard, 1987, pp. 38–44).[8] However, the LAMA has not freed African women from the constraints of legal minority in any straightforward way (Mpofu, 1983, p. 10; Ranger, 1987, p. 17). Even though the recent Matrimonial Causes Act (1985) concerning divorce, and the Succession Bill (1986) concerning widows' rights of inheritance, do stand to benefit women, it is unlikely that they will have great effect in the rural areas (May, 1983; Kazembe, 1986, p. 395; Pankhurst, 1986b, p. 48).

Given women's legal status and the lack of employment opportunities for them in towns – even domestic work was monopolised by men – they became (and yet again, remain) largely encapsulated in the Reserves, later known as Tribal Trust Lands, and now as Communal Areas. In 1969, approximately sixty-three per cent of the population lived in Communal Areas (Passmore, 1972, p. 1); an estimate made in 1962 suggested that eighty-two per cent of the population in Communal Areas were women and children under fourteen (Folbre, 1983, p. 23).

In many areas, women became the main farmers when large numbers of able-bodied men worked elsewhere, sending home remittances when they chose to. Subsistence agriculture became 'feminised' both as a result of male migration and because of the enforced change from shifting cultivation to sedentary agriculture. Changes in the traditional gender division of labour operated so as to increase women's share of work. For instance, the establishment of permanent arable and grazing areas meant that men's work of clearing land was lessened, and male absence meant that women assumed tasks such as ploughing. The poor land in the Reserves meant in most cases that little surplus could be grown for cash. Thus rural wives' dependence upon remittances from husbands increased and male prestige was enhanced. Men's contribution to agriculture came to be, increasingly, to earn cash (Pankhurst, 1986b, p.11). It would seem, then, that rather than the Communal Areas subsidising capitalist accumulation on mines and plantations by obviating the need to pay a family wage – as argued by Wolpe (1972) – instead, people in the Communal Areas became dependent upon wage remittances in order to subsist. This dependence upon remittances is now well-documented for Zimbabwe (Bush and Cliffe, 1984; Harris and Weiner, 1986; Leys, 1986; Bush, Cliffe and Jansen, 1986; Pankhurst, 1986b). The Communal Areas are not 'tribal' in spite of the use of non-capitalist forms, but have been incorporated into capitalist production.

As farming became a less important activity and one subordinate to the main business of wage-earning, it also became feminised in the sense that women took on the burden of work. It seems to have become the norm in the Reserves that women performed most agricultural labour (Weinrich, 1975; Muchena, 1982, pp. 30–1; Callear, 1981, p. 22; Zimbabwe Women's Bureau, 1981). However, this should not be taken to mean that women gained overall control of agricultural production. Despite feminisation of the workload, men retained rights to make decisions about their land, even about issues such as the type of crops to plant, and the amounts to sow, as well as nearly all other major household decisions. Such factors vary among households, of course, so that in some, women were able to gain control to match their competence as farmers. Callear (1982), for instance, found in Wedza Communal Area that women were highly involved in decision-making when their husbands were engaged in migrant labour. But other accounts disagree with this evidence and hold that in many, and probably most, cases women risked being beaten or divorced if they took decisions about their husbands' land on their own authority, even in cases of the husband's prolonged absence (Mubi *et al.*, 1983; Pankhurst, 1986b; Pankhurst and Jacobs, 1988).

In some areas, however, agriculture remained a 'masculine'

concern for some time, at least in the sense that it was seen as important and valued, although it is not known what the extent of male agricultural activity was in such circumstances. At the beginning of the colonial era, male Shona peasants responded to the opportunities provided by the new European market by an expansion of cash-cropping: African agriculture had to be actively *suppressed* both by expropriation of the best land and by a variety of discriminatory measures.[9] Ranger documents the continued survival of African agriculture and of the 'peasant option' in most areas into the 1930s; in some districts, such as Makoni, which is near the area of this study, peasant agriculture underwent a revival in the late 1930s (Ranger, 1985, pp. 58 and 78). And Folbre, quoting R. W. Johnson, notes that foreign workers from Malawi, Zambia and Mozambique have long comprised a large proportion of the wage labour force in Zimbabwe (Folbre, 1987, p. 17).[10] It seems that, in areas where for ecological and political reasons agriculture remained viable, male Zimbabwean peasants may have chosen not to migrate.

In any case, choice of the 'peasant option' became more and more constrained as the quality of land deteriorated and as official intervention in African agriculture grew. Expropriation of African territory and racial reservation of land caused overcrowding and soil erosion in the Reserves. Erosion was blamed on poor African farming methods; official concern over conservation grew during the 1930s and continued thereafter, at times reaching almost hysterical proportions (Beinart, 1984; Ranger, 1985; Phiminster, 1986). Official schemes to maximise production and to train Africans in 'proper' techniques were launched, and farmers – including some women – who successfully completed the scheme after three years, were issued with 'Master Farmer' certificates. Master Farmers were better off than other peasants, but were never able to grow into a consolidated *kulak* stratum.

Other attempts were made to allow for the development of layers of middle and wealthier peasants. The system of 'tribal' tenure in the Reserves and their general impoverishment meant that such development could more easily occur outside them, and Native Purchase Areas (later African Purchase Areas and now Small Scale Commercial Farms) were set up on about eight per cent of land. In these, male peasants could obtain title deeds. However, the potential emergence of an African petty bourgeoisie was greatly feared by white settlers, so its development was contained within well-defined limits. Lack of credit helped to hold back the development of a *kulak* class.

The one major attempt to undermine the migrant labour system and to implement capitalist reforms was the 1951 Native Land Husbandry Act. In the Reserves (or Tribal Trust Lands, now Communal Areas), chiefly allocation of land was to be ended and individual male cultivators were to be given land titles and rights to buy land. These measures encouraged class polarisation – the only way to designate landowners entailed designating the landless – and women especially were deprived of access to the means of subsistence (Bush and Cliffe, 1982, p. 5). Compulsion in the use of approved farming methods was stepped up: this, and the erosion of land rights, engendered opposition, and attempts to implement the Act were abandoned in 1962 (Callear, 1982).

The victory of the Rhodesian Front represented the defence of white settler interests against the Todd government's attempts at multiracialism. The 1967 Tribal Trust Land Act and then the 1969 Land Tenure Act further reinforced the tribal tenure system of the Reserves and the migrant labour system dependent upon it. Land remained racially divided. Whites were allotted 46·9 per cent and 133 million hectares, while blacks were allocated 48·6 per cent on a communal basis in 165 Tribal Trust Lands and 4·5 per cent in African Purchase Areas (Stoneman (ed.), 1981, p. 132).

Land resettlement

The ecological, economic and political situation the government faced at independence made land reform a priority. The land resettlement programme is one of the most visible manifestations to date of the pledge made by the liberation movement, and then by the new government, to restructure Zimbabwean society. Aside from this redistribution of land, the main change occurring in Zimbabwean agriculture is that some large-scale farm land is passing from the hands of white to black commercial farmers: Moyo estimated in 1986 that some 300 Africans of a total of 4,400 commercial farmers owned large-scale estates (Moyo, 1986, p. 188). However, this racial reform does not signal any change in capitalist production relations *per se*.

Government plans and intentions for land resettlement are set out in a series of policy statements. In *Growth with Equity*, paragraph 22 states the overall aims for agriculture: a fair distribution of land, reduction in poverty levels, increases in productivity of land and labour, and development of human resources (Government of Zimbabwe, 1981). Six models of resettlement have been put forward, of which the most significant politically and in terms of numbers of people resettled is Model A, a scheme of individual family farming.[11]

In this model, land is redistributed in five-hectare or twelve-acre plots, with variable grazing rights and with small plots for houses and gardens. Landholding is based upon a series of permits potentially retractable by government. The permits are held by the 'household head', usually deemed to be the male spouse both by government and by popular opinion, male and female. Settlers should be aged twenty-two to fifty-five and should be married (or widowed) with dependents. Unless 'widowed' (the term used in Shona also applies to divorcees), women are normally unable to settle in their own right because they are not household heads. Settlers are not permitted to hold any formal sector employment, must live on the land, and are meant to relinquish any rights they hold to land in the Communal Areas from which they come.

Model A Resettlement Areas are at present independent of neighbouring District and Rural Council structures of local government, although there exist plans for their incorporation in future. They are administered by Resettlement Officers who hold a good deal of administrative and quasi-judicial power.

The land resettlement programme has been a large and rapidly conducted enterprise (Kinsey, 1982), but it has not been able to meet the ambitious official targets set. The Transitional National Development Plan of 1982/3 – 1984/5 set the number of families to be resettled at 162,000 by the end of 1984; however, by December 1984, 34,000 families had been resettled (AGRITEX, 1985, p. 15). A year later, approximately 38,000 families had been resettled, 35,000 being on Model A schemes (Hanlon, 1986, p. 8). Even if the high targets mentioned were to be met, however, this would not greatly alleviate the massive need for land in the Communal Areas.

The programme has suffered from various types of limitations. One is the speed with which 'white' commercial farmland can be and has been acquired. The main constraint has been the Lancaster

House Agreement, under which land must be purchased on a 'willing-buyer/willing-seller' basis: this clause has been interpreted to mean that only land voluntarily offered or abandoned could be acquired. This interpretation has probably slowed the pace of resettlement and may have contributed to the quality of land acquired, most of this being in the more arid ecological regions (Natural Regions III and IV) (Weiner *et al*, 1985, pp. 12–13). By the end of 1984, the government had acquired land amounting to over fifteen per cent of commercial farmland (ZANU, 1985, p. 2). Model A individual family resettlement has been favoured but the programme, as a whole, was affected by severe budget cuts during the financial years 1982/3 and 1983/4. These occurred partly because of external pressures (Green and Kadhani, 1986; Davies and Sanders, 1987) and partly because of internal political conflicts (Hanlon, 1986; Bratton, 1987, pp. 187–90). However, in 1985–6, resettlement received funding again and a target of 15,000 resettlement families was set (Cliffe, 1986, p. 13). Annual targets for the next two years were set higher, to reach 35,000 per year after 1987/8 (Hanlon, 1986, p.10). While it has various limitations, the land reform programme does signal important changes in the relations of production and reproduction of labour in the countryside.

One such change is an effect of the stipulation preventing migrant labour, mentioned above. This aims to establish a stratum of permanently-settled peasants and to encourage 'family reunification'. This stipulation has important implications for the economic standing of settler households as well as for gender relations. It means, first, that the main source of wage remittances – husbands' wage labour – is no longer permitted on any regular basis. Second, in attempting to end (albeit on a limited scale) a system which divides families geographically and socially, it has also established a situation in which agricultural work is again becoming more 'masculinised'. It should also be remembered that the aspect of 'permanence' mentioned here applies only to those settlers considered household heads. Married women, in resettlements as elsewhere, always stand at risk of divorce, be this upon traditional grounds[12] or at the arbitrary whim of the husband. Aside from the destitution and the loss of custody over children which, for women, frequently attend divorce (May, 1983; Mpofu, 1983), resettled women also lose rights to resettlement land when divorced.

A clear aim of resettlement is to create a group of permanently-settled cultivator household heads and their families and therefore to begin to reverse the trend which occurred with colonialism, but what 'class' positions[13] these settlers may attain through land reform is less clear. It is useful to separate two dimensions of class differentiation, one being background prior to resettlement and the other, processes of differentiation that occur within resettlements.

Class differentiation: social background and current processes

It is true that the pre-independence situation in Zimbabwe was one in which the peasantry was relatively homogeneous, since the white settler administration had set itself against the development of any black bourgeoisie, rural or urban, and with the exception of the Native Land Husbandry Act, pursued policies to undercut any such possible development. However, some differentiation nonetheless occurred. For instance, African Purchase Area farmers (now, Small Scale Commercial Farmers) do constitute a rural petty bourgeoisie or (in some cases) a small bourgeois stratum, owning on average 200 – 250 acres of land (Cheater, 1985) and hiring labour or else using that of wives in polygynous marriages. These farmers exist alongside rural businessmen (and a few businesswomen) and a small 'white collar' grouping, mainly of school teachers and district or regional officials. Within the smallholding worker-peasantry, there also exists differentiation. Several studies undertaken since independence in different areas of the country are in broad agreement about the main lines of class division within this grouping (Bush and Cliffe, 1982; Bush *et al.*, 1986; Leys, 1986; Pankhurst, 1986b; Harris and Weiner, 1986). All identified either three or four subdivisions, with households having access to regular wage remittances generally being the best off. In the more fertile agricultural areas, households which are agriculturally self-sufficient also ranked as well-off. People who have achieved Master Farmer status tend to fall into this category: on average they employ some labour and cultivate twelve to fifteen acres (Mukora, 1983). In all regions, the most impoverished groups include widows and divorcees with no male present; they have little or no access to remittances and tend to lack agricultural inputs and sufficient labour.

Differentiation does exist, then, within Zimbabwean Communal Areas, even if for historical reasons it has not become as extreme as in many societies. Resettlement policy aims both to distribute land to the land-hungry and to establish a stratum of rural petty-commodity producers or small-scale capitalist farmers who can viably farm the twelve-acre plots. It would not be surprising, then, to find some acceleration of the process of class differentiation: indeed, signs of it are appearing. The following data come from a survey conducted on two resettlement schemes; the sample population consisted of 100 married women, sixty-six married men and forty-one widows/female household heads.

Settlers are differentiated both in 'social' (for example, religious, educational, national) terms – of which more later – and in class terms. Most settlers are from Communal Areas. Nationally, the figure for people resettled from Communal Areas is slightly over sixty per cent of total resettlement (Moyo, 1986; Geza, 1986); in this sample, sixty-eight per cent of settlers had previously lived in a Communal Area, most of these being nearby the Resettlement Area. Slightly under thirteen per cent were previously commercial farm labourers. Approximately fourteen per cent lived previously in townships or mines, with the rest of the sample living either in 'keeps' (so-called protected villages), on Small Scale Commercial Farms or else outside of the country.

Another feature of this sample population is that under twenty per cent[14] of households studied had previously been split through male migration to jobs in urban areas and in mines, or abroad. A small group of men were employed in wage labour within the Communal Areas themselves, and so lived permanently at home. The Zimbabwe Energy Accounting Project also found that in the more favoured agro-ecological regions – in two of which this study was conducted – rates of migrant labour were lower than in the rest of the country (Harris and Weiner, 1986, p. 42).

Preliminary findings from the Central Statistical Office allow some comparison between the general population of the communal Areas and this sample in terms of previous holdings of land and of cattle ownership.[15] In the Communal Areas of Mashonaland East, 10·6 per cent of the population is landless, with another eighteen per cent having less than two acres (Central Statistical Office, 1985, p. 12). A far higher proportion of this sample, twenty-three per cent, were landless, with another thirty-one per cent holding less than two acres. The overall average landholding figure prior to resettlement was 4·1 acres, slightly less than the 4·5-acre average in Mashonaland East and neighbouring Manicaland Province (Central Statistical Office, 1984, p. 12; and 1985, p. 12). This may partly reflect that some settlers depended mainly on other sources of income for their livelihoods and partly that priority is given to the land-hungry. On the other hand, in some respects, people in this sample are better off than 'average' Communal Area dwellers. In Mashonaland East, nearly fifty-five per cent of people have no cattle, with twenty-six per cent having between one and five head. In my study, approximately a third of people interviewed held no cattle, with thirty-seven per cent holding between one and five head.[16] Given that over sixty per cent of settlers also owned one or more ploughs, as well as other implements, this meant that well over half (fifty-six per cent) of the sample population could be considered to be at least 'self-sufficient' in ability to plough. This finding is consistent with the idea that an important aim of Model A resettlement is to establish a stratum of petty bourgeois or small capitalist farmers.

People come to resettlement, then, with varying and unequal amounts and types of resources, including land and cattle which may continue to be held outside resettlements. Many do come without any livestock or agricultural equipment, and these tend to constitute the poorest groups after settlement. Interestingly, in this sample, although about forty per cent of 'widows'/female household heads interviewed were very impoverished, the others were spread across class groupings, with some being fairly well-to-do. According to their class positions, households (or, more accurately, household heads) may either hire out or hire in draught animals and implements: seven per cent of household heads hired out equipment whereas over thirty per cent had to hire in equipment. Households may either hire in labourers or hire out family labour (the latter often illicitly). Landholdings within resettlements should be strictly equal, since all households are allocated twelve-acre plots. However, share-cropping arrangements have already developed, so that settlers unable to farm all their land, at times, and illegally, hire out portions of their own land for others to cultivate. In this way, five per cent of settlers had access to up to thirty-seven acres of land, [17] while others cultivated less than half the land allotted.

The effect of the processes of class differentiation upon women is mediated by marriage. The rate of polygamy in this sample is quite high: that is, twenty-seven per cent of men have two or more wives. While this does not compare to the extremely high rates of polygamy found in some Purchase Areas (Weinrich, 1975, p. 162), where one strategy of accumulation is for men to exploit the labour of wives (Cheater, 1981, 1985), it is still high compared to the rate of ten per cent which Weinrich estimated to be average for rural Shona people (Weinrich, 1982, p. 142). The highish polygamy rate was accounted for by men classed as middle or better-off peasants; among 'poor' male peasants, the rate of polygamy was five per cent. Preliminary comparison of indices of 'class' and of 'wifely power' indicates that in this population such power is lowest among groups in the middle of the class range.[18] The wife's perceived power was usually higher in monogamous households.

Women's Clubs

As well as the survey data mentioned above, I collected data on women's opinions of resettlement from discussions held in Women's Club meetings.[19] Twenty-five discussion meetings were held, eighteen in Model A villages, one in a study centre in Harare, the capital (on a course for resettled women), and six on co-operatives. The meetings lasted from one to three hours and attendance varied from fifteen to eighty women; a total of approximately 650 –700 women were contacted in this manner.

Women's Clubs today constitute the main forums in which rural women can meet together without men to discuss their projects, problems and concerns.[20] Women's Clubs originally had the functions of teaching African women (Western-style) home-making skills and of helping them with income-generating projects. These functions remain now that the clubs fall under the jurisdiction of the Ministry for Community Development and Women's Affairs, although there is now more emphasis on women helping to educate each other. The Ministry has little to do with the everyday running of the clubs and, although in some areas the Women's Leagues of ZANU – the governing political party – are significant,[21] Women's Clubs are still the main arenas in which women can meet democratically and discuss their family and personal problems.

Even though this research was carried out in areas of very recent settlement, nearly all villages and co-operatives studied had established clubs, most meeting once or twice weekly. The main overt focus of activity in clubs is women's projects or other means for the group to generate income. Projects ranged from vegetable gardening (with land allocated to the group by the Resettlement Officer), to sewing and knitting, bakery and pottery-making. Many women wished to expand into more ambitious projects such as poultry-keeping. The clubs usually attempt to market goods produced, although in resettlements they often meet difficulties in transport and distribution which are even greater than those in the Communal Areas, as well as familiar problems of lack of credit and finance.

The rubric of 'learning how to live well with our husbands' legitimises the collective discussion of personal and family problems in the club settings. Such discussions are not always held openly, but most groups have created the traditional practice of appointing elder women to give advice to their juniors. The presence of elders appears to facilitate and to further legitimise discussion. In roughly one-third of meetings, women said explicitly that they would not discuss such matters openly with one another and that they could not always trust other women 'not to go to their husbands with tales'. The extent to which women discussed personal matters, then, varied a good deal: certainly some clubs appeared to provide networks in which women could express themselves freely. In any case, the continued existence of clubs alongside ZANU Women's Leagues, the frequency of their meetings and the importance with which projects are viewed, all attest to their continued strength, at least within these settlements.

The discussions at the meetings convened at my request generally concerned topics of immediate interest to the women involved: for example, club projects, income generation and problems faced because of the immediate situation of resettlement. However, more general questions and issues, such as those of women's needs and priorities, of migrant labour and of family unification, were also touched upon. The following sections draw both on data from the survey and from Women's Club meetings.

Gender division of labour and land

Division of labour

Processes of division of labour within households have an important bearing upon reproduction of labour, upon the development of class divisions and upon the creation of gender inequalities. With resettlement, a shift in the gender division of labour has occurred. Married men now take a more active role in field labour than most did while living in the Communal Areas, where, as noted, women bear the main burden of field-work. The process of resettlement entails clearing of land and building of huts before field-work can begin properly. Women in the Women's Club meetings said that this initial preparatory work 'should be men's', although about sixty-two per cent of married settlers interviewed said that in fact the work of clearing was shared.

The change in the division of labour is particularly evident with regard to ploughing. For instance, no one reported that women ploughed by themselves; this would have been common in Communal Areas. Nearly seventy per cent of women surveyed said that they and their husbands ploughed together, and sixteen per cent said that the men ploughed alone. The great majority of women attending meetings also said that men ploughed or that men and women ploughed together. This does not seem to be a situation in which men are mainly responsible for the tasks customarily seen as theirs; in fact, most field-work seems to be shared between the sexes.[22] As an indication: between eighty-five and ninety per cent of married settlers interviewed said that both husband and wife/wives were responsible for sowing, weeding and harvesting of crops. This does represent a change from the situation in the Communal Areas, where the latter tasks fall primarily to women. Men do not commonly assist with domestic duties in Resettlement Areas, but women in the Women's Club meetings held that husbands assisted with housework and child care a good deal more often than in their previous situations. Although no man admitted to helping his spouse/s with housekeeping, cooking, or bathing children, three per cent of married women reported that 'both husband and wife' performed these tasks; two per cent of both sexes said that men sometimes fed children. These figures should probably be interpreted to mean that men sometimes help out with these tasks when the wife is ill or otherwise occupied, rather than that men do domestic work and child care on any regular basis. Tasks such as fetching firewood and playing with children appeared to be more socially acceptable for men, with about three per cent of settlers reporting that men had main responsibility for these, and forty-one per cent (in both cases) reporting that spouses shared them. The fact that even a very small proportion of men do participate in housework is significant, given the stigma that attaches to men performing 'women's' tasks. Women commonly said, 'in twelve acres [that is, resettlement], we work together here as a unity'. However, this phrase should not be taken too literally. It is clear that women's burden of work is still heavier than men's, given that the sharing mentioned takes place mainly in field-work and only occasionally in domestic labour. Nevertheless, women's relative burden of agricultural labour has been, for the most part, lightened, and so women experience this as betterment of their position.

Decision-making, land and income for women

The fact that women and men now commonly work together more does not automatically imply that women have control over agricultural production. As has been pointed out, married women in Zimbabwe in most walks of life, who make decisions autonomously, risk not only antagonising their husbands but also being beaten or even divorced. However, some – although by no means all or most – women whose husbands were long-term migrant labourers previously, probably did have a measure of autonomy over everyday decision-making. Indeed, some women interviewed in a national survey shortly after independence preferred a migrant labour system because of the autonomy it afforded them (Muchena, 1982, p. 38). It is very difficult to make comparisons between Resettlement Areas and Communal Areas on this point (and on many others), given the lack of available research. What information is available (Callear, 1981; Muchena, 1982; Mubi *et al.*, 1983; Pankhurst, 1986a) is somewhat contradictory but tends to indicate that this is an exceptional situation for women in Communal Areas, and that husbands continue to make most major decisions concerning agriculture and other spheres.

Resettlement has not changed women's position of structural dependence upon men. For instance, where women hold land, then this is because it has been allocated to them by their husbands. In this sample, thirty-seven per cent of married women had been allocated land. The largest holding was four acres, and the average among those with land was 1·6 acres. The crop most commonly planted was the traditional groundnuts, with finger millet, sunflowers, sorghum and soya beans being poor seconds.

Again, because of lack of proper data for the Communal Areas, it is impossible to determine whether this extent of landholding represents a gain, a loss or little change. Certainly in some Communal Areas, it is reported that women hold no land at all (Pankhurst, 1985), but it is likely that this is not the case in other areas. Since the general situation in Zimbabwe concerning land tenure is now very chaotic and uneven as a result of the war and of the preceding years of Rhodesian intervention, the situation concerning women's land rights is likely to be similarly variable. My impression, however – and it can be little more than that – is that the extent of women's landholding and cropping is no less than, and possibly more than, that in nearby Communal Areas.

Many women, in the meetings as well as in the survey, expressed the wish to have access to their *own* sources of income, as well as their own land, held independently of husbands. In both rural and urban Zimbabwe, women's access to most sources of income is at best extremely limited. Bujra (1978) has pointed out that the sphere of petty commodity production is one which may offer possibilities for women seeking independent incomes, and indeed this factor accounts for the popularity in Zimbabwe of Women's Club projects. In resettlements, as in Communal Areas, without direct access to land or to produce or crops, possibilities of petty commodity production for women are very much curtailed. In resettlements, marketing of any goods for most settlers is made difficult by poor transport and by the isolated position of many villages in what are large tracts of ex-commercial farmland. So resettled women, like women elsewhere, need cash in general and, particularly, independent sources of cash. They have little access to this vital resource for a variety of reasons, some being specific to resettlements (lack of transport, banning of migrant labour) and one being general throughout Zimbabwe. This general problem is that men are likely to appropriate the proceeds of labour of household members as their own, including the proceeds of their wives' independent activities (May, 1983; Mpofu, 1983; Pankhurst and Jacobs, 1988). Given the newness and limited nature of women's projects so far, resettled women are likely to have access to adequate amounts of cash only if their households have been successful in producing and marketing cash crops[23] and their husbands are willing to redistribute some of the proceeds to them; or, much more rarely, if they have access to other sources of cash, most or part of which the man does not appropriate.

If resettled women work with men 'as a unity', then the unit is still a male-dominated one. Having said this, however, it remains the case that settlers both in Women's Clubs and survey settings held that women's influence in decision-making has increased with resettlement. A large majority of people – eighty-eight per cent of men and sixty-five per cent of women – said that both husband and wife take decisions over crops, including which crops to plant, crop siting and crop rotation. Concerning general decisions on budgeting, fifty-seven per cent of women and forty-eight per cent of men said that husband and wife decide together. Nine per cent of women and twenty-four per cent of men said that women took such decisions alone. These responses should not be taken to mean that women are now equal to men; however, it may be that, within what is basically a patriarchal unit, women's influence is increasing.

Community, kin and personal networks

Prior to resettlement, most settlers lived in kraals in the Communal Areas, in townships, in wartime 'keeps' or else in compounds as agricultural workers. The formation of resettlement villages entails a new type of living arrangement for Zimbabweans, since customarily households are widely spaced-out rather than organised in villages. This means that most settlers live in closer proximity to others than they have been used to. Some feel resentment at this, and this sentiment is exacerbated because people must live, in the main, with unfamiliar neighbours who come from many different parts of the country. Difficulty in getting on with people was often expressed as being because of differences between the customs of different regions. Another consequence of the mixing of people from different areas concerns the ancestral spirits: some settlers felt there to be confusion with regard to people not living in their own ancestral lands – the war, after all, being fought for these lands – and this was thought to be displeasing to the spirits.

However, meetings of different sorts, concerning building, farming, government instructions, ZANU as well as Women's Club meetings, do take place regularly so settlers do have opportunities for contact with one another. Indeed, settlers sometimes complained that meetings took them away from work. Many people have formed friendships within their new villages, although men form these more frequently and also report that they have more friends. For women, an institutionalised pattern of 'best' friendship seems to be important in these resettlements; that is, women tend to have one female 'best friend' who is an important contact outside the home.

Resettled women report that they do help one another in times of illness and trouble. I observed this to be the case, and the survey results reinforce this impression. But I also had the impression that there often exists a lack of informal networks of solidarity for women beyond the individual friendships they form. Such networks are particularly important for widows and divorcees, who may be isolated and may lack access to labour. Depending upon whether they develop into bureaucratised structures, Women's Clubs may offer the possibility of consolidating women's networks of communication in newly-formed villages.

In general, resettled people do not now live in extended three-generation family structures. Couples, or polygamous families, do not always settle alone; about half of settler households included dependents outside the nuclear family. However, these consisted most commmonly of other relatives' children and of siblings, cousins and in-laws of the same generation. About twelve per cent of households contained relatives of the parents' generation. Although some settlers did report missing the support of the extended family, especially in times of illness and of labour shortage, most were greatly relieved to be freed of it. Men were most in favour of the nuclear family, with seventy per cent considering it the best unit in which to live, but sixty per cent of married women also held this view. Widows were most likely to miss the extended family, but even among them well under half – thirty-seven per cent – expressed such a sentiment. These responses are remarkable, especially given the Shona emphasis on politeness and a tendency not to disagree in public. Both men and women frequently made comments such as 'you may end up hating each other if you stay in the extended family'. Although some resented the drain on resources which the extended family can entail, a much stronger reason for its unpopularity was the perceived interference of the older generation in what are now seen to be individual or nuclear family matters. It is likely that men and women have somewhat different reasons for their views; for instance, men are likely to resent interference in their freedom to spend money as they like or in their dealings with wives, while women are likely to resent the authority of mothers-in-law. Nevertheless, the sexes converge in their dislike of what is seen as an oppressive structure and in a growth in feelings of individuality.

Women's needs

Women's Club meetings, as mentioned, provide forums in which women can discuss their specific needs as women, as well as issues such as general problems in resettlement. I have divided the issues discussed into 'the material' and 'the personal', although in practice they overlap. Here, reference to recent debates between First and Third World feminists about the nature of feminism and stances concerning issues of race/ethnicity and class is relevant (cf., for instance, Hooks, 1981; Anthias and Yuval-Davies, 1983; Roberts, 1984; Brittain and Maynard, 1985; Barrett and McIntosh, 1985; Amos and Parmar, 1986; Ramazanoglu *et al.*, 1986; Bhavani and Coulson, 1986). Some Third World/black feminists have held that, for Third world or minority women, questions of sexuality and/or family oppression are very much secondary to other, non-gender forms of oppression and to basic material needs. Some First World feminists, on the other hand, have at times considered issues of sexuality to be paramount for all women, not always with due regard to difference of social, and especially ethnic, circumstances. One must be careful not to polarise positions too much: Third World feminists have taken up questions of family structure and of sexuality, and Western feminists are not all insensitive to questions of race and imperialism. Nevertheless, some division between positions still exists.

Some of the difficulty encountered in this debate lies in the conceptualisation of economic and of sexual and personal concerns as if they were separate. For most women, such concerns are, and are experienced as, intertwined: biological reproduction is both sexual and material, and relationships within households involve a series of economic and sexual transactions, although women are usually unequal partners within these. Certainly, for many women with whom I spoke, I found the problem of needs not to be amenable to conceptualisation in terms of any simple dichotomies. The divisions made below are not meant to reflect any simplistic dichotomy, but are made for ease of discussion.

Property, income and family unity

These needs have been touched upon earlier. Women in resettlement may desire land, but they have no more right to it than do women elsewhere in Zimbabwe. As noted, due to lack of comparative data, it cannot be determined whether the women in this sample hold more or less land than those in Communal Areas; though I feel that it is likely that the resettled women I interviewed have no less land than do women in neighbouring Communal Areas. However, most of the plots held are very small, and they hold this land only with their husbands' consent. Women typically produce crops to supplement the family diet rather than for cash sales. But even where land is held and cash crops are grown by women, marketing opportunities are extremely limited because of the lack of transport facilities and of shops and marketing centres. In addition, because of the lack of well-established Women's Club projects in new Resettlement Areas, other opportunities for income generation are limited.

This situation accounts for the strongly felt need for cash. Cash is necessary in order to purchase such items as soap, oil, salt, sugar and tea, which are now essentials. Payment of school fees also constitutes a major expense for some, and is a source of great anxiety for many women. In some families, women do make decisions over the allocation of income to various types of expenditure, either alone or together with husbands; but the norm remains that men make such decisions, and it is certainly their right to do so. So many resettled women, like others, struggle both with an absolute shortage of cash and with husbands' frequent failure to allocate them enough of what is available to buy household items and for child care. Compared with the situation in Communal Areas, this seems to have eased somewhat in resettlement, possibly due to generally greater affluence. Nevertheless, lack of allocation of cash by husbands remains a great problem.

Another factor specific to Model A resettlements is that migrant labour is prohibited. A minority of settlers still receive regular remittances, usually from sons. The stipulation concerning migrant labour is exceedingly unpopular and, reportedly, is sometimes officially ignored (Weiner, 1987). I was surprised to find, in Women's Club meetings, that some women felt so strongly about the need for migrant labour that they brought up the subject even in the two meetings which a Resettlement Officer attended. My surprise was in part because migrant labour is strictly illegal in Resettlement Areas, as settlers must be full-time farmers. It also had another basis: when I began research, I had supposed, following the above line of exchanges between Third and First World feminists, that rural Zimbabwean women would wish above all to have united families. Contrary to my expectations, about half of the women in meetings and a large minority in the sample called for migrant labour to be allowed. This desire to retain a migrant labour system does not necessarily signal any rejection of family unity *per se*, especially in this population, in which only about twenty per cent of men had been migrants in any case. Rather, it indicates the overriding importance of cash, which implies wage labour, in order to meet families' basic needs. Settler women were aware of the importance of remittances in the determination of their own class positions and those of their families. A minority of women preferred a migrant labour system because of the relative independence it afforded from male controls (at least of the immediate sort); however, others had strong preferences to live with their husbands. Regardless of their wishes in this regard, women's urgent need for cash generally outweighed any desire for family unity.

Rights of person

Family unity is, of course, a mixed blessing for women (and many men!) throughout the world, and this is no less the case for Zimbabwean women. For rural women, lack of such can mean loneliness, labour shortages and nearly complete dependence upon wage remittances. But family unity may also mean subordination to the husband, a lack of personal and sexual autonomy and subjection to violence. Violence against women is quite common in Zimbabwe, and if within marriage and not extreme – that is, not causing severe injury or disablement – is usually seen as 'normal'. Resettled women were quite aware of these contradictions and did raise issues to do with sexuality and with personal – literally, bodily – autonomy frequently and without prompting. Three topics of concern were: first, the need for safe, effective child-spacing methods which would not be *visible* to men; second, the right to refuse sex. Refusal of sex with husbands was one of the chief causes of wife-beating. Reasons given for refusal to have sexual relations were avoidance of pregnancy and expression of anger. Such refusal is an important, if individualised, site of resistance in a society in which the social means of resistance for women are very limited. It is also one proscribed strongly by African custom, particularly as interpreted by many elder women advisers and as violently enforced by some men. Thirdly, the associated problems of adultery/prostitution and of male drinking habits. It was reported that husbands' drunkenness and wives' enquiries about men's use of money and about extra-marital affairs often led to instances of violence.

These issues were seen as crucial, and not as ones of low priority or as imposed by Western feminist values. But it can also be said that women saw such issues as strongly related to and dependent upon the sphere of production. A commonly expressed feeling was, 'without food, there is no love'.

Resettlement and women's oppression

The concerns discussed above are, of course, not specific to Zimbabwean resettlement areas or to Zimbabwe: problems such as rights over sexuality and biological reproduction, violence towards women, and men's use of cash for personal, non-essential consumption, are common themes for women in many situations and societies. Although resettled women emphasised these issues in their discussions, the general consensus was that such problems have diminished with resettlement and that women's lot has improved.

Before discussing the changes which have occurred, it would be well to emphasise again how difficult it is to make comparisons between Resettlement and Communal Areas in the country, on the basis of what is at best patchy, and at worst non-existent, data. The generalisations made here about 'resettled women' cannot, of course, be extended to all resettled women, although findings from this study may be indicative of changes in other areas.

The improvement in women's position mentioned is, in fact, quite a contradictory one. On the one hand, women are better off in material terms, mainly because their households have more land to cultivate and because, it seems, husbands in general are redistributing no less to wives – of land, crops and cash – than they did previously. In general, resettled men are perceived and perceive themselves to work harder in agriculture, and they divert fewer resources away from the agricultural unit to personal consumption (Pankhurst and Jacobs, 1988). On the other hand, women are at least as dependent upon men as they were in the Communal Areas: they have no rights, as such, to land or other property except perhaps to their own cattle and some personal possessions, and so are entirely dependent upon their husbands' goodwill and upon their ability to please or at least not to antagonise them. However, in this they do not differ greatly from women in the Communal Areas, except that migrant labour being more common in Communal Areas, *some* women gain a measure of autonomy in agriculture during the absence of their husbands. Even though women's position of legal and economic dependence has not been altered, the balance of these factors means that they are better-off in terms of the burden of work and of living standards. In addition, and in spite of the present lack of services in most Resettlement Areas, the prospect of greater future material prosperity in 'twelve acres' appeals to the hopes and ambitions of most men and women.

At the same time, most resettled women say that they are better treated and more highly regarded by husbands in resettlement. Women see their husbands as moving nearer to an ideal of the 'good husband' because they work harder, spend less money on women outside the household, drink less and beat wives less often. This change is indeed an important one and one which improves the quality of women's lives in crucial respects. There are several possible explanations for the change in men's behaviour.

One set of factors could be temporary and contingent: beer halls are usually much farther away, and opportunities of adulterous relationships perhaps less (although, of course, men are still free, in practice, to take second and third wives under Customary Law). A more lasting factor may be that sharing of agricultural work has given men greater respect for women. The predominance of the nuclear over the extended family may have improved women's position within the family, at least within monogamous households with more modern views. In the absence of other relatives, and in the context of 'living among strangers', husband and wife may have had to draw closer together. It may also be the case (although this is difficult to discuss in concrete terms) that altered familistic ideology as well as 'Comrade Mugabe's ideas' have led to wives being perceived by husbands more as partners.

Perhaps most importantly, both men and women know that their behaviour is scrutinised by Resettlement Officers who hold a great deal of power, and that they stand to lose their plots if they are not 'on good behaviour'. (In practice, settlers are only removed for gross misbehaviour, but the *possibility* of removal and the insecurity of their tenure appear to be deterrent enough.) In this case, social and state control of a very direct kind has operated to the benefit of women.

The case of Zimbabwean land resettlement helps to highlight the complex determinants of women's social position, and the contradictory effects of one set of policies. Resettlement has altered and improved women's lives in many ways. At the same time, all of the structural components of their subordination remain, so that they are still the dependents of men. This situation accounts for the common thread in the demands they make. All these, be they to do with needs for cash, land, reproductive rights or freedom from male violence, have to do with personal autonomy – that is, with the crucial rights they do not yet have despite the gains made. Without these, it is difficult to speak of any substantial lessening of women's subordination, for the economic improvements written of depend upon husbands' actions and attitudes. Whether such rights for resettled women and other will be achieved in policy and in practice depends both upon the direction that state policies take and upon struggles which women collectively and individually wage on their own behalf.

Notes

1   First (1983) used these descriptive terms, and they have been used by Bush and Cliffe (1984), as well as by others. The terms refer to the fact that the categories of 'workers' and 'peasants', and 'farmers' and 'housewives' cannot be easily or usefully separated in the southern African labour reserve context.

2   In particular, the Legal Age of Majority Act (1983), the Matrimonial Causes Act (1985) and the Succession Bill (1986) give women limited rights such as the right to vote, (implicitly) the right to have custody over children, the possibility of no-fault divorce, and the right to inherit intestate property of husbands.

3 In the past, African women could become 'emancipated' if they could show that they had means of support and were of a 'civilised' lifestyle. However, obviously, only a few women met these criteria. Similarly, today, a tiny minority of black women with independent incomes and property holdings escape such inequality.

4 There are three main linguistic or 'tribal' groupings in Zimbabwe, of which the Shona-speaking groups constitute the largest, being eighty per cent of the population. The Ndebele (or Sindebele-speaking) peoples constitute the second largest group – fifteen per cent of the population – and live mainly in the west and southwest. The smaller Tonga grouping lives mainly around Lake Kariba in the north (Weinrich, 1982). This research refers only to Shona peoples.

5 Bride-wealth, or *lobola* as it is known throughout the region, entails a payment from the husband's family to the wife's, or to her guardian. The payment often takes place over a long period – that is, up to 20–25 years; today, it nearly always includes cattle and substantial sums of cash. Through the bride-wealth payment, the man and his lineage gain rights to the woman's work, to her sexuality and to her reproductive capacity. Divorce entails a return of *lobola*, the amount being determined according to who is the 'guilty' party.

6 This was known as her *mavoko* property, literally, 'of her hands'. Today, interpretations of Customary Law often mean that the husband lays claim to such property.

7 The first and predominant wage labour opportunities for Zimbabwean women were in prostitution, particularly on mining compounds and in towns (cf. van Onselen, 1980, pp. 174 – 82). Even today, wage labour and urban life bear, for women, an association with 'loose morality'. It is not clear why women were not, by and large, incorporated into 'female' sectors such as domestic work, as they were in neighbouring territories.

8 Some see the LAMA as amounting to a total emancipation of women from legal minority status (Kazembe, 1986) while others, including the author, see it as being of significant but limited impact (Mpofu, 1983; Ranger, 1987; Jacobs and Howard, 1987).

9 The Maize Control Act of 1931, for instance, established a two-tier pricing system for African and for European products, with European returns being subsidised while African returns were reduced. The burden of the economic slump of the 1930s and 1940s was effectively shifted to African agriculture, while Europeans were able to obtain state subsidies.

10 The foreign-born comprised more than half of the wage labour force until 1950 (Folbre, 1987, p. 17).

11 Six models of resettlement exist, including Model A (individual family farming). The others are: *Model B*: collective production co-operatives, in which land is state-owned and state-operated but communally-held and managed. Women can be full members of co-operatives in their own right. *Accelerated Resettlement* (in both Models A and B): an attempt to respond to urgent needs for land, especially on the part of rural squatters. Here, farmers are given land but no infrastructure is provided in the short term. *Model C*: individual family holdings attached to a core estate, run either co-operatively by the farmers themselves or as a state farm. At the moment three such schemes exist. *Model D*: the incorporation of nearby ranches as extended grazing areas for Communal Area farmers in the arid regions of the west and south (that is, mainly in Matabeleland). *Model F*: the incorporation, in 1982, of new criteria for some settlement, so that experienced and usually fairly well-off Master Farmers (that is, farmers who have obtained official certificates) could be resettled, in addition to the most needy.

12   In Shona Customary Law, just causes for divorce of women included: failure to keep house or to cook properly; failure to feed the family; repeated adultery; infertility; witchcraft; insubordination (including, for example, public disagreement with the husband, argumentative behaviour, rudeness to the husband's relatives); and refusal of sexual relations with the husband (Holleman, 1952; Goldin and Gelfand, 1975; Bourdillon, 1982; May, 1983).

13   I place the term 'class' in quotation marks here, since what I actually refer to when writing of differentiation within resettlements is of differences of strata among peasant cultivators. Some cultivators are 'poor' both in income terms and in the sense that they cannot plough self-sufficiently. At the other extreme, some settlers own many head of cattle, more than the minimum amount of equipment needed to plough, hire labour and cultivate more land than they have been allotted. Nevertheless, no fully-fledged proletarians and capitalists exist.

14   Among other women interviewed in Women's Club meetings (discussed later in the chapter), the proportion of ex-migrant labourer husbands was higher, being around a quarter.

15   Available CSO reports cover Mashonaland East Province, in which part of this study was conducted, and Manicaland Province, where some of the Women's Club meetings were conducted. Figures are not available at present for Mashonaland Central, where several meetings and half of the survey took place.

16   Some of these cattle could have been acquired after resettlement but this seems unlikely to be the general case, as most Agricultural Finance Corporation (a para-statal body) debts are for fertilizers, seeds and equipment rather than for animals.

17   This arrangement is strictly illegal, and so its incidence may be underreported.

18   The variable 'class' was computed from five other variables, including extent of ownership of cattle and ploughs, participation in wage labour or in hiring labour, and amount of land cultivated. The variable 'wifely power' was computed from twenty-eight questions covering a range of topics.

19   Between February and October 1984, on several schemes in Mashonaland East and Central, and in Manicaland Province.

20   Women's organisational advisers were first posted to villages in 1968, in order to encourage the formation of clubs and to encourage women

to help their families to rise 'above subsistence level' (Passmore, 1972, p. 156).

21 ZANU Women's Leagues have some functions parallel to those of Women's Clubs but also exist to promote the interests of ZANU among women, to interject women's concerns into ZANU policy and to organise women in more overtly 'political' ways. Soon after independence, there occurred moves for ZANU Women's Leagues to supersede Women's Clubs, but such moves appeared to have receded during the time of study.

22 The research of Henny Henson (Institute of Political Studies, University of Copenhagen) in Mufurudzi district also supports this view.

23 As many peasant households have been, contributing to the widely-reported post-drought boom in peasant agriculture and production during the 1984–86 period.

References

AGRITEX (1985), *Aspects of Resettlement*, Ministry of Agriculture, Harare.

Amos, V., and Parmar, P. (1986), 'Challenging imperial feminism', *Feminist Review*, no. 23.

Anthias, F., and Yuval-Davies, N. (1983), 'Contextualising feminism – gender, ethnic and class divisions', *Feminist Review*, no. 15.

Arrighi, G. (1970), 'Labour supplies in historical perspective', *Journal of Development Studies*, vol. 6, no. 3.

——(1973), 'The political economy of Rhodesia', in G. Arrighi and J. Saul, *Essays on the Political Economy of Africa*, Monthly Review Press, New York.

Barrett, M., and McIntosh, M. (1985), 'Ethnocentrism and socialist feminist theory', *Feminist Review*, no. 19.

Beinart, W. (1984), 'Soil erosion, conservationism and ideas about development: a southern African exploration', *Journal of Southern African Studies*, vol. 11, no. 1.

Bhavnani, K., and Coulson, M. (1986), 'Transforming socialist feminism: the challenge of racism', *Feminist Review*, no. 23.

Bourdillon, M. (1982), *The Shona Peoples*, Mambo, Gweru.

Bratton, M. (1987), 'The comrades and the countryside: the politics of agricultural policy in Zimbabwe', *World Politics*, vol. 39 no. 2.

Brittain, A., and Maynard, M. (1985), *Sexism, Racism and Oppression*, Blackwell, Oxford.

Bryan, B. (ed.) (1985), *The Heart of the Race: Black Women's Lives in Britain*, Virago, London.

Bujra, J. (1978), 'Female solidarity and the sexual division of labour', in P. Caplan and J. Bujra (eds), *Women United, Women Divided*, Tavistock, London.

Bush, R., and Cliffe, L. (1982), 'Labour migration and agrarian strategy in the transformation to socialism in Southern Africa: Zimbabwe as a case', paper presented to *Review of African Political Economy* Conference, Leeds.

——(1984), 'Land reform or transformation in Zimbabwe?', *Review of African Political Economy*, no. 29.

Bush, R., Cliffe, L., and Jansen, V. (1986), 'The crisis in the reproduction of migrant labour in Southern Africa', in P. Lawrence (ed.), *World Recession and the Food Crisis in Africa*, Currey, London.

Callear, D. (1981), 'Zimbabwe: some agricultural issues a year after independence', *Food Policy*, August.

——(1982), 'Small Farmer Maize Production in Wedza Communal Area, Zimbabwe', unpublished report for UNESCO.

Central Statistical Office (1984), *Zimbabwe National Household Survey: Report on Demographic Socio-Economic Survey: Communal Lands of Manicaland Province, 1983/84*, Harare.

——(1985), *Zimbabwe National Household Survey Capability Programme: Report on Demographic Socio-Economic Survey of the Communal Areas of Mashonaland East Province, 1983/84*, Harare.

Cheater, A. (1981), 'Women and their participation in commercial agricultural production', *Development and Change*, vol. 12, pp. 349–77.

——(1985), *Idioms of Accumulation*, Mambo, Gweru.

Chigwedere, A. (1982), *Lobola*, Books for Africa, Harare.

Clarke, D. G. (1977), *Agricultural and Plantation Workers in Rhodesia*, Mambo, Gwelo.

Cliffe, L. (1986), 'Prospects for agricultural transformation in Zimbabwe', unpublished report submitted to Government of Zimbabwe.

Davies, R., and Sanders, D. (1987), 'Stabilisation policies and the effects on child health in Zimbabwe', *Review of African Political Economy*, no. 38.

Duggan, W. R. (1980), 'The Native Land Husbandry Act and the African middle classes of Southern Rhodesia', *African Affairs*, no. 79.

First, R. (1983), *Black Gold: The Mozambiquan Miner*, Harvester, Brighton.

Folbre, N. (1983), 'Zimbabwe and the lineage of patriarchal capitalism', [mimeo.], Amhurst, Massachusetts.

——(1987), 'Patriarchal social formations in Zimbabwe', in S. Stichter and J. Parpart (eds), *African Women in the Household and Workplace*, Sage, New York.

Geza, S. (1986), 'The role of resettlement in social development in Zimbabwe', *Journal of Social Development in Africa*, vol. 1, no. 1.

Goldin, B., and Gelfand, M. (1975), *African Law and Custom in Rhodesia*, Juta, Cape Town.

Green, R. H., and Kadhani, X. (1986), 'Zimbabwe: transition to economic crises, 1981–83: retrospect and prospect', *World Development*, vol. 14, no. 8.

Government of Zimbabwe (1981), *Growth with Equity*, Salisbury.

Government of Zimbabwe, Ministry of Lands, Resettlement and Rural Development (1981), *Intensive Resettlement: Policies and Procedures*, Salisbury.

Government of Zimbabwe (1982), *Transitional National Development Plan: 1982/3–1984/5*, vol. I, Salisbury. *Ibid.* (1983), vol. II, Harare.

Government of Zimbabwe, Ministry of Manpower Planning and Development (1983), *National Manpower Survey*, vols. I–III, Harare.

Hanlon, J. (1986), 'Producer cooperatives and the government in Zimbabwe', [mimeo.], London.

Harris, T., and Weiner, D. (1986), 'Wage labor, environment and peasant agriculture in the labor reserves of Zimbabwe', [mimeo.], Worcester, Massachusetts.

Hobsbawm, E., and Ranger, T. O. (1983), *The Invention of Tradition*, Cambridge University Press, Cambridge.

Holleman, J. (1952), *Shona Customary Law*, Oxford University Press, Cape Town.

Hooks, B. (1981), *Ain't I a Women*, Pluto, London.

Jacobs, S. (1984), 'Women and land resettlement in Zimbabwe', *Review of African Political Economy*, no. 27/8.

Jacobs, S., and Howard, T. (1987), 'Women in Zimbabwe: stated policy and state action', in H. Afshar (ed.), *Women, State and Ideology*, Macmillan, London.

Kazembe, J. (1986), 'The woman issue', in I. Mandaza (ed.), *op. cit.*

Kinsey, B. (1982), 'Forever gained: resettlement and land policy in the context of national development in Zimbabwe', *Africa*, vol. 32, no. 3.

——(1983), 'Emerging policy issues in Zimbabwe's land resettlement programme', *Development Policy Review*, vol. 1, no. 2.

Leys, R. (1986), 'Drought and drought relief in Southern Zimbabwe', in P. Lawrence (ed.), *World Recession and the Food Crisis in Africa*, Currey, London.

Makamure, N. (1984), 'Women and revolution: the Women's Movement in Zimbabwe', *Journal of African Marxists*, no.6.

Mandaza, I. (ed.) (1986), *Zimbabwe: The Political Economy of Transition*, Codeseria, Dakar.

May, J. (1983), *Zimbabwean Women in Customary and Colonial Law*, Mambo, Gweru.

Milroy, R. (1982, 1983), *The Herald* (Salisbury), 31 October 1982 and 27 February 1983.

Moyo, S. (1986), 'The land question', in I. Mandaza (ed.), *op. cit.*.

Mpofu, J. (1983), 'Some observable sources of women's subordination in Zimbabwe', Centre for Applied Social Studies, University of Zimbabwe.

Mubi, M. *et al.* (1983), 'Women in agricultural projects in Zimbabwe: final report', AGRITEX, Harare.

Muchena, O. (1982), 'Report on the situation of women in Zimbabwe', [mimeo.], Ministry of Community Development and Women's Affairs, Harare.

Mukora, C. (1983), private correspondence, 8 March.

van Onselen, C. (1980), *Chibaro: Mine Labour in Southern Rhodesia: 1900–33*, Pluto, London.

Palmer, R., and Parsons, N. (eds) (1971), *The Roots of Rural Poverty in Central and Southern Africa*, Heinemann, London.

Palmer, R. H. (1977), *Land and Racial Domination in Rhodesia*, Heinemann, London.

Pankhurst, D. (1985), private correspondence, 20 February.

——(1986a), 'Women's control over resources: implications for development in Zimbabwe's communal lands', paper presented to *Review of African Political Economy* Conference, Liverpool.

——(1986b), 'Wives and husbands: rules and practice', [mimeo.], University of Liverpool.

Pankhurst, D., and Jacobs, S. (1988), 'Land tenure, gender relations and agricultural production: the case of Zimbabwe's peasantry', in J. Davison (ed.), *Women and Land Tenure in Africa*, Westview, Boulder.

Passmore, G. (1972), *The National Policy of Community Development in Rhodesia*, University of Rhodesia Press, Salisbury.

Phillips, A. (1987), *Divided Loyalties: Dilemmas of Sex and Class*, Virago, London.

Phiminster, I. (1986), 'Discourse and disciplines of historical context: conservationism and ideas about development in Southern Rhodesia: 1930–50', *Journal of Southern African Studies*, vol. 12, no. 2.

Ramazanoglu, C. *et al.* (1986), 'Feedback: feminism and racism', *Feminist Review*, no. 22.

Ranger, T. O. (1985), *Peasant Consciousness and Guerilla War in Zimbabwe*, Currey, London.

——(1987), 'Thirty-third review of the Zimbabwean press: 6 June–10 July 1987', [mimeo.], Charlbury.

Roberts, P. (1984), 'Feminism in Africa: feminism and Africa', *Review of African Political Economy*, no. 27/8.

Seidman, G. W. (1984), 'Women in Zimbabwe: post-independence struggles', *Feminist Studies*, vol. 10, no. 3.

Stoneman, C. (ed.) (1981), *Zimbabwe's Inheritance*, Macmillan, London.

Weiner, D., Moyo, S., Munslow, B., and O'Keefe, P. (1985), 'Land use and agricultural productivity in Zimbabwe', *Journal of Modern African Studies*, vol. 23, no. 2.

Weiner, D. (1987), private correspondence, 9 August.

——(1988), 'Land and agricultural development', in C. Stoneman (ed.), *Zimbabwe's Prospects*, Macmillan, London.

Weinrich, A. K. H. (1975), *African Farmers in Rhodesia*, Oxford University Press, Oxford.

——(1979), *Women and Racial Discrimination in Rhodesia*, UNESCO, Paris.

——(1982), *African Marriage in Zimbabwe*, Mambo, Gweru.

Wolpe, H. (1972), 'Capitalism and cheap labour in South Africa: from segregation to apartheid', *Economy and Society*, vol. 1, no. 4.

Yudelman, M. (1964), *Africans on the Land*, Harvard University Press, Cambridge, Massachusetts.

ZANU (1985), *Zimbabwe at Five Years of Independence*, ZANU Department of Information and Publicity, Harare.

——(1986), 'Comrade E. Zvobgo explains new divorce law', *Zimbabwe News*, vol. 17, no. 3.

Zimbabwe Women's Bureau (1981), 'Black women in Zimbabwe', Salisbury.

——(1982), 'We carry a heavy load: rural women in Zimbabwe speak out', Harare.

The limits to women's independent careers: gender in the formal and informal sectors in Nigeria

Women in Yoruba society in south-west Nigeria are customarily expected to earn an income of their own from which a substantial proportion of household expenses may be met. They typically aspire to do this through independent self-employment in the informal sector[1] (a 'career'). The problem they face is accumulating the necessary savings, skills and contacts.

This chapter examines how gender relations structure women's participation in the urban formal and informal sectors in southern Nigeria, shaping the extent to which women can achieve independent careers, in the context of the specific political economy of Nigeria. Particular attention is paid to how women's ability to use industrial wage employment as a springboard for profitable self-employment compares with that of men, drawing on a case study of workers in a textile plant. The chapter ends with a consideration of the prospects for women's independent careers in the context of economic crisis and structural adjustment in the 1980s.

Women in the economy of southern Nigeria

There was considerable variation between pre-colonial Nigerian societies in terms of size, specialisation and gender division of labour. But in all of them, the household was the primary productive unit within which women were responsible for both reproductive and productive labour. Within such households there was no absolute distinction between domestic and productive labour, but children, and wives newly married into the household, were most likely to be responsible for 'domestic' tasks, leaving older women with more managerial responsibilities and, in some

societies, more specialised income-generating activities. As all these
societies were primarily agricultural, the most important
productive work done by women was in agriculture (Perchonok,
1985; Afonja, 1981). Yoruba communities tended to be larger than
in other Nigerian societies, and in the large urban centres it was less
common for women to work on their husbands' farms and more
usual for them to engage in craft production or trade. For a small
minority of Yoruba women, this developed during the nineteenth
century into food wholesaling, and into forms of trade with a higher
rate of return such as gold or cloth trading.

The household responsibilities of women were widely defined to
include providing, as well as preparing, many of the most important
consumption goods of a household. This wide definition of
women's household responsibilities appears to have been
characteristic of many southern Nigerian societies and is illustrated
by women's important agricultural duties and their responsibility
for marketing agricultural surpluses. This tendency to define
women's domestic duties to include income generation is especially
characteristic of Yoruba society and is likely to be related to the
greater size of Yoruba settlements; residential patterns in which
farmers lived for a large proportion of the year in towns; and, in
particular, the development of a few large urban settlements such as
Ibadan and Abeokuta which provided a great range of production
and trading opportunities through which women could contribute
materially to a household (Aronson, 1971; Mabogunje, 1962, 1968;
Peel, 1983).

The pattern of settlement may have provided the necessary
opportunities for this particular conception of women's household
responsibilities to develop, but kinship and marriage patterns
provided the necessary impetus to income generation for individual
women. Yoruba kinship varies from one area to another but by
comparison with other patrilineal societies, bride-wealth tends to
be relatively low and the links retained by a woman with her own
family, relatively strong. The low bride-wealth increases the
possibilities of men contracting polygynous marriages. This in turn
has tended to reduce the stability of marriage (Caldwell, 1968;
Lloyd, 1968). The widespread expectation among Yoruba women
that their marriage will turn out to be either 'officially' or
'unofficially' a polygynous one, makes the achievement of an
independent source of income especially important, both to

safeguard her position within her husband's family or as the head of her own household unit, and to provide the material basis to establish a social position independent of her husband, which is necessary in a polygynous marriage.

The historical participation of women in productive labour in both rural and urban communities means that there is no 'tradition' in the south of Nigeria that women should be excluded from income-earning opportunities nor that they should seek these opportunities only within the household. The rate of women's labour force participation (as currently measured) is somewhat higher than for other sub-Saharan African countries. For instance, in 1980 the female labour force participation rate in Nigeria was reported to be 28·6 per cent, whereas in Kenya it was 23·8 per cent (World Bank, 1984, p. 69). The average rate for Africa in 1975 was reported to be 24·4 per cent (ILO/INSTRAW, 1985, p. 18). The majority of those women are working in agriculture or the informal sector, with a small but significant proportion in salary-earning employment, either in public sector services or industry. The factor that has primarily determined their access to a salaried income has been their access to education. As in many other countries, the access to education of girls has lagged behind that of boys and has served to exclude them from important new sources of employment. The income-generating opportunities open to women in the informal sector depend on access to supplies, markets and capital, an access which is mediated by gender relations. The access of women to an independent income is also crucially determined by the structure of the political economy and the dominant processes within it, particularly the relationship between the formal and the informal sectors. The manner in which the relationship between the formal and the informal sectors has been structured by the growth of the petroleum-dominated economy in Nigeria, and the impact of the economic crisis and international indebtedness on women's income-generating possibilities will be discussed below.

Women's construction of a 'career'

The concept of a career will be used to explain the relationships between income generation, reproduction and the obligations created by marriage and child-bearing which are central to the experience of Yoruba women. The sociological concept of a career has developed from the secularisation of Weber's concept of a 'vocation'. It is generally understood to apply to paid employment, structured by reference to the existence of a ladder of advancement and promotion, the criteria for which are understood by those working within a particular organisation or sector (Gerth and Wright Mills, 1967). It has been used for some time as a means of identifying the differences between the work experience of the middle and working classes in industrial societies (Beynon, 1973; Goldthorpe, 1969; Willis, 1976), and also, for example, to distinguish the work experience of female and male industrial workers in less developed countries (LDCs) (Humphrey, 1987).

This concept, with its implications of a systematic progression in a working life, moving up steps on a ladder, is potentially useful but needs to be modified in order to assist the analysis of Nigerian perceptions of possible advancement at work and, in particular, the work experience of Yoruba women. First, this is a society in which the objective of the majority of individuals, both men and women, is to establish themselves as owners of an independent business (Peace, 1979; Barnes, 1986). Their ability to do so depends on their access to sources of capital, to other inputs and to markets. This in turn depends on the establishment of a network of relatives, friends and acquaintances. Access to salaried employment can form an important part of this process. The concept of a career in this context cannot, therefore, be narrowly defined in terms of work experience in one sector of the economy or for one employer. It is necessary to include within it all the stages which are intended to lead to the establishment of a viable informal sector enterprise. Second, for both men and women, the ability to build up such networks is based on participation in ethnic and religious associations and the rituals of kinship. This in turn is dependent on the possession of material resources and the recognition obtained from being married, having children, the occupational achievements of those children, having grandchildren, and possibly taking a chieftaincy title (Eades, 1980; Henderson, 1972). Thus the concept of a career needs to be modified to include those elements of personal biography which cannot be directly classified as 'work' but are crucial to the achievement of successful income generation in the informal sector and also those stages of personal biography which help to determine an individual's ability to build up and manipulate the necessary kinship and friendship networks for this purpose.

A tentative model of the preferred career, in this wider sense, to which Yoruba women aspire can be constructed as follows: a woman is trained by her mother to trade; she marries, and her husband provides her with the initial capital to establish herself as a trader, in foodstuffs, for example. In the first years after her marriage, she has young children and domestic responsibilities within the household: cooking, child care and providing hospitality for her husband's relatives, which leave her with limited time for her own trade. However, she does trade and invest her profits and, as her children grow older, she is able to devote more time to her trade and to move into more lucrative types of trade requiring more capital, such as the trades in cloth and gold. She uses her money to assist the formal education of her children, especially that of her daughters for which her husband may be less willing to provide money than for the education of their sons. This helps the daughters to obtain qualifications for salaried occupations.

By the time she reaches the menopause or her daughters and daughters-in-law have begun to bear children, her husband marries again. The new young wife soon has children and is expected to assume the direct domestic responsibilities of child care and assisting in feeding the household, which leaves little time for income-earning activities. The household assistance provided by the second wife leaves the first wife time to concentrate on her trade. As a prosperous trader, she has the financial resources to become a substantial figure in her own right at the church or mosque. This provides her with a circle of friends and supporters, gives her social recognition in spite of her husband's absence and thus makes it possible for her to take the socially approved attitude of acceptance of his second marriage. As she has been able to ensure that her children received an education, they are likely to achieve success in formal sector careers, which increases her own social recognition. When they marry and have children, she is able to exercise considerable influence in her sons' households; and as her daughters have salaried occupations and, therefore, independent financial resources, they are able to provide for her when she is too old to work.

This ideal career, which is often assumed to be the actual experience of most Yoruba women, in fact depends on the class position of a woman's natal family and that of her husband. In agricultural communities, a woman is likely to be fully occupied working on her husband's farm, for which she will be compensated but will not obtain a guaranteed, regular income (Babalola and Dennis, 1988; van den Driesen, 1971; Afonja, 1984). If her husband or her own family is unable or unwilling to provide her with the initial capital, she may never be able to establish her own independent enterprise. She will thus possess very limited resources to invest in her children's, especially her daughters', education. As she gets older, her husband is likely to take a younger wife which releases her from many domestic responsibilities but, without capital, she is not in a position to take advantage of the extra time she now has at her disposal. Without an independent source of income, she is unable to establish an independent social position so that she remains dependent on the goodwill of her husband's family for her social recognition, with the additional problem of a new wife also competing for such recognition. As she has been unable to contribute significantly to the education of her children, they are unlikely to possess the resources to assist her. It is also likely to be difficult for such a women to maintain substantive links with her own family, which makes the possibility of going back to them problematic. This alternative model demonstrates the difficulties faced by a woman without an independent income as she becomes older. This is a society which respects age but expects a man or woman to accumulate the socially approved characteristics of the old: wealth, children and a network of kin and friends to support them (Barber, 1981; Lawuyi, 1988; Eades, 1980). The problem for a woman is dependence on husband or her own family in starting accumulation.

Access to salaried employment might enable women to overcome that handicap, a handicap which has increased as the process of incorporation of Nigeria into the world economy, and of capitalist penetration, has produced an increasing polarisation in what is loosely described as the informal sector. The requirements of initial set-up capital, and on-going resources of working capital, to establish and maintain a viable trade, service or production enterprise are continually increasing. Formal employment for a salary is perceived as a means of accumulating that capital. It may also be perceived as a source of a continual, reasonably secure, if low, income, over a long period of time; providing a cushion if an individual business is not sufficiently well established to generate a high enough, stable income. Such employment, in addition, is perceived as creating new skills, new contacts and access to potential suppliers and markets. In practice, the conventional women's occupations in the public sector, notably clerical work, teaching and nursing, do generate savings potential and offer some possibility of using the experience gained on the job to establish a private nursery, school or clinic; but entry to these occupations is based on educational qualifications which are not available to all women. Industrial employment, which does not usually require such high educational qualifications, is potentially a way by which other women may earn a salary, and use that salary as the basis of systematic income generation in the informal sector in the future.

Thus, the definition of women's reproductive responsibilities in Yoruba society creates a need for them to possess an independent source of income generation; and the expectations of a polygynous marriage make it desirable to use the ability to generate an income as the basis of a career which incorporates paid work, the fulfilment of marital obligations and the construction of an autonomous social position. The majority of Yoruba women aspire to do this by setting up their own businesses. In a situation in which the capital requirements of this are increasing, industrial employment is perceived as providing both an independent income and a source of capital accumulation.

The political economy of Nigeria

This section will focus on those elements of Nigerian political economy which are most relevant to understanding the limits on Nigerian women's ability to construct a career. These are the historical development of a particular type of peripheral economy; and the results of the rise of the 'petrol economy' and the expansion of the industrial sector. The impact of the present economic crisis and the Structural Adjustment Programme will be considered in a later section.

The economic relationship established with metropolitan societies, particularly Britain, throughout the pre-colonial, colonial and post-colonial periods, created in Nigeria a cash crop economy similar to that of other West African states but more diverse because of the size of the country and the variations within it of ecology and social structure (Hopkins, 1973; Crowder, 1968; Onimode, 1982). All these economies were marked by a growing commoditisation of agricultural production and the substitution of non-food cash crop production for food production. This led to growing disparities between food crop and cash crop regions in terms of income and investment (Watts, 1983). But as the taxes on cash crops have been spent on infrastructure and social projects in urban centres, the result has been growing disparities between rural and urban areas and an increasing rate of rural-urban migration (Onimode, 1982). The emphasis on urban social and infrastructural investment has over time increased the advantages of living in a city. The relative returns to urban, formal sector salary earnings have led to an overwhelming popular demand for an expansion in educational facilities to make possible the escape from peasant farming to such salaried employment. Educational facilities, especially in towns but also in rural areas, have expanded hugely since independence (Williams, 1970; van den Berghe and Nuttney, 1971). Thus the major social investment by government in rural areas in Nigeria has facilitated, even encouraged, the migration from the countryside and agriculture to the towns and to salaried employment.

The process by which Nigeria was incorporated into the world economy transformed the structure of agriculture; women were incorporated into this process as workers on family-owned farms. They were more likely to obtain returns in kind from food production, and the increasing returns to cash crop production were overwhelmingly retained by male farmers. As explained above, in pre-colonial Nigeria, especially in the large towns of Yoruba and Hausaland, there was considerable development of craft manufacture and trade. In Yoruba communities, women were important in particular areas of trade and craft production. The import of cheap manufactured cloth and household goods undermined the position of those engaged in the local craft manufacture and trade in such goods, an important proportion of whom were women.

In the economy of colonial and post-colonial Nigeria, this trading tradition became the foundation of an informal sector trading indigenous and imported goods to an increasing urban population and adopting new forms of craft manufacture (Hill, 1966; Hopkins, 1973; Gertzel, 1962). The potential importance of salaried employment as providing the basis for self-employment was established very early for men, and the combination of investment in educational qualifications and private entrepreneurship provided the foundations for the development of the Nigerian bourgeoisie, especially in Yorubaland.

Those women who lived in urban areas had new opportunities within this emerging informal sector if they were able to obtain access to capital, which was more difficult for them than for men, and to markets. Their access to salaried employment was determined by their more limited access to educational facilities (Awe, 1982; Dennis, 1987; Agheyisi, 1985).

The Nigerian economy is distinguished from other West African cash crop economies by the importance of the petroleum extraction sector since the 1970s (Pearson, 1970; Usman, 1979). This phenomenon served to intensify, in a very short period, developments which were inherent in the structure of the Nigerian economy as outlined above. First, the exploration of petroleum resources was carried out by multinational companies which paid their exploration fees and royalties to the Federal Government (Turner, 1976; Onimode, 1982; Freund, 1978). This concentration of proceeds from the sale of oil in the hands of the Federal Government increased greatly the existing disparity between the funds available for capital and 'development' projects to the Federal Government and to State and Local Governments. These capital resources were spent mainly on large capital projects such as the construction of Federal roads and on expanding educational provision at all levels (Onimode, 1982; Ogunsheye, 1982; National Planning Office, 1981). This type of expenditure was concentrated in urban areas, apart from the investment in large-scale irrigation projects, and thus tended to increase the previously mentioned disparity between the standard of living attainable in rural and urban areas. Also, the expansion of education at primary and, later, secondary level, rapidly increased the number of men and women who expect wage-earning employment which can only obtained in in towns, and thus increased the rate of rural-urban migration.

The period of the petrol economy saw a drastic movement in the terms of trade against agriculture and rural areas, which made more desperate the problem of generating an income from cash and food crops, particularly for women working in the agricultural economy as producers of food or workers on cash crop farms owned by men. The expansion of the educational sector and other areas of social expenditure created large numbers of public sector jobs to which women had access, to the extent that they had access to educational institutions in order to obtain the necessary qualifications. This, in turn, expanded the urban informal sector which catered to the needs of urban wage-earners.

One result of the growth of the Nigerian oil extraction sector in the 1970s was the expansion of Nigeria's industrial base. The size of Nigeria's population by comparison with that of other African countries means that Nigeria has potentially a large domestic market for manufactured goods. The expansion in Federal Government infrastructural and social expenditure, as a result of their receipt of oil revenues, led to an increase in the numbers of salary-earners, thereby increasing the actual market for manufactured consumer goods. In addition, the Nigerian Federal Government and the governments of the individual states pursued very active policies of industrialisation by offering generous incentives and concessions to prospective investors and by themselves establishing joint ventures with individual industrialists (Collins, 1979; Akeredolu-Ale, 1976). The industrial enterprises which have been established as a result of these inducements are mainly concentrated in a few large ports such as Lagos, Port Harcourt and Calabar, and large urban centres like Kano, Kaduna and Ibadan. They ranged from branches of multinational companies, such as Volkswagen and Coca Cola, operating in joint ventures with the Federal Government, and smaller foreign companies in partnership with State Governments, to small private foreign and Nigerian entrepreneurs making short runs of plastic goods or clothing. Although manufacturing industry provides only a small proportion of the Nigerian GDP, in the major urban centres in which factories have been established, it is an important source of wage employment.

The labour force employed in industry in Nigeria as a proportion of the total labour force, increased from ten per cent in 1960 to nineteen per cent in 1981 (World Bank, 1984, p. 69). The structure of ownership of Nigerian industry means that the nature of industrial employment also varies. A simple classification of differences in industrial employment would start from the evidence that in multinational firms, wages tend to be higher than for other forms of industrial enterprise; although there are also significant differences in wages and training opportunities between, for example, vehicle assembly plants and soft-drink bottling plants within the multinational sector. The available evidence suggests that women are concentrated in jobs defined as unskilled or seasonal in plants producing basic consumer goods. There does not appear to be a tendency for particular types of manufacturing to be dominated by female employment, as all types of industrial employment, apart from the most seasonal or insecure, in Nigeria are perceived as being desirable by male workers (Di Domenico, 1983; Dennis, 1984). The ability of women to use such industrial work as the basis of independent income generation depends on the wages and training offered, which in turn depends on the pattern of ownership, range of goods produced and the manner in which women are incorporated into the industrial labour force.

The development of the oil extraction sector and its effect on Nigerian government spending had important implications for the structure of the informal sector in Nigeria, revealing the heterogeneity of the sector and illustrating the looseness of the category 'informal sector' (Gerry, 1975; Bienefeld, 1975). The most profitable trading activity in Nigeria has been through obtaining government contracts, symbolised by the 'sole agent' who has a monopoly right to import a particular product and negotiate its price with the relevant government department. The most profitable sections of the informal sector merge into the activities of an emerging comprador bourgeoisie (Usman, 1984; Onimode, 1982). This type of activity requires political influence to obtain contracts and a particular relationship with the bureaucracy and government to establish agreement on prices and the various rates of return on contracts. Its development implies a polarisation of trade in the informal sector between large-scale and small-scale trading.

In Nigerian 'folklore', the characteristic place of women in the informal sector is as the wife of an influential man, preferably an army officer, using her access to influence to obtain contracts in the public sector; 'bottom power' (Women in Nigeria, 1984, pp. 104–6). This depicts Nigerian women as not only having access to an independent income but using this opportunity to subvert the structure of Nigerian society through influence and corruption. In fact, the majority of Nigerian women in the informal sector are engaged in petty trade (Sudarkasa, 1973; Trager, 1981), which became more difficult to enter as the inflation of the oil boom years raised the capital requirements and political influence became necessary in order to secure access to imported and locally produced consumer goods (Usman, 1984; Ihonvbere, 1985).

The post-independence Nigerian economy has exemplified a long-term trend towards the marginalisation of the agricultural sector. In both the industrial and informal sectors, particular patterns of ownership and concentration of capital have developed in which access to those with political power can be converted into economic resources. This serves to divide the experience of women in different classes. It has had particularly important negative implications for the ability of women whose husbands cannot provide substantial resources of capital or political influence to generate an income in the informal sector.

Industrial employment and resource accumulation for self-employment

The above analysis of Nigerian political economy and the place of women within it has indicated that the development of the petrol extraction economy led to the growth of some types of industrial investment and thus to the growth of industrial employment. Women were incorporated into this industrial structure by being recruited into 'women's work' as an unskilled labour force in plants producing basic consumer goods. At the same time, the historical development of the informal sector, the cultural significance of 'trading' and the growth of opportunities for provisioning the state sector in the 1970s meant that to be a businesswoman or businessman, owning one's own enterprise, remained a goal of the majority of Nigerians. The growth of industrial employment with its relatively secure wages was seen as permitting accumulation of transferable resources and thus bringing the possibility of going into business on their own account close to those Nigerians with the necessary educational qualifications living in large towns (Peace, 1979; Di Domenico, 1973). How realistic was this expectation that industrial employment would provide the basis for self-employment?

The 'realism' of the aspiration to self-employment on the part of Nigerian industrial workers depends primarily upon the structure of the Nigerian political economy and the most important tendencies within it and, secondarily, upon the ability of the individual to manipulate those structures. The analysis of Nigerian political economy above suggests that the possibility of securing a substantial income from the informal sector, especially through obtaining government contracts, increased dramatically. However, at the same time, there was a process of concentration of capital going on in the informal sector which made it necessary to make higher and higher initial capital investments to secure the desired rate of return. The most important question then becomes: how far was it possible to accumulate the necessary capital through industrial employment? It is difficult to secure quantitative data on this, but impressionistic evidence would suggest that the level of industrial wages and inflation rates in Nigeria during the 1970s made this increasingly difficult and that this difficulty has been greatly intensified in the 1980s with economic crisis and structural adjustment. Thus in the 1970s, and much more so in the 1980s, the need to secure a non-salary income has intensified at the same time as it has become increasingly difficult for those without greater and greater capital resources.

The experience of some of the difficulties in accumulating resources for self-employment modifies the ambition of many industrial workers: their aspiration is not to move into complete self-employment but to supplement industrial wages by additional self-employment as a trader or craft worker. In times of increased capital requirements and difficulty of access to raw materials, this is likely to be a more realistic ambition that complete self-employment. As a survival strategy, it has the advantage of spreading risks between the formal and informal sectors.

However, a successful transition to self-employment, even on a part-time basis, also requires the establishment of the necessary contacts to create obligations which will in turn secure suppliers, membership of the necessary associations, a favourable site and regular clients. This requires time and resources and a concept of a career much wider than that of wage-earning employment. A crucial question is whether industrial employment hinders or assists this process of establishing trading networks (Peace, 1979).

Constructing a trading network requires the investment of a great deal of time both to cultivate contacts and to lay the foundation of the prospective enterprise. The access of the industrial worker to the necessary time depends partly on the structure of the shifts in particular factories; but also on access to housing, which affects the duration of the journey to work and the ease of access to prospective trading contacts. The greatest disadvantage in this respect is likely to be experienced by immigrant industrial workers in large cities like Lagos and Kano, where workers have to live long distances from work and where the cost of transport is high in terms of time and money.

Those aspiring to self-employment also need to acquire the skills relevant to their chosen enterprise. Under some circumstances, industrial employment may itself provide these skills. Otherwise, access to the necessary skills is in turn dependent on access to time and money.

If industrial work potentially provides access to the accumulation of capital and the opportunity to obtain skills and contacts, the question arises as to whether women and men have equal access to this potential accumulation of capital, skills and contacts. Women tend to be concentrated in insecure, unskilled sectors of industrial employment, which is likely to have a significant influence on the extent to which they are able to use industrial employment as a springboard to self-employment. The problems they encounter are illustrated by the following case study.

Women workers in the Odua'tex textile factory

The Odua'tex factory, which was opened in 1966, spins cotton thread and weaves cotton cloth for local consumer markets, and for uniforms for schools and the police force. It is situated in Ado-Ekiti in what was until the 1960s a relatively underdeveloped area of Yorubaland.

Research[2] conducted in 1972 revealed that out of a labour force of 1,262, there were sixty-two women workers. All the women were interviewed, and a random sample of 371 men workers. The personal histories of the women, forty-three of whom were unmarried, were significantly different from those of the men. The former were all younger than thirty-five. They had higher levels of education: of the workers interviewed, eighty-two per cent of the women as compared to sixty-four per cent of the men workers had received some form of secondary education. Their previous work experience was different from that of the men; twenty-nine (forty-six per cent) of the women as compared to 157 (thirty-four per cent) of the men had not been previously employed; and twenty-four (thirty-eight per cent) as compared to eighty-seven (eighteen per cent) had been non-manual clerical workers. Very few of the women had been petty traders and 'traditional' weavers. Thus, in a society in which women have an obligation to contribute materially to their households and especially to the maintenance of their children, very few of these relatively well-educated young women had, prior to their employment at Odua'tex, been able to secure an independent source of income and therefore establish the basis of a careers to generate income to meet their future responsibilities. This is reflected in the reasons they gave for taking the job and whether or not they were satisfied with it. The reasons for seeking employment at Odua'tex and for their degree of job-satisfaction nearly all centred around their need for an income; in many cases expressed as a desperate need which meant that whatever the conditions of work at Odua'tex, they had to be satisfied with any work which gave them an income. This was especially true of the married women with children.

Apart from cleaning and clerical work, almost all the women shop-floor workers were employed in the doffering department, in which the cotton thread is prepared for the looms, and the relevant colours for each pattern are laid down. This job had in practice become 'women's work' and was carried out in a room separated from the weaving shed and marked out as a room occupied by women. There were no women employed in the weaving shed except as cleaners.

The most highly-prized position open to workers without previous supervisory experience at the Odua'tex factory was as a mechanic or electrician. The next most sought after position was as a weaver. Weavers were recruited from workers who had no previous experience of working in textile factories, and received higher levels of pay than those available in the spinning or dyeing sheds. Weaving was perceived as a 'technical' occupation, which provided valuable experience in working with machinery. The electricians and mechanics were recruited from among the weavers when, as frequently occurred, applicants with previous experience were not available. Electricians and mechanics received higher wages and also had greater autonomy at work than the machine-minders. The ability to move around the factory without direct supervision was highly valued. In addition, the training as an electrician or mechanic provided workers with the basis for establishing part-time enterprises. The opportunities for successfully combining full-time industrial employment and part-time informal sector entrepreneurship were greater in Ado-Ekiti than Lagos. The market for the skills and products was smaller but the skills were scarcer, business premises cheaper, distances and time spent travelling between work and home less, and relatives were more readily available to look after such businesses during factory shifts. The possibility always existed that if sufficient capital was accumulated or a sufficiently fortunate opportunity presented itself, the worker concerned could move from factory employment and the basic security it provided into full-time informal sector income generation.

The pattern of recruitment and deployment of male workers in the textile factory meant that for them a ladder of skill accumulation existed, to which access was controlled by initial educational qualifications, work experience and the influence of foremen. The possibility of attaining the position of weaver, the first stage on the ladder, was relatively open. For the smaller number of weavers who received training as electricians or mechanics, not only did their working conditions in the factory change but the training provided the basis of a supplementary occupation now and possible self-employment later. The possibility of doing this is enhanced by the support of kin and friends and ease of transport within Ado-Ekiti. Thus in the best case, work in the textile industry provides for male workers both the skills and capital for establishment as an individual businessman.

The relationship between working in a textile factory and their potential income-generating ambitions was different for the women workers. For the majority of them, their educational qualifications and their previous work experience as traditional weavers, traders and clerical workers did not appear to provide the basis for allocating them to work within the factory. The jobs to which they did have access were defined as 'women's jobs' and were low paid and with limited opportunities for training and promotion. They did not have access to the jobs with the highest pay and greatest autonomy and lack of supervision. Thus for women, work at Odua'tex did not provide training, skills and equipment they could use to establish their own independent income-earning activity, nor did it provide them with a career in the factory itself. The most it did was to provide them with a relatively stable income, which they hoped would enable them to accumulate sufficient capital to enter trade or petty commodity production. The realisation of this possibility depended upon general trends within the Nigerian economy and became more remote as the rapid inflation of the oil boom years steadily increased the capital required to enter the informal sector.

The pattern of recruitment of women into the labour force in the Odua'tex textile factory in low-paid jobs without access to training or promotion is consistent with other research findings (Humphrey, 1984; Lim, 1980). This pattern, combined with the trends in the informal sector, suggests that women were being incorporated as marginal workers in industry at the same time as the requirements for entry into the informal sector were becoming more difficult. Together, the two factors make it far less likely that women will be able to construct an independent career by using industrial employment as the basis of self-employment, than will male workers.

Women's independent careers in conditions of economic crisis and structural adjustment

The economic crisis affecting the Nigerian economy since 1981 has intensified both women's need for an independent career, and the difficulties most women face in securing one. Difficulties in importing essential supplies and raw materials, owing to shortage of foreign exchange, have led to industrial plant being operated at far below capacity levels, or closing down altogether, and workers being retrenched. Indebtedness and falling oil revenues have led to cut-backs in public expenditure. In the public sector, workers have been retrenched, or salaries simply not paid; and the recurrent budgets for social expenditure by Federal and State Governments, such as those for health and education, have not been honoured (Dennis, 1986). This in turn reduced the market for informal sector products and services, as the numbers and incomes of wage-earners were cut. At the same time, the growing insecurity and fall in purchasing power of wage employment has made access to an informal sector income an important survival strategy. Despite the cut-backs in government expenditure, it has remained the case that the most profitable informal sector activity is trading in the interstices of government expenditure.

The structural adjustment programme (SAP) imposed by a military government in response to the crisis has, if anything, made things worse (Onimode, 1987). The SAP has reduced the protection enjoyed by the industrial sector, a policy which has had particularly serious consequences for Nigerian industry with its narrow bias towards luxury production. This has led to increasing levels of unemployment of industrial workers (Bangura, 1987). Savage cuts in government expenditure have continued. There has been much talk of the need to impose 'discipline' on the Nigerian people; which in practice has been interpreted as meaning the need to secure higher levels of productivity from workers, particularly in the public sector; and the necessity of controlling and confining the informal sector (Dennis, 1987). Inflation has continued to increase with a massively devalued currency, causing large increases in food prices. This combination of pressures is felt most severely by lower-income urban households (Weeks, 1986).

The recession and the SAP have had a particularly severe impact on lower-income urban women. Official explanations of the economic crisis appear to take the view that women play a special role in promoting national indiscipline, and the military government has implemented policies on the price of food and other essential commodities which identify women traders in the informal sector as being the 'cause' of the problem and involve high levels of harassment of such women (*West Africa*, 1984a, p. 126; 1984b, p. 148). Evidence that is becoming available suggests that within poor households, it is women who bear the burden of a decrease in capacity to generate a sufficient income to sustain a household and of the increasing price and scarcity of essential commodities (Dennis, 1987). This crisis has shown how close is the relationship between access to income in the formal and informal sectors for the survival of households, and the particular significance of careers in the informal sector as a source of income generation for women. But it has also intensified the difficulties of women in pursuing such careers.

Conclusion

Yoruba women have the responsibility and the need to secure for themselves their own source of income to survive in a polygynous society, to fulfil their duties to their children, and to retain links with their own families. The range of income-generating opportunities open to women in southern Nigeria has been wider than in many other sub-Saharan African societies; and women aspire to independent self-employment in the urban informal sector. However, these opportunities remain limited by dominant perceptions of appropriate gender roles. Yoruba women have to negotiate their careers within this structure, in which their ability to accumulate the required resources is largely determined by the socio-economic position of their husbands.

The growth of industrial employment for women has not changed that dependence. As the textile industry case study illustrates, there is male bias in the construction of the gender division of labour in industry, enabling men to use industrial employment as a springboard to desired forms of self-employment, but not affording women the same opportunities. Although wage employment seemingly has the potential to offer women a source of income for establishing an enterprise independently of the husband, usually required to provide the initial loan for such purposes, this potential has not been fulfilled.

The deterioration of Nigeria's economy in the 1980s, and related adjustment measures, have intensified women's need for an independent income in the informal sector, but have made it much harder for most women to enter the profitable parts of this sector. The common male assumption that urban Yoruba women are all typically able to achieve the socially approved career as a successful independent trader is increasingly at odds with the experience of a growing number of Nigerian women.

Notes

1   The term 'informal sector' is notoriously loose and covers a wide range of different activities. In the Nigerian context, it is generally used to designate petty commodity production and petty trade. It is perceived in terms of self-employment rather than waged work, and is viewed positively, as a means to socio-economic advancement. Thus the characterisation of the informal sector in Nigeria differs from that current in most work on Latin America and Asia, in which the informal sector is assumed to consist largely of low-paid, low-skilled casual work (see Scott, ch.5, this volume).

2   The results discussed in this section are taken from a research project carried out by the present author and Dr S. A. Afonja on social change and industrialisation in Ado-Ekiti. For a more detailed presentation of the research, see Dennis, 1984; Afonja and Dennis, 1976.

References

Afonja, S. A., and Dennis, C. (1976), 'Social aspects of rural industrialisation: the Ado-Ekiti example', Proceedings of Conference on Social Research and National Development in Nigeria, Ibadan.

Afonja, S. A. (1981), 'Changing modes of production and the sexual division of labour among the Yoruba', *Signs*, vol. 7, no. 2, pp. 299–313.

——(1984), 'Land control: a critical factor in Yoruba gender stratification', in C. Robertson and I. Berger (eds), *Women and Class in Africa*, Africana Publishing Company, New York.

Agheyisi, R. U. (1985), 'The labour market implications of the access of women to higher education in Nigeria', in Women in Nigeria (eds), *Women in Nigeria Today*, Zed Books, London.

Akeredolu-Ale, B. (1976), 'Private foreign investment and the underdevelopment of indigenous entrepreneurship in Nigeria', in G. Williams (ed.), *Nigeria: Economy and Society*, Rex Collings, London.

Aronson, D. R. (1971), 'Ijebu Yoruba urban-rural relationships and class formation', *Canadian Journal of African Studies*, vol. 5, no. 1, pp. 263–79).

Awe, B. (1982), 'Formal education and the status of Nigerian women: an historical perspective', in F. Ogunsheye, K. Awosika, C. Dennis, and C. Di Domenico (eds), *Nigerian Women and Development*, Ford Foundation, Ibadan.

Babalola, S., and Dennis, C. (1988), 'The returns to women's labour in cash crop production: tobacco in Igboho, Oyo State, Nigeria', in J. Davidson (ed.), *Women and Land Tenure in Africa*, Westview Press, Boulder.

Bangura, Y. (1987), 'Workers' struggles in vehicle assembly plants, Nigeria', *Review of African Political Economy*, no. 39, pp. 4–22.

Barber, K. (1981), 'How man makes god in West Africa: Yoruba attitudes towards the Orisa', *Africa*, vol. 31, no.3, pp. 724–45.

Barnes, S. (1986), *Patrons and Power: Creating a Political Community in Metropolitan Lagos*, Manchester University Press, Manchester.

van den Berghe, P. L. and Nuttney, C. M. (1971), 'Some social characteristics of University of Ibadan students', *Nigerian Journal of Economic and Social Studies*, vol. 42, pp. 44–56.

Beynon, H. (1973), *Working for Ford*, Penguin, Harmondsworth.

Bienefeld, M. (1975), 'The informal sector and peripheral capitalism: the case of Tanzania', *I.D.S. Bulletin*, vol. 16, no. 3.

Caldwell, J. C. (1968), *Population Growth and Family Change in Africa*, Australian National University Press, Canberra.

Collins, P. (1979), 'The political economy of indigenisation', *African Review*, no. 4.

Crowder, M. (1968), *West Africa Under Colonial Rule*, Hutchinson, London.

Dennis, C. (1984), 'Capitalist development and women's work: a Nigerian case study', *Review of African Political Economy*, no. 27/28, pp. 109–19.

——(1986), 'The economic crisis in Africa and women's health:

constructing its effect on Nigerian women', African Studies Association, UK Conference, University of Kent, 17–19 September.
——(1987), 'Women and the state in Nigeria: the case of the Federal Military Government 1984–85', in H. Afshar (ed.), *Women, the State and Ideology*, Macmillan, London.
Di Domenico, C. M. (1973), 'Nigerian industrial recruits: a case study of new workers at the Nigerian Tobacco Company in Ibadan', PhD Thesis, Ibadan University.
——(1983), 'Male and female workers in Ibadan', in C. Oppong (ed.), *Female and Male in West Africa*, Allen & Unwin, London.
van den Driesen, I. H. (1971), 'Some observations on the family unit, religion and the practice of polygyny in the Ife division of western Nigeria', *Africa*, vol.42, pp. 44–56.
Eades, J. (1980), *The Yoruba Today*, Cambridge University Press, Cambridge.
Freund, B. (1978), 'Oil and crisis in contemporary Nigeria', *Review of African Political Economy*, no. 13.
Gerry, C. (1975), 'Petty producers and capitalism', *Review of African Political Economy*, no. 3.
Gerth, H. H., and Wright Mills, C. (1967), *From Max Weber*, Routledge & Kegan Paul, London.
Gertzel, G. (1962), 'Relations between African and European traders in the Niger Delta, 1880–96', *Journal of Historical Society of Nigeria*, vol.24.
Goldthorpe, J. *et al.* (1969), *The Affluent Worker in the Class Structure*, Cambridge University Press, Cambridge.
Henderson, R. (1972), *The King in Every Man: Evolutionary Trends in Onitsha Igbo Society and Culture*, Yale University Press, New Haven.
Hill, P. (1966), 'Landlords and brokers: a West African trading system', *Cahiers d'Etudes Africaines*, vol. 6, pp. 349–66.
Hopkins, A. G. (1973), *An Economic History of West Africa*, Longmans, London.
Humphrey, J. (1984), 'The growth of female employment in Brazilian manufacturing industry in the 1970s', *Journal of Development Studies*, vol. 20, no. 4, pp. 224–47.
——(1987), *Gender and Work in the Third World*, Tavistock, London.
Ihonvbere, J. (1985), *The Rise and Fall of Nigeria's Second Republic 1979–84*, Zed Books, London.
ILO/INSTRAW (1985), *Women in Economic Activity: A Global Statistical Survey*, ILO, Geneva.
Lawuyi, O. B. (1988), 'The world of the Yoruba taxi driver', *Africa*, vol. 58, no. 1, pp. 1–13.
Lim, L. (1980), 'Women in the redeployment of manufacturing industry to developing countries', UNIDO Working Papers on Structural Change, no. 18, Vienna.
Lloyd, P. C. (1968), 'Divorce among the Yoruba', *American Anthropologist*, vol. 70, pp. 67–81.
Mabogunje, A. L. (1962), *Yoruba Towns*, Ibadan University Press, Ibadan.
——(1968), *Urbanisation in Nigeria*, University of London Press, London.

National Planning Office (1981), *Fourth National Development Plan, 1981–85*, Federal Ministry of National Planning, Lagos.

Ogunsheye, F. A. O. (1982), 'Formal education and the status of women in Nigeria', in F. A. O. Ogunsheye, K. Awosika, C. Dennis, and C. M. Di Domenico (eds), *Nigerian Women and Development*, Ford Foundation, Ibadan.

Onimode, B. (1982), *Imperialism and Underdevelopment in Nigeria*, Zed Books, London.

——(1987), 'The African crisis and Nigeria', in Institute for African Alternatives, *Africa's Crisis*, IFAA, London.

Peace, A. (1979), *Choice, Class and Conflict: A Study of Southern Nigerian Factory Workers*, Harvester, Brighton.

Pearson, S. R. (1970), *Petroleum in the Nigerian Economy*, Stanford University Press, Stanford.

Peel, J. D. Y. (1983), *Ijeshas and Nigerians: Incorporation of a Yoruba Kingdom, 1890s–1970s*, Cambridge University Press, Cambridge.

Perchonok, N. (1985), 'Double oppression: women and land matters in Kaduna State', in Women in Nigeria (eds), *Women in Nigeria Today*, Zed Books, London.

Sudarkasa, N. (1973), *Where Women Work: A Study of Yoruba Women in the Market Place and in the Home*, Museum of Anthropology, University of Michigan, Ann Arbor.

Trager, L. (1981), 'Customers and creditors: variations in economic personalism in a Nigerian market system', *Ethnology*, vol. 20, no. 2, pp. 133–46.

Turner, T. (1976), 'Multinational corporations and the instability of the Nigerian state', *Review of African Political Economy*, no. 5.

Usman, Y. B. (1979), 'Petroleum in the economy of Nigeria', in Y. B. Usman, *For the Liberation of Nigeria*, New Beacon Books, London.

——(1984), 'Middlemen, consultants, contractors and the solution to the current economic crisis', in Nigerian Political Science Association, *Debate on the Nigerian Economic Crisis*, Zed Books, London.

Watts, M. (1983), *Silent Violence: Food, Famine and the Peasantry in Northern Nigeria*, University of California Press, Berkeley.

Weeks, J. (1986), 'Vulnerable segments of the labour market: urban areas of the African region', Seminar Paper presented to Project Planning Centre, University of Bradford.

West Africa, (1984a), no. 3465, 16 January.

West Africa, (1984b), no. 3476, 2 April.

Williams, G. (1970), 'The social stratification of a neo-colonial economy – western Nigeria', in C. Allen and R. W. Johnson (eds), *African Perspectives*, Cambridge University Press, Cambridge.

Willis, P. (1976), *How Working-Class Kids Get Working-Class Jobs*, Centre for Contemporary Cultural Studies, University of Birmingham.

Women in Nigeria (1984), 'Press releases', *Review of African Political Economy*, no. 31, pp. 104–6.

World Bank (1984), *World Tables*, vol. II, Johns Hopkins University Press, Baltimore.

Informal sector or female sector?: gender bias in urban labour market models

The informal sector paradigm has provided the basis for studies of urban poverty in less developed countries (LDCs) for almost twenty years now. During that time there have been many criticisms and modifications of the original model and there are now a number of different versions available. As a result of this theoretical pluralism it has been possible to contain most of the initial criticisms, and the paradigm has become widely used even within Marxist circles (Portes and Walton, 1981; Smith, 1986). However, a new challenge to the paradigm has come from recent studies of the position of women in these labour markets. It has been accused of male bias because of a failure to notice the substantial numbers of women in the sector and to appreciate the significance of their work for the economic survival of the urban poor and the wider functioning of the labour market as a whole. However, in drawing attention to these factors, the importance of gender divisions in the labour market has paradoxically been both overstated and understated. The argument to be put forward in this chapter is that the male bias in the informal sector paradigm lies not so much in the underestimation of women as a particular group within the informal sector – whose size may actually have been exaggerated – but in the faulty characterisation of the model itself, which is in a much more profound sense gender-blind.

In the course of the development and differentiation of the informal sector paradigm most of the early criticisms – the excessive stress on duality, the neglect of linkages between sectors and the problem of heterogeneity within them[1] – have been taken on board. Most contemporary work now assumes that it is polarisation rather than dualism that we are talking about; that there is a continuum rather than an abrupt discontinuity between the opposite poles; and that diversity is important within the sectors, as are the linkages between them. While most models share similar assumptions in these respects, the differences between them lie in the degree of emphasis given to particular causal factors: for example, the role of technology, institutional intervention (unions, labour legislation), market fragmentation (capital and financial markets, consumer goods markets), and the supply characteristics of labour.[2] They vary, too, in the degree to which the existence of the informal sector is seen as a manifestation of exploitation or as a positive feature, the source of future growth.[3] As Dennis shows in chapter 4, in Nigeria the informal sector is widely perceived as offering advancement through an independent career.

However, leaving aside differences in explanations and evaluations, the basic characterisation of 'formal' and 'informal' employment in most research , especially on Latin America and Asia, has remained remarkably stable over the years. For the most part, the paradigm assumes that there is a broad correspondence between scale of production, employment categories and labour markets. Production is polarised between large and small enterprises, and whereas employment in the former is mainly based on wage and salaried labour, in the latter it consists of self-employment, family labour and quasi-wage workers such as apprentices, outworkers and domestic servants. Within this structure, the 'formal' sector is defined as the labour market most associated with large capital-intensive enterprises, where in relative terms workers are highly paid and highly skilled, well protected by unions and labour legislation, and have high job stability and good career prospects. On the other hand the 'informal' sector is associated with small labour-intensive enterprises and consists of low-paid, low-skilled, casual workers with few career prospects. Admittedly, this characterisation is ideal-typical rather than real, and it is recognised that the variables are much less clear-cut and shade into one another in real life; the purpose of the ideal type is to identify the specific behavioural characteristics of different segments of the labour market prior to analysing the more complex interrelationships between them. The most important feature of this characterisation is the assumption that there is a *single* axis of segmentation in the urban labour market which underlies all the variables that differentiate the two sectors. It is this assumption that is called into question by the data on gender, and as a result, the basic characterisation of the two sectors is in jeopardy.

Women in the informal sector

The early work on the informal sector barely mentioned the presence of women, indeed in Sethuraman's review of nine city studies conducted by the International Labour Organisation(ILO) during the 1970s, he states that 'female participation in the informal sector seems surprisingly small' (Sethuraman, 1981, p. 190).[4] However, Mazumdar (1975) had noticed that women were an important group within the sector, along with the young, the old and the transient. His paper was one of the first to shift the focus of interest away from enterprise characteristics towards the supply conditions of labour in the informal sector, arguing that it was the low opportunity cost of labour that accounted for the low wages there. He argued that all of the groups identified had a lower commitment to the labour force and were more prepared to accept low wages. This argument was followed by a number of studies that focused on the heterogeneity of labour in the informal sector (for example, Squire, 1979; Morley, 1982); however, there was little examination of the structural basis of this.

Feminist work has taken up these questions, focusing attention on specific groups of women workers such as outworkers, street-sellers and domestic servants, and emphasising the linkages between these jobs and women's role in the family. It has pointed out that a much greater proportion of women are concentrated in the informal sector than men because of family constraints, and that the size of female participation in the informal sector may have been underestimated in official statistics because so much of women's work is carried out in the home and is not perceived as 'work'. Many studies have explored the theoretical significance of women's paid and unpaid work for the wider functioning of the urban economy (for example, Young and Moser, 1981; Roldan, 1985; Babb, 1986; Buechler, 1986). It has been argued that women's informal sector work acts as a 'subsidy' to the formal sector in that it enables men to subsist on lower wages than might otherwise be possible; it provides a reserve of flexible and cheap labour that can be drawn into production at particular times of the year when demand is high (such as Christmas); it enables firms to bypass institutional regulation in the formal market (through outwork); and above all, it provides the means whereby men's labour is serviced or 'reproduced' for further economic participation (see Redclift (1985) for a review of these issues).

Whether one agrees with such ideas or not, these studies have been extremely important in correcting the bias inherent in previous work, which tended to focus solely on men's informal sector activities. However, there is a danger that the bias can now go in the other direction: the impression is given that women are the dominant group within the sector and the men have been forgotten; women's functions as a source of cheap or unpaid labour are made to appear so crucial to the urban economy that it would seem that the entire system depended on it. Whereas formerly the informal sector was a 'male' sector in terms of interest and emphasis, it has now become a 'female' sector.

It is important to place these questions in the perspective of the overall economy, where it can be seen that this picture is mistaken. In Lima, Peru, the female participation rate is still too low for women to be able to dominate a segment of the labour market as large as the informal sector (which is nearly half of total employment); although they are overrepresented in the informal sector in relation to their overall share of employment and in comparison with men, they do not dominate it – men are still the majority work-force there. The contribution of women's cheap labour to the economy either in the form of a reserve wage-force or as a quasi-proletariat (in outwork) is small in relation to the exploitation of male labour. Even amongst poor families, the majority of wives do not have paid employment, so while those who do undoubtedly enable *particular families* to survive, the reproduction of their class or the system as a whole cannot be said to depend on it. The contribution of women's *unpaid* labour to the day-to-day maintenance of the family and its economically active members is undisputed and clearly has important system-wide functions; but this cannot be said of women's participation in *paid* employment.[5]

On the whole, the feminist work mentioned above has tended to work *within* the informal sector paradigm, drawing attention to the role of women and providing new explanatory variables, rather than challenging the basic framework as such. Moreover, the focus on the role of the family in structuring the female work-force is consistent with conventional supply-oriented models (for example, Squire, 1979; Morley, 1982). The effect is to expand and deepen the informal sector model rather than to invalidate it. However, in other social science fields, such as class and the state, the effect of the inclusion of gender has been much more revolutionary. It has lead to a questioning of the most basic concepts and methodologies.[6] This is largely because they are gender-focused rather than women-focused. The analysis of differences between men and women reveals a gender bias in *all* activities, not merely those involving women, and requires revision of the way we think about these activities themselves. My view is that a gender-focused analysis has a similar revolutionary effect on the informal sector paradigm because it actually invalidates it in its present form. The reason for this is the profound segregation between men and women within both sectors and the differences between men's and women's work there. This combination of segregation and differentiation has several implications: first, it means that the ideal-typical characterisation of 'formal' and 'informal' only ever applies to one sex and excludes the other; second, it is not solely supply-determined but is a fundamental part of the structure of demand; and third, since gender crosscuts the formal/informal sector division, rather than running in parallel with it, one cannot maintain that there is a single axis of segmentation in the labour market – there are two.[7]

In the pages that follow I shall provide empirical evidence from Lima, Peru, to support these arguments. The data are from the period 1972/74, years that came at the end of a long period of industrial and urban growth which created a sizeable informal sector. I use these data because it is the period I know best and for which there is reliable information. However, I shall make reference to data from the 1981 period so that the changing position of women in the informal sector in the aftermath of a severe recession can be assessed. (See Scott, (1986a and 1986b) for brief background data.)[8]

Two methodological provisos are in order at this point. First, the data refer to the capital city, Lima, rather than national level data; second, in most of the analysis that follows I shall refer to the *manual* labour market only, which will exclude white-collar or middle-class employment. This is in order to remove the occupational bias in the formal sector, which prevents the two sectors from being strictly comparable.[9] Note that I shall occasionally refer to manual workers and their dependents as the 'working class'; this term includes informal sector workers such as domestic servants, street-sellers and outworkers, rather than being restricted to wage-labourers.

Gender and the informal sector in Lima, Peru

According to the 1972 census, the female labour force participation rate in Lima was twenty-two per cent (population of six years and over) and women were around twenty-eight per cent of the metropolitan work-force. The male participation rate was fifty-six per cent, and men were seventy-two per cent of the work-force. Survey data show that women were a similar proportion of the manual work-force.[10] If we define the informal sector in terms of enterprise work-force size, with a cut-off point of five workers, it accounted for forty-five per cent of total employment. If we define it in terms of employment categories consisting of self-employment, family labour and domestic service, it was thirty-two per cent of total employment.[11] Women were disproportionately concentrated in the informal sector compared with men; on the latter definition, forty-seven per cent of all working women were in this sector compared with only twenty-three per cent of men (census data). The disproportionate concentration of women was even more marked in the manual labour force; survey data show that seventy-five per cent of manual women were in the informal sector compared with only thirty-six per cent of manual men. If we include wage-workers in enterprises with less that five workers, the figures rise to eighty-four per cent and forty-nine per cent respectively (see Table 1).

However, men were still the majority in the sector and they dominated all categories of informal employment except domestic service. On the wider definition used above, men were fifty-four per cent of the manual informal sector work-force, but if we exclude domestic service, which accounted for nearly half of women's informal sector employment, male dominance rises to sixty-seven per cent. The numbers of manual women in small-scale manufacturing, on which much of the case for the reserve-army function of women has been made, was very small indeed. Only eleven per cent of informal sector women were in this category of production and they accounted for only a quarter of total informal manufacturing. The major reason for women's concentration in the

Table 1   *Employment status of the manual labour force, Lima, Peru, 1973*

Employment status	Distribution of labour force			Women's share in each category (%)
	Men (%)	Women (%)	Men and women (%)	
Self-employed	29·8	38·1	32·6	39·1
Family labour	5·1	5·7	5·3	35·7
Domestic servants	1·4	31·3	11·4	91·9
Wage-workers in informal sector*	11·5	8·6	10·8	n.a.
Wage-workers in formal sector	41·2	6·1	29·2	n.a
Salaried employees**	10·5	9·5	10·1	31·5
Unspecified	0·5	0·7	0·6	42·9
Total	100·0	100·0	100·0	33·5
(Number in sample)	(1,581)	(796)	(2,377)	

* establishments with less than five workers.
** refers to employees with white-collar status (for social security purposes), principally shop-workers.
n.a. = not available
Source: Ministry of Labour Urban Employment Survey, 1973 (unpublished).

informal sector was domestic service, an occupation that consisted largely of young unmarried women rather than spouses who were supplementing their husband's income. These data show that in 1973/4, when there was still considerable growth in the economy, with rising real incomes and expanding job-opportunities in both the formal and informal sectors of the economy, women's contribution to the informal sector was less than men's as far as aggregate employment was concerned; their role in petty manufacturing was small and limited to a few specific industries, and their role as contributors to family incomes was also relatively minor given the low female participation rates. In the shanty-towns, typically only a third of wives were in paid employment. Of course these figures may be liable to some undercounting, but the margin is probably small, certainly not sufficient to overturn the massive male majority in most informal occupations, nor substantially to alter the level of household income.[12]

If we look at the situation in 1981, after five years of acute economic crisis, we find the situation still remarkably similar. Women's general level of labour-force participation moved up less than one percentage point, much less than might have been expected if the reserve-army or the subsidy effect had been operating, and the structure of women's participation in the informal sector did not show major changes, but was merely in line with long-run trends (Scott, 1986b). There is evidence at the micro-level that for *some families* women's work was crucial for the maintenance of the family income, but this could not be generalized to all others in the working class.

However, even though they were a minority in the informal sector, it is clear that women worked under very different conditions from men. On all the major indicators of informal sector employment – income, education, skill and occupational mobility – we find noticeable differences between men and women. Let us look first at incomes. Table 2 gives mean monthly earnings as a proportion of the minimum wage by enterprise size. The first category, with one to four workers, includes domestic servants, outworkers, the self-employed and wage-workers in small enterprises. The table shows the general correlation between levels of earnings and enterprise size predicted by the informal sector model. This correlation held for both men and women but there were enormous sex differentials in earnings in each enterprise size group and these differentials increased with scale of production. Note that the average earnings of women were below the minimum wage level in all enterprises with less than fifty workers, whereas the figure for men *never* fell below the minimum wage level. Women had to secure employment in enterprises with a hundred workers or more before they could reach the level of earnings of men in the smallest enterprises.

Let us turn now to education, which is often held to be a barrier to formal sector employment and hence a reason for the concentration of relatively uneducated workers in the informal sector. There used to be significant educational inequalities between men and women in Peru, and these differentials were especially pronounced in the working class. However, there has been considerable improvement in educational levels in recent years, with a narrowing of the differential between men and women amongst younger age groups (Scott, 1986a). It is not surprising then, that educational

Table 2 *Average monthly earnings (expressed as a proportion of the minimum wage)* of manual workers, by enterprise size, Lima, 1973*

Enterprise size (no. of workers)	Men		Women		Women's earnings as % of mens'
	% distri- bution	Earnings	% distri- bution	Earnings	
1–4	47·8	136	83·7	62	45·6
5–9	8·9	135	5·2	78	57·8
10–19	6·6	139	1·8	99	71·2
20–49	6·5	149	1·7	98	65·8
50–99	4·7	149	1·9	117	78·5
100 +	25·5	190	5·7	144	75·8
Total	100·0	150	100·0	71	47·3
(Number in sample)	(1,489)		(775)		

*the minimum monthly wage in 1973 was 2,400 Peruvian soles.
Source: Ministry of Labour Urban Employment Survey, 1973 (unpublished).

differentials between men and women were small, far smaller than the income differential. While it is true that levels of education were lower in the informal sector than in the formal, and they were lower amongst women than men there, the differentials were slight compared with the earnings figures. On average, women had 4·3 years of education compared with men's 5·8 years, but women's monthly earnings were only forty-four per cent of men's. Especially noteworthy is the fact that there was *no difference* in the educational levels of men and women in the formal sector (both had 6·1 years of schooling), yet it was in this sector that the male-female differentials were widest (Scott, 1986a, table 8.19).

In fact, formal education only acts as a screening device in the manual labour market and has relatively little relevance to informal sector work. Vocational skills are far more important, and these are largely transmitted through work-place training and apprenticeships. Such training is reflected in skill divisions which carry formally recognised labels such as 'maestro' (master), 'operario' (journeyman) and 'aprendiz' or 'ayudante' (apprentice, helper). Unfortunately, the Ministry of Labour does not collect information on this aspect of skill, although my own case studies did. These data show that vocational skill was much more strongly associated with levels of earnings than formal education. Table 3 presents some of these results; it shows that both the informal and formal sectors were very heterogeneous in terms of skill, and this was the case amongst the self-employed and informal wage-workers. Vocational skill made a great difference to the level of earnings in the sector, and this was true for women as well as men. It is interesting to note the very high earnings of skilled men (more than double the level of the minimum wage) whatever their category of employment or enterprise size. Self-employed skilled men earned considerably more than semi-skilled workers in the formal sector and marginally more than skilled ones. In fact, when skill is taken into account, the earnings differentials between small and large enterprises fall significantly. These data confirm the oft-noted heterogeneity of the informal and formal sector work-forces and show how misleading is the portrayal of informal sector work as unskilled. However, there are some significant anomalies between men and women in this respect. Although skilled women earned more that unskilled ones, they were likely to earn more if they worked in a factory than if they were self-employed. This may be an effect of shorter hours amongst the latter group and of the premium that was paid to the skilled workers in otherwise unskilled clothing sweatshops. Note that skilled women earned far less than skilled men, and subsequent analysis showed this to be true even when the number of hours worked was held constant. This suggests that female skills had less economic power than male skills; whether this was due to technical differences between the two or was a reflection of the lower worth of women's work is a question worth considering. I shall come back to this question later.

Job stability is another variable that is expected to be associated with the formal-informal division in the labour market. Yet here again we find some surprises. In the first place, contrary to what is often assumed, the general level of job stability was high compared with advanced industrial societies. The average number of jobs held during the decade 1963–73 was 1·8, and fifty per cent of the manual work-force had only held one job.[13] Moreover, age and sex did not affect the level of job stability as much as in the USA; in fact, job-changing was less pronounced amongst teenagers than amongst older groups. Since women were more concentrated in these younger groups than men, their level of stability was actually higher than men's: sixty per cent of them had only had one job in the last decade compared with forty-five per cent of men. However, even

Table 3 *Average daily wage** of manual workers, by enterprise size, skill and sex, Lima, 1974*

Level of skill	Men			Women			Total			
	S.E.	WW <5	WW 5+	S.E.	WW <5	WW 5+	S.E.	WW <5	WW 5+	(N)
Skilled	248	200	236	99*	–	141*	221	200	230	66
Semi-skilled	126*	125	179	96*	83*	127*	113	120	168	51
Unskilled	109*	40*	127*	81	50	–	88	48	127*	59
Total	203	133	199	89	52	131	155	94	190	
(N = Number in sample)	33	31	52	24	28	8	57	59	60	176

S.E. = self-employed
WW < 5 = wage-workers in establishments with less than 5 workers
WW 5+ = wage-workers in establishments with 5 workers and over
 * note very small numbers in these cells (< 10).
** the minimum daily wage in 1974 was 100 peruvian soles.
Source: author's case study data (weighted).

amongst older age groups, women's job stability was higher than men's. Finally, there was very little difference in average levels of job stability between informal and formal sectors. There were differences between occupations and employment categories within the sectors, with wage-labour (for example, domestic service and construction workers) being more unstable than self-employment, but they tended to cancel each other out in the end.

There were, however, noticeable differences in the direction of movement of men and women between jobs. Much has been made of the process of movement between the formal and informal sectors, which was ignored in the early models. It is often maintained that movement between sectors is a vehicle for upward mobility, providing a means for acquiring skill and improving incomes (for example, Balan, Browning and Jelin, 1973). However, case study data show that it was men who were most likely to move between sectors and to improve their position in the labour market as a result. Women had much less mobility between the sectors and such movement as did occur was likely to be a lateral movement between unskilled jobs rather than an upward career progression. Looking at all job moves in the work history, only twelve per cent of men had been confined to the informal sector throughout their lives, compared to forty-six per cent of women. Moreover, forty-one per cent of the men had experienced upward movement into the skilled category, whereas only fourteen per cent of the women had.

In summary then, when we look at the characteristics of men's and women's employment in the informal sector, we find that it was *women's* employment that conformed to the ideal-typical conception of unskilled and poorly paid and dead-end jobs, and this was true of their situation in both formal and informal sectors. Men tended to have skilled jobs with relatively high incomes and good career prospects, and this too was true in both sectors. In other words, as currently characterised, 'formal' jobs corresponded to men's jobs and 'informal' jobs correspond to women's jobs. Moreover, this characterisation applied regardless of the size of enterprise or category of employment. It is in this sense that the informal sector could be portrayed as a 'female' sector, not because it was dominated by women but because it described the characteristics of female employment.

Does this mean that gender should replace enterprise/ employment status variables as the major axis of segmentation in the labour market? No, it does not, for *within* the male and female labour markets, there were differences in skill, earnings and job mobility associated with conventional formal/informal sector variables. Gender was *crosscutting* enterprise and employment characteristics, creating a double axis of segmentation. Just as the gender division was internally segmented by enterprise size and employment status, the formal/informal division was internally segmented by gender. One implication of this is that gender inequalities within the informal sector cannot be explained by the informal sector model itself; a more complex analysis of gender is required. In order to examine these questions further, let us now look more closely at the nature of gender segregation within the informal sector.

Gender segregation within the informal sector

Occupational segregation by sex is normally thought to account for much of the inequality between men and women in the labour market because it creates a barrier between male and female labour markets preventing women from obtaining access to the better jobs and confining them to the worse ones.[14] The reasons for this are generally attributed either to supply factors which can be traced to the different positions of men and women in the family, or to demand discrimination by employers or by male employees who for various reasons see women as a threat to their own employment status, or to the more nebulous dissuasive powers of occupational sex-typing. However, there is a problem in applying these explanations to the analysis of segregation within the informal sector since they have been developed in advanced industrial societies where production is organised on formal sector lines. There is a separation between the work-place and the home and production is based on the wage relation. In the informal sector, many activities are of a type that can be dovetailed with women's domestic responsibilities, thus resolving some of their supply constraints. Relations of production are based on self-employment or family employment where demand discrimination is less easy to explain. In analysing gender segregation within the informal sector then, we are faced with two tasks, first to document gender differences through the systematic comparison of men's and women's employment (rather than focusing on one sex or the other), and second, to search for explanations that are appropriate to the specific characteristics of informal sector production. A further methodological point is that since the informal sector is enmeshed within a wider economy rather than operating as an autonomous unit, and gender crosscuts the sectoral division rather than running in parallel with it, the analysis of gender segregation has to be set within the wider context of formal/informal sector relations rather than confined to the informal sector alone.

In the analysis below I shall therefore start with an examination of the way in which patterns of gender segregation relate to the informal/formal sector division. This analysis is based on an examination of the sex ratio of occupations described at the three-digit level of classification. In order to stress the polarization between 'formal' and 'informal', I have used two categories of analysis, enterprises with less than five workers and those with over a hundred.

In Lima, the occupational structure was highly segregated between the sexes. Most occupations were dominated by one sex or the other and four-fifths of the work-force was employed in heavily gender-typed occupations (Scott, 1986a). The manual labour market was much more highly segregated than the non-manual one.

At the level of skilled manual work there was a proliferation of occupations almost entirely dominated by men such as mechanics, electricians, plumbers, shoemakers, tailors, carpenters, and so on. There was only one skilled female occupation, dressmaking, and this was exclusively filled by women. At the unskilled level there was segregation between caretakers, sweepers, office-cleaners and stevedores, who were all male: and domestic servants, laundresses and boardinghouse-keepers, who were all female. Only one occupation appears to have had no segregation – street sellers – but here the polarization was manifested in terms of sales lines rather than occupational titles; men were concentrated in the more lucrative lines which involved more capital outlay and hence greater profitability, while women were in the more marginal lines such as perishable foodstuffs (cf. Moser, 1977, 1981; Bunster and Chaney, 1985).

Few of these occupations were confined totally to the informal sector. However, the degree of concentration in either sector varied. There were three groups: one with a clear predominance in the informal sector, one with concentration in the formal sector, and an intermediate group that was distributed almost equally in both sectors (see Table 4). Interestingly, there were manufacturing and service occupations in all groups, although more service occupations in the informal-oriented group and more manufacturing ones in the formal-oriented group. The relevance of this will become apparent below. In general, the work-force was more heavily concentrated in occupations that had higher than average informal sector concentration, with about a third in the intermediate group and only eighteen per cent in the one with greater formal sector concentration. However, the distribution of men and women in these groups was quite different. Nearly half of the men were in the intermediate group, with a quarter in each of the two extreme groups, whereas the women were much more heavily concentrated in the informal-oriented group. A look at the particular occupations held by women shows that they were the ones where informal sector concentration was most extreme and the female to male ratios highest.

These data show that (1) most manual occupations had a clear predominance of one sex rather than the other; (2) this intense segregation applied to occupations in both formal and informal sectors; (3) men's occupations tended to straddle the formal/

Table 4 *Relative concentration of male and female manual workforces in formal and informal sectors, by occupation, Lima, Peru, 1973*

Occupations	% occupational workforce in: I.S. (<5)	% occupational workforce in: F.S. (100+)	Female to male ratio %	% all women workers	% all men workers	% all workers
*Occupations with higher than average I.S. concentration**						
Street pedlars	96·1	1·1	42·3	9·7	6·6	7·7
Domestic servants	94·7	0·9	88·9	36·3	2·3	13·7
Barbers, hairdressers	92·3	–	53·8	1·8	0.8	1·1
Retail sales	91·4	1·4	50·9	14·4	7·0	9·5
Boardinghouse-keepers	82·6	17·4	95·7	2·8	0·1	1·0
Laundry workers	71·4	21·4	76·8	5·4	0·8	2·4
Jewellers	71·4	9·5	4·3	0·1	1·4	1·0
Garment workers	64·6	8·9	64·2	13·3	3·7	6·9
Shop assistants	63·6	4·5	45·8	5·5	3·3	4·0
(subtotal)				(89·3)	(26·0)	(47·3)
*Occupations with half to average I.S. concentration***						
Carpenters	56·9	10·8	1·5	0·1	4·2	2·9
Butchers, bakers, etc.	50·9	12·7	21·1	1·5	2·8	2·4
Drivers	50·8	32·2	0·5	0·1	12·1	8·1
Painters	45·8	20·8	–	–	1·9	1·3
Metal workers	44·8	29·9	–	–	4·4	2·9
Bricklayers	43·9	26·2	1·7	0·3	7·5	5·1
Shoemakers	43·1	17·6	9·3	0·6	3·1	2·3
Other manufacturing	35·1	13·5	10·0	0·5	2·3	1·7
Waiters, waitresses	34·1	14·6	13·6	0·8	2·4	1·9
Cooks	33·3	14·8	35·7	1·3	1·1	1·2
Electricians	33·3	47·2	–	–	4·7	3·1
Apprentices	30·6	25·0	5·1	0·3	2·3	1·6
(subtotal)				(5·5)	(48·8)	(34·5)

Contd. overleaf

Table 4 cont'd.

Occupations	% occupational workforce in:		Female to male ratio %	% all women workers	% all men workers	% all workers
	I.S. (<5)	F.S. (100+)				
Occupations with less than half the average I.S. concentration***						
Caretakers	28·3	48·3	2·9	0·3	4·3	2·9
Cleaners	26·9	53·8	–	–	1·6	1·1
Mechanics	26·8	32·5	2·3	0·4	8·1	5·5
Stevedores	25·0	53·6	–	–	1·8	1·2
Textile workers	22·2	57·1	26·1	2·3	3·2	2·9
Printers	10·7	35·7	10·3	0·4	1·6	1·2
Potters, glass workers	9·5	47·6	9·1	0·3	1·3	0·9
Postmen	9·5	52·4	4·8	0·1	1·3	0·9
Packers, labellers	5·6	58·3	31·0	1·6	1·8	1·8
(subtotal)				(5·4)	(25·0)	(18·4)
Total	60·1	18·7	35·5	100·2	99·8	100·2

* the average I.S. concentration = 60·1%, i.e. the proportion of the total workforce employed in establishments with less than five workers.
** 30–60%.
*** <30%.
I.S. = Informal Sector: establishments with less than five workers
F.S. = Formal Sector: establishments with more than one hundred workers
Source: Ministry of Labour Urban Employment data (unpublished). (Number in sample: 2377)

informal divide while women's were much more heavily confined to the informal sector; and (4) within the informal sector, women were in occupations that were almost exclusively 'female'. Domestic servants, boardinghouse-keepers, laundresses and garment workers were all over two-thirds female and these four occupations alone accounted for fifty-eight per cent of the entire female manual work-force. Table 5 shows the association between informal sector concentration and sex-ratios. The greater the informal sector concentration, the higher the predominance of women, and the more occupations straddled the two sectors the greater the presence of men. Table 6 gives the actual distribution of men and women in these categories and shows the same polarization.

Let us look now at the consequences of this polarization for gender inequality. One outstanding characteristic of the male occupations compared with the female ones is that the former had a greater range of skill levels than the latter. Almost all women's occupations, with the exception of garment workers, were generally classified as unskilled. Men's occupations, on the other hand, included a number of artisanal trades that carried the label of 'maestro', as well as industrial occupations that were classified as skilled. Most of these occupations fell into the intermediate group which bridged the two sectors, thus facilitating movement between them. In general, earnings tended to be highest in those occupations that had the highest skill levels and the greatest possibilities for bridging between the two sectors. It was this combination of skill hierarchy and sector-overlap that accounted for gender inequalities in informal sector earnings. It also provided the basis for the greater career mobility of men, enabling them to increase their earnings, capital and job security. Women had few such possibilities. Their occupations did not form part of a skill hierarchy and did not straddle the formal/informal sector divide. There was little opportunity for career progression and job movement was confined to exchanging one unskilled, low-paid job for another. The one exception to this was in the clothing industry: dressmaking was a recognised craft skill that carried the status of 'maestra'; women could acquire it through apprenticeship in the informal sector or in factories and sweatshops, and they often moved from the latter into self-employment or outwork in their own homes. However, according to Table 4 only thirteen per cent of manual women fell into this category.

Note that a number of occupations in the third group, that with greater than average formal sector concentration, were unskilled (caretakers, office cleaners, and packers and labellers). All of these were dominated by men, although there was one group with significant numbers of women: packers and labellers. Because of their low level of skill, these occupations had low earnings in comparison with the more highly-skilled formal sector jobs, but most were covered by minimum wage legislation which put them well above the incomes of similar occupations in the informal sector. Male office cleaners and laundry workers, for example, had more than double the incomes of female domestic servants and laundresses in the informal sector.

Table 5 *Manual occupations by degree of informal sector concentration and female concentration, Lima, 1973*

	Degrees of female concentration in occupation				
Degrees of concentration in informal sector	*Almost exclusively male (0–10% F)*	*Below average female share (11–32% F)*	*Above average female share but absolute minority (33–49% F)*	*Absolute majority of women (50–89% F)*	*Almost exclusively female (90–100% F)*
Above average concentration in I.S.(61% +)	Jewellers		Street pedlars Shop assistants Barbers, hairdressers*	Retail stores Laundry workers* Garment workers*	Boardinghouse-keepers Domestic servants
Half to average concentration in I.S. (30–60%)	Carpenters Drivers Painters Metal workers Bricklayers Shoemakers Electricians Apprentices Other operatives	Butchers, bakers Waiters, Waitresses*	cooks*		
Less than half average I.S. concentration (<30%)	Caretakers Cleaners Mechanics Stevedores Printers Potters, glass workers Postmen, messengers	Textile workers Packers, labellers			

* these occupations are internally segregated but cannot be disaggregated because already coded.
Source: Ministry of Labour Urban Employment Survey, 1973 (unpublished).

Table 6 Distribution of men and women manual workers by degree of concentration in informal sector and female concentration of occupation, Lima, Peru, 1973

Degrees of I.S. concentration		Almost exclusively male (0–10% F)		Below average female share (11–32%)		Above av. female share, but abs. minority (33–49% F)		Absolute majority of women (50–89%)		Almost exclusively female (90–100% F)		Total		Grand total
		F	M	F	M	F	M	F	M	F	M	F	M	
Above average (61% +)	F	0·1		—		17·0		33·2		39·1		89·4		
	M		1·4		—		10·7		11·6		2·3		26·0	47·2
Half to average (30–60%)	F	1·9		2·3		1·2		—		—		5·4		
	M		42·6		5·3		1·1		—		—		49·0	34·4
Less than half the average (<30%)	F	1·3		3·9		—		—		—		5·2		
	M		20·0		5·0		—		—		—		25·0	18·4
Total	F	3·3		6·2		18·2		33·2		39·1		100·0		
	M		64·0		10·3		11·8		11·6		2·3		100·0	100·0
Grand total		43·7		8·9		14·0		18·8		14·6				100·0

(Number in sample: 2,377)
Source: Ministry of Labour Urban Employment Survey, 1973 (unpublished).

In summary then, much of the inequality between men and women in both formal and informal sectors was occupationally based. It was women's confinement to unskilled occupations, occupations that were restricted to the informal sector, which accounted for their low levels of income and their low opportunities for mobility. Although men also worked in the informal sector, indeed predominated there, they had access to occupations that facilitated skill acquisition, accumulation of savings and movement between formal and informal sectors; hence a stronger position in the labour market overall. Therefore, as in any society, the sex-segregation of occupations had serious consequences for women, but in one that was also segmented by the formal/informal sector division, they were doubly disadvantaged.

Explaining gender segregation in the informal sector

These data raise two important questions. Why were women restricted to these occupations and why were women's occupations not represented in the formal sector? As already discussed, whereas it might be possible to explain sex-segregation in the formal sector in terms of women's domestic constraints or employer discrimination, it is not easy to explain segregation within the informal sector. It might appear 'natural' that women should have become domestic servants, laundresses or boardinghouse-keepers because these activities replicated their own domestic responsibilities and were largely carried out in their own or other peoples' homes. But why did they not gain access to some of the skilled informal sector occupations, such as shoemaking, tailoring, jewellery, metal-working or painting, which were also carried out in the home? In many cases, apprenticeships were served in artisanal workshops appended to the household, and the family was the major source of access to tools, credit and clients. Could not girls have had access to these resources as well as boys? In fact, it often *was* the case that girls and women were involved in such workshops; I have known women who helped their husbands to stitch the soles to the uppers of shoes and to machine the seams of garments prepared for tailoring. Why then was this work not recognised publicly, why could they not set up in these trades on their own?

The answer to this lies in the family, not as an institution that differentiated the supply of male and female labour to the market, but as one that affected the entire organisation of small-scale production; which handled resource allocation in a much wider sense and designated certain activities as appropriate for men and other activities as appropriate for women. The family was the basis for the division of labour and resource allocation within the domestic sphere, but it also played a similar role within small-scale production. It affected the apprenticeship system, the distribution of credit, tools and client networks. Because it played this role in the organisation of the domestic economy as well as petty commodity production, and because both often took place in the home and involved similar activities, there was a transference of the domestic division of labour to that of small-scale production.

Ironically, kinship traditions amongst peasants and urban workers in Peru embodied expectations that women should contribute economically to the household, have access to economic resources and a degree of economic autonomy. There was also the expectation that women should have educational and mobility aspirations. The gender ideology of many working-class families did not correspond to the stereotypical image of women's low investment in human capital and unstable attachment to the labour force. However, there was a very marked segregation within the family between male and female roles and this segregation carried over into small-scale production. Thus men did not cook, even though they sold cooked food; women did not do construction work even though they were accustomed to hard physical labour; nor did they make men's suits even though they were dressmakers. The male sphere was also the public sphere where authority and control were exercised and where large-scale commercial transactions took place. Women's authority was confined to the domestic sphere, to control over other women and children but not men; their commercial transactions were of the small-scale daily housekeeping type. This restricted their capacity to manage large amounts of capital or to control workshops staffed by male journeymen. One of Grompone's informants, who was the recently widowed wife of a garage owner, tells of the difficulties she had in carrying on the business after his death. Even though she had effectively run it for years after he had become an alcoholic, she was now unable to exercise independent authority in her own right. It was difficult for her to maintain control over the mechanics and to establish credibility with clients (Grompone, 1985, pp. 258–61). Lobo gives an indication that property inheritance in the shanty-towns followed gender lines, in the case cited, the house and contents of the deceased went to the wife, whereas his work tools and equipment went to the brother-in-law (Lobo, 1982, p. 89).

The family undoubtedly did play a role in differentiating women's availability for work because of their responsibilities for child care, and this would have limited the extent to which they could participate in the formal sector. However, as far as the informal sector was concerned, it played a part in *excluding* them from certain resources and activities which might have been compatible with their domestic responsibilities. It was also influential in defining the status of activities that were designated for men and women – that is, their skill, commercial roles, and so on – thereby affecting the actual structure of informal sector activities. This partly explains why female activities such as cooking were not conceived as skilled and why the trade of dressmaking, even though skilled, was not accorded as much status as its male equivalent, tailoring. The higher status of male artisanal trades relative to female was also an effect of the historical actions of urban guilds, which defended them via negotiations with the municipal authorities. This was, above all, a public sphere dominated by men, for the gender ideology of the urban middle classes as well as the peasantry and urban working class excluded women from participation in formal politics. Wilson (1986) notes that women had very little representation in urban guilds in the provincial town she studied, even though similar activities to the men's were being carried out by women in the surrounding rural areas. In summary, the family influenced gender segregation within the informal sector because it affected the way production was organised and defended economically and politically.

This might explain women's exclusion from certain informal sector activities and their concentration in others, but we are still left with the question of why *women's* activities are confined to the informal sector. To answer this would require a more detailed analysis of the economics of women's work than I can provide here, but let me offer some suggestions. First, it is well known that commodity production is more amenable to increasing scales of operation than personal services. Table 4 shows that most of the occupations that straddled the two sectors were commodity-producing activities, while those that were confined to the informal sector consisted of personal services. Although there were some service occupations in the formal sector they consisted of services to firms rather than to individuals. The fact that women's activities consisted of personal services, mainly to homes, made them less feasible for formal sector production. Second, women's services were partly a product of the low cost of female labour and the low incomes of consumers. With increased economic growth it is more likely that such services would be automated out of existence (that is, by washing-machines and other domestic appliances) rather than organised on a formal sector basis. Alternatively, if the incomes of the poor began to rise significantly, boardinghouses and the sale of cooked food would be replaced by hotels and cafes staffed by men rather than women.[15] Women's activities were therefore concentrated in the informal sector because of the high service content; because such services were mainly offered in the private sphere and occupied a specific niche that would be more liable to total substitution than to expansion in scale of operation; and finally, because when such activities did enter the formal sector, they tended to become the property of men.

Conclusion

This chapter has argued that conventional models of the informal sector can legitimately be accused of male bias, but this bias has less to do with the underrepresentation of women and ignorance of their role there than with the characterisation of the sector itself, which is gender-blind. The lack of awareness of gender segregation in the sector, and of the substantial differences in the circumstances of men and women there has meant that the ideal-typical characterisation of the sector is partial.

It mainly applies to women and is seriously misleading as a description of men's employment. Similarly, the characterisation of 'formal' employment applies to men rather than women. Although women are only a small part of the formal sector work-force, nevertheless their role as a casual and cheap source of labour there is not to be underestimated, particularly in certain industries. In the informal sector, however, men are the majority work-force; therefore, if the ideal-typical description does not apply to them, it seriously invalidates the model. A further point is that if the characterisation of 'formal' and 'informal' applies to men and women *regardless* of the size of enterprise or employment status, the explanatory power of such variables is undermined.

One might wonder why these issues have not been realised before now, given the proliferation of empirical studies which have supported the general correlation between enterprise size and earnings, notwithstanding internal diversity. A major reason, in my view, is that not enough attention has been paid to the occupational basis of the formal/informal sector division. In the analysis here, non-manual employment has been excluded in order to provide greater comparability between the two sectors, but in most studies this is not the case. Yet non-manual occupations fall exclusively into the formal sector, and in Lima represented over half of total employment there. The high incomes and better working conditions in occupations such as the professions and high-level administration accounted for a considerable amount of the variation between formal and informal sector incomes, overshadowing internal differences. A second reason has to do with aggregation – the fact that the contrasting employment situations of diverse groups within sectors can cancel each other out when submitted to statistical averaging.

In any event, it is clear that any comprehensive analysis of segmentation in urban labour markets in developing countries must abandon the assumption that there is a single axis of segmentation. Gender cannot replace enterprise size as this axis, for it is not the case that all the men are in the formal sector and all the women in the informal one; although the balance is not even in either sector, both sectors contain men and women. Moreover, within male and female labour markets there is differentiation according to enterprise size. The important point here is that gender *crosscuts* enterprise size as an axis of segmentation. This means that the ideal-typical model has to be made more complex so as to avoid partiality; and more explanatory variables have to be included so that the variation within sectors can be explained as well as that between them.

New models of segregation and discrimination are required that can take account of the specific conditions of informal sector production. Conventional employer discrimination hypotheses are inapplicable, and only small mileage is to be had from conventional supply variables. As we have seen in the Peruvian case, the gender ideology of working-class families did not fit the middle-class stereotype of housebound, economically-dependent wives. There was ample evidence that working women did have a continuous commitment to the labour force, very nearly the same level of education as men and a capacity for entrepreneurial activity akin to that of peasant women.[16] The fact that they were forced into the stereotypical mould had more to do with discriminatory constraints than lack of motivation or ability. It was discrimination within the family – which played a crucial role in the organisation of informal sector activity – coupled with that in the state and the formal labour market, that accounted for women's reduced employment options. Paradoxically then, although the family might have encouraged women to contribute economically to the household, and indeed some poor families may have depended on their support, it was this same institution that confined their options and reduced their capacity to make significant contributions. Conventional informal sector models therefore need to examine the causes and effects of gender segregation in the labour market and remove any biases that may have resulted from ignoring this factor. However, the more recent feminist work also needs to take on board the contradictions within the family that place limits on the extent of women's participation in the informal sector and their capacity to subsidise male wages and family income. It is important to avoid female bias as well as male bias.

Notes

1 For critiques and reviews see the articles in Bromley, 1978, 1985; Bromley and Gerry, 1979; Nelson, 1979.

2 The supply characteristics of labour usually refer to personal variables and include, for example, sex, race, age, length of residence. See Mazumdar (1981) for a good case study analysis of supply variables, and Squire (1979) for a review.

3 For an example of the exploitation approach, see Portes and Walton (1981). The positive approach was featured in some of the earliest work on the informal sector such as the ILO report on Kenya (1972). More recently, it has been espoused by libertarian right-wing economists, for example, De Soto (1986).

4 The low representation of women in the studies reported by Sethuraman was largely the product of a survey methodology that focused on enterprises rather than households. This would have excluded many activities taking place in the home, such as outwork.

5 There is some confusion over whether the term 'informal' is applied to women's paid or unpaid work. In advanced industrial societies it is often used to refer to women's unpaid labour in the home or paid work that is

unregistered officially and hence 'illegal'. In the LDCs it usually refers to paid work that is reported in official government surveys, but which is in non-wage relations or in small-scale enterprises. In this paper I am using the latter definition.

6   See, for example, the articles in Crompton and Mann (1986).

7   There may also be other axes of segmentation, such as race.

8   For the analysis of the 1972/74 period I use three main data sources: (1) the national population census of 1972; (2) two Ministry of Labour employment surveys, one in 1973 and another in 1974. These two surveys use the same methodology and give coverage of a large sample population (*c.* 7,000 individuals of working age and *c.* 3,500 economically active individuals); (3) 192 case studies collected by myself, selected from the 1973 sample for reinterview. There is a comprehensive evaluation of the first two of these sources in Scott (1988). The census data suffer from a slight underestimation of married women's work, in comparison with the survey data. My view is that the degree of underestimation in the Ministry of Labour data is relatively small due to its highly trained and experienced interviewing staff. Most of the data presented in this paper are the results of my own computations of the Ministry survey data.

9   In a segmentation analysis the assumption is that comparable jobs have different levels of earnings because of enterprise or institutional variables which prevent competition between groups that would otherwise be seeking the same jobs. In Peru, the gap between manual and non-manual labour is so large that one cannot assume that the two are competing groups. In manual employment, however, this is more feasible given internal job mobility. The definition of 'manual' employment was made on the basis of a detailed scrutiny of the physical content of work in occupations described at the three-digit level of classification.

10   More detailed figures are provided in Scott (1986a and 1986b).

11   These two definitions have different theoretical origins, although they are interconnected. The enterprise size definition originates from a concern with the technological and financial structure of the enterprise while the employment status definition relates to the role of labour in the process of accumulation. The numerical difference between the two definitions is due to the position of wage workers in enterprises with less than five workers. These would have been apprentices, 'helpers' on construction sites, fares collectors on buses, etc. Amongst women, they would have been apprentices in clothing workshops and sales assistants in small shops. Many of these men and women would have been relatives and probably were paid partly in cash and partly in food and accommodation. There is therefore a good case for including them in the informal sector, in spite of the wage component, since their conditions of work differed substantially from formal sector wage-workers. However, it is not possible to identify such workers in the censuses since they did not collect information on enterprise size. The Ministry of Labour did have this information, and for all subsequent analysis it is the wider definition that is used.

12   The problem of undercounting applies mainly to married women's work and would have included mainly casual jobs with very low earnings.

The figures on the number of married women in paid employment are relatively constant even in anthropological monographs that would have been less susceptible to undercounting.

13 Compare this with thirty-six per cent in a similar study carried out in the USA (Bendix and Lipset, 1964, p. 159). Note, however, that these figures included non-manual employment.

14 By 'better jobs' I mean jobs with higher incomes, more skill, better working conditions and good chances of upward mobility.

15 In the peasant and working-class family, food has important symbolic value as the basis for domestic relationships and wider social networking; and women have a particularly strong association with it. Women have the exclusive obligation to prepare food and to serve it to the members of the household or their guests. Yet in the formal sector, men are the cooks and the waiters. Similarly, women are the caretakers of their own homes or even employers' homes, yet formal sector caretakers are all men.

16 Peasant women are known for their energy as traders. Because of bilateral inheritance systems, they have access to land and associated resources and these are often channelled into transport and trading ventures.

References

Babb, F. (1986), 'Producers and reproducers: Andean marketwomen in the economy' in J. Nash and H. Safa (eds) *Women and Change in Latin America*, Bergin & Garvey, Massachusetts, pp. 53–63.

Balan, J., Browning, H. L., and Jelin, E. (1973), *Men in a Developing Society*, Latin American Monographs No. 30, University of Texas Press, Austin, Texas.

Bendix, R., and Lipset, S. M. (1964), *Social Mobility in Industrial Society*, University of California Press, Berkeley.

Bromley, R. (ed.) (1978), 'The informal sector: critical perspectives', special issue of *World Development*, vol. 6, no. 9/10.

——(1985), *Planning for Small Enterprises in Third World Cities*, Pergamon, Oxford and New York.

Bromley, R., and Gerry, C. (eds) (1979), *Casual Work and Poverty in Third World Cities*, John Wiley, Chichester and New York.

Buechler, J.-M. (1986), 'Women in petty commodity production in La Paz, Bolivia', in J. Nash and H. Safa (eds) *Women and Change in Latin America*, Bergin & Garvey, Massachusetts, pp. 165–87.

Bunster, X., and Chaney, E. M. (1985), *Sellers and Servants: Working Women in Lima, Peru*, Praeger, New York.

Crompton, R., and Mann, M. (1986), *Gender and Stratification*, Polity Press, Cambridge.

De Soto, H. (1986), *El Otro Sendero*, Editorial El Barranco, Lima, Peru.

Grompone, R. (1985), *Talleristas y Vendedores Ambulantes en Lima*, DESCO, Lima, Peru.

ILO (International Labour Office) (1972), *Employment, Incomes and Inequality: A Strategy for Increasing Productive Employment in Kenya*, ILO, Geneva.

Lobo, S. (1982), *A House of My Own: Social Organization in the Squatter Settlements of Lima, Peru*, University of Arizona Press, Tucson, Arizona.

Mazumdar, D. (1975), 'The urban informal sector' World Bank Staff Working Paper No. 211, Washington DC. Also published in *World Development*, vol. 4, 1976, pp. 655–79.

——(1981), *The Urban Labor Market and Income Distribution: A Study of Malaysia*, published for the World Bank, Oxford University Press, Oxford.

Morley, S. A. (1982), *Labor Markets and Inequitable Growth*, Cambridge University Press, Cambridge and New York.

Moser, C. (1977), 'The dual economy and marginality debate and the contribution of micro analysis: market sellers in Bogota', *Development and Change*, vol. 8, no. 4, pp. 465–89.

——(1981), 'Surviving in the suburbios', *IDS Bulletin*, vol. 12, no. 3, pp. 19–29 (special issue on Women and the Informal Sector).

Nelson, J. M. (1979), *Access to Power*, Princeton University Press, Princeton, NJ.

Portes, A., and Walton, J. (1981), *Labor, Class and the International System*, Academic Press, New York.

Redclift, N. (1985), 'The contested domain: gender, accumulation and the labour process', in N. Redclift and E. Mingione (eds), *Beyond Employment*, Basil Blackwell, Oxford, pp. 92–125.

Roldan, M. (1985), 'Industrial outworking, struggles for the reproduction of working-class families and gender subordination', in *ibid.*, pp. 248–85.

Scott, A. MacEwen, (1986a), 'Economic development and urban women's work: the case of Lima, Peru', in R. Anker and C. Hein (eds), *Sex Inequalities in Urban Employment in the Third World*, Macmillan, London, pp. 313–65.

——(1986b), 'Women and industrialisation: examining the "female marginalization" thesis', *Journal of Development Studies*, vol. 22, no. 4, pp. 649–80.

——(1988), 'Peruvian employment statistics since 1940: an evaluation', University of Liverpool, Institute for Latin American Studies, Working Paper No. 8.

Sethuraman, S. V. (1981), *The Urban Informal Sector In Developing Countries*, ILO, Geneva.

Smith, C. A. (1986), 'Reconstructing the elements of petty commodity production', *Social Analysis*, no. 20, December, pp. 29–46.

Squire, L. (1979), 'Labour force, employment and labour markets in the course of economic development', World Bank Staff Working Paper No. 336, Washington DC.

Wilson, F. (1986), 'Urban craftsmen and their struggle against capitalism: a case study from Peru', *Social Analysis*, no. 20, December, pp. 69–78.

Young, K., and Moser, C. (eds) (1981), *Women and the Informal Sector*, *IDS Bulletin*, vol. 12, no. 3.

Male bias and women's work in Mexico's border industries

This chapter charts the trajectory of women's employment in Mexico's border industries and critically examines some interpretations of its significance. It argues that the female work-force should not be viewed as an undifferentiated mass of women all sharing the same characteristics, and highlights important differences between the female work-force in electronics and garment factories. It also shows how women in both sectors have largely been confined to low-paid jobs without prospects at the bottom of the production hierarchy. The growth in recent years of jobs requiring technical and administrative skills is shown to be associated with a fall in the female share of the labour force. Male bias has structured both the way in which women have been incorporated into the border industries, and the appraisal of the significance of this growth of industrial jobs for women.

The development of the border industries

Since the mid-1960s women have formed the major part of the industrial labour force in the border states of northern Mexico. The 'maquiladora'[1] or border industries are largely labour-intensive industries typical of the offshore manufacturing or 'export processing'[2] which has been the dominant feature of Third World industrialisation in the 1970s and early 1980s. Although there has been some diversification in the type of industries operating within the border areas, women continue to form the majority of those employed.

The preference for women workers for labour-intensive assembly operations in industries around the world is widely acknowledged.[3] However, it is interesting that in the early stages of the Border Industrialisation Programme (BIP), the employment of women was not anticipated. The programme was initiated by the Mexican government in 1965 as part of a series of measures to offset the adverse effects on the Mexican economy of immigration control and protectionist policies in the United States.

The economy of Mexico's northern states over the last hundred years has been more integrated with the economy of the southern states of the USA than with the rest of Mexico. Mexico's post-Second World War expansion of import-substituting industrialisation was not extended to the border states; and a large proportion of the consumption expenditure in this area goes directly on US goods (SIC, 1974).

The border between Mexico and the United States is of comparatively recent creation. It was not until 1851, with the annexation of Texas, that the USA finally halted its territorial expansion which had already forced Mexico to cede to its more powerful northern neighbour, the States of California, Arizona and New Mexico: thus losing more than fifty per cent of the territory which comprised the Republic of Mexico in 1821.

The border has remained a source of conflict between the two countries. In some senses it constitutes an artificial barrier which has been overridden when the dynamics of accumulation in the agricultural, industrial and service sectors in the USA have required access to the pool of cheap labour from Mexico. Migration from Mexico – often seasonal labour for agriculture and construction projects, as well as casual labour for the manufacturing sector and domestic and other low-paid service jobs – has been a constant feature of the economy of the south west of the USA throughout this century, in spite of periodic attempts to restrict immigration by the US government. The willingness and ability of Mexicans to migrate, often illegally, is partly a reflection of the fact that the population of the south-west of the USA is predominantly of Hispanoamerican origin (Flores Cabellero, 1982). It also reflects the high levels of unemployment in Mexico and the failure of the industrialisation programmes of the 1950s and 1960s to generate sufficient employment opportunities to absorb the growing population throughout Mexico.

The BIP was directly stimulated by a US Congress decision in 1964 to rescind the legislative basis of the 'Bracero' programme, by which a fixed number of Mexicans were permitted to migrate across the border for specified employment. This left the Mexican government with a serious crisis. Not only did the flow of potential migrants continue to head for the frontier cities in spite of the fact that there were no further legal opportunities to work in the USA; in addition, the Mexican economy stood to suffer from the drying-up of the flow of remittances from immigrants working in the USA, which in some years had contributed up to forty per cent of foreign exchange inflows. At the local level there was a rapid increase in population in the northern border cities, where officially estimated unemployment rates ran as high as forty to fifty per cent by 1966.

The Mexican government had made previous attempts to solve the chronic unemployment problem in the border towns, which acted both as a pole of attraction for rural migrants and those migrating from towns in the interior of Mexico, and as a stepping-stone and negotiating post for those intending to continue their journey north to seek work in the USA. In 1961 PRONAF (Programa Nacional Fronterizo) was launched with the aim of modernising northern cities, cleaning up their image as Rest and Recreation posts for troops serving in Panama and elsewhere in the region, and encouraging a higher participation of Mexican-produced goods in the commercial transactions of the areas (NACLA, 1975).

PRONAF resulted in the establishment of hotels, trailer camps and parks for North American tourists, and the construction of commercial complexes and shopping centres, but no significant industrial activity was inaugurated. The programme was ineffective in developing an industrial alternative to absorb the growing population of the urban areas, swelled by rural migrants displaced by the intensifying pace of mechanisation and concentration of ownership in agriculture, especially in the states of Baja California, Sonora and Chihuahua.

The BIP, which led to the development of the border industries, was thus intended as a substitute for emigration, as much to replace lost foreign exchange transfers as to provide employment opportunities. The basic idea of the programme was to encourage foreign (primarily American) firms to establish labour-intensive manufacturing activities in Mexico where they could profit from the differential between the cost of labour there and in the USA. Such a policy was seen as attractive both to the Mexican government, which stood to gain foreign exchange as US companies converted dollars to pay for Mexican workers and local inputs of goods and services, as well as employment creation within Mexico; and to the American companies which had been deprived of their legal access to cheap Mexican labour as the result of US labour union pressure. The initiative for the programme came from the Mexican government, following visits to East Asian countries where such labour-intensive manufacturing industries producing for the export market had been established for some years; and where such activity was frequently located in specially created Free Trade Zones.

For American firms, the possibility of taking advantage of the lower wage rates in Mexico (and in Asia), was enhanced by the introduction of certain special clauses in the US Tariff Schedule. These allowed American firms to export partially processed products or components for further processing and assembly abroad, and re-import them into the USA, with import duties only payable on the value added abroad – that is, primarily on the labour cost of the overseas operation.

Because of Mexico's proximity to the USA, it was argued that there were special advantages for American firms relocating part of their production process to the Mexican border areas rather than to more distant Third World countries, even though labour costs in Mexico were higher than those in South East Asia and Central America. First, the nearness to the US domestic market means that transportation costs are lower. This is particularly important for products which have a high weight to value ratio and accounts for the fact that there is a greater variety of goods produced by maquiladora industries than in many Free Trade Zones elsewhere. A second advantage is the possibility that firms can operate 'twin plants' – that is, a firm located in one of the US border towns can establish an assembly plant on the Mexican side of the border and run both plants as an integrated operation using a single management, technical and personnel structure.[4] Both the geographical proximity and the direct control available through twin plants make production in Mexico more flexible: for instance, when the dictates of fashion or unseasonal weather alter the predicted demand for certain lines in the apparel industry, it is easier to change the orders to a Mexican sub-contractor than to a plant located in Hong Kong or the Philippines.

In spite of these attractions, it took three or four years of official encouragement from the US government (NACLA, 1975), and considerable changes in the Mexican investment regulations for the area, before the maquiladora plants established themselves in Mexico in any significant numbers.[5] The Mexican government enacted a series of special measures which enabled foreign manufacturers to import components and export the finished goods incorporating them, under a bond system without incurring customs duties. In addition, machinery could be imported duty free on a temporary basis. Both the Federal government and individual states also introduced a number of fiscal incentives, including exemption from some local and national taxes, and some state governments initiated the construction of special industrial parks, complete with required utilities, telecommunications facilities and road networks (Carillo and Hernandez, 1985, pp. 94–89).

Mexico had to compete as a location for offshore processing with other Third World countries where wages were considerably lower. Whilst hourly wage rates in Mexico were less than twenty-five per cent of US unskilled wage rates, they were still considerably higher than those quoted for East and South-East Asian countries which were already exporting to the USA under items 807 and 806.30 of the US Tariff Schedule (USITC, 1975). However, the advantages of Mexico, in terms of the nearness to the final market, the reduction in transport costs both of materials and components and of assembled goods for re-export to the USA, together with the incentive package offered by Mexico and her long record of political stability, eventually proved sufficient inducements for US investments in the northern border area.

The BIP got off to a slow start as the administrative and infrastructural framework spread slowly across the major border towns. In December 1965 there were only twelve maquiladora plants, employing some 3,000 people; but by 1970 the official total was 120 plants, with a workforce of 20,000 (see Table 1). In the early 1970s the overall level of employment continued to increase until the sharp recession in the American economy led to employment cut-backs in 1975. A strong body of US entrepreneurial opinion, widely shared in Mexican government circles, held that escalating labour resistance in Mexico, as workers organised to demand better wages, fringe benefits and working conditions in many of the larger plants, was 'forcing' American firms to abandon production in

Mexico for other locations where the work-force was more amenable to the conditions and remuneration they offered.

Table 1   *Growth of the maquiladora industry in Mexico 1968–88*

Year	Number of plants	Total labour force
1968	112	11,000
1969	108	15,900
1970	120	20,300
1971	251	29,200
1972	n.d.	48,100
1973	247	64,300
1974	455	76,000
1975	454	67,200
1976	448	74,500
1977	443	78,400
1978	457	90,700
1979	540	111,400
1980	620	119,500
1981	605	131,000
1982	585	127,000
1983	600	151,000
1984	672	199,700
1985	760	212,000
1986	987	268,400
1987	1055	290,579
1988	1450	330,579

Sources: Sklair, 1989, table 8–1; Carillo and Hernandez, 1985, fig 1, table III–I; SIC, 1974.

The Mexican government was sufficiently alarmed by the current and threatened scale of cut-backs in the maquiladora plants in the mid-1970s to offer an improved package of incentives to American firms, although there is little hard evidence that many of the companies withdrawing from Mexico actually did set up replacement operations in other Third World countries. New regulations increased the tax holidays enjoyed by the plants; reduced their obligations to pay social security quotas and other local taxes; extended the period during which workers could be legally kept on temporary contracts; and allowed a more liberal interpretation of the laws about 'justifiable dismissal of workers' (Carillo and Hernandez, 1985, p. 93). In 1976 the Mexican peso was substantially devalued, which reduced labour costs in dollar terms by approximately 100 per cent at a stroke. As the US economy started to recover from the recession, the maquiladora plants began to increase and expand employment again. The Mexican government was so convinced of the benefits of this type of industrial activity that the legal and administrative basis of the programme was extended to the interior and south-east of the country, though some ninety-five per cent of employment continued to be located in the northern border region.

Indeed, for some time after the 1976 currency devaluation, Mexico's competitive position *vis-à-vis* competing locations improved. The dollar cost of wages and salaries fell from US$215 million in 1976 to US$200 million in 1977, even though the total number employed rose by 4,000 in that year. One estimate indicates that the average savings per worker, compared with costs in the USA, increased from US$6,000 in 1972 to US$10–12,000 in 1978 (Fernandez-Kelly, 1978, cited in Carillo and Hernandez, 1985, p.100). In dollar terms the minimum wage paid to maquiladora workers had fallen to ten per cent of daily wage minimum rates in the USA by 1983, compared with a level of twenty per cent in 1969–78, (*ibid.*, p. 131). In spite of the fears of increased workers' militancy in 1975, Mexico regained a more stable political image with the ending of the Echeverria presidency in 1976, and with this the promise of a more stable economic and industrial relations environment. From 1979, the maquiladora regulations were extended beyond the border states to cover the whole country. Again in the early eighties, inflation and instability temporarily halted the expansion of the programme, but devaluation in 1982 again ensured a continuing growth of both employment and number of plants which continued unabated up to 1988 (see Table 1).

Gender composition of the labour force

In 1975, the overwhelming majority (78·3 per cent) of unskilled production workers ('operators') employed in the maquiladora plants were women (Table 2). No detailed breakdown of the gender composition of technical, administrative and managerial staff is available, but it is known that few women were employed at these levels. Women operators constituted 64·5 per cent of the total maquiladora labour force in 1975. Women's share of employment has been declining in the 1980s (see Table 2) for reasons that will be discussed later, but even in 1987, women constituted over two-thirds of operators, and female operators constituted over half of total employment in the maquiladora plants. Despite the declining share, the absolute level of women's employment has continued to rise, the number of women operators almost tripling in the decade 1975–85.

A study undertaken in 1975 by the Institute of Research on Labour (INET, 1975) gives more detailed information about the gender composition of the labour force in plants registered as maquiladoras in the municipalities of the six most important centres in northern Mexico. In these plants taken together, women comprised seventy-five per cent of the total labour force, but the proportion of women varied between plants in different industrial sectors.

Confirming the findings of other research, this study showed that women were concentrated in electronics, clothing, shrimp and other food processing, toymaking and coupon-sorting, where they comprised up to ninety per cent of the total labour force. Mexican government statistics indicate that in 1975, women comprised 81·6 per cent of the production workers in the electrical and electronics sector, 82·5 per cent in the shoes and garments sector, [6] and 73·5 per cent in the food products sector, but only 64·4 per cent in the miscellaneous sector, which includes metal processing and transportation equipment and components (SIC, 1974).

The INET study also indicated that men were the preferred labour force in maquiladora firms making transportation equipment, leather and synthetic goods including shoes, wood and metal furniture, photographic, sporting and paper goods. In two of these sectors – furniture, and transport and machinery – men comprised 96·5 per cent and 72·3 per cent of the labour force, although employment in these sectors was only 3·5 per cent of the total.

Thus in the sectors which accounted for the major part of employment, women made up eighty per cent of the total labour force. In those sectors which are untypical of export processing activities elsewhere in the world, and, until recent years, not extensive even in Mexico – that is, transportation equipment, wood and metal furniture – the percentage of men employed matched that

Table 2 *Gender composition of Maquiladora labour force, 1975–87*

	Total employment	Operator employment					Technical staff	Salaried (admin/manag)
		A Total	*B Male*	*C Female*	*D Female as % of total operator employ-ment*	*E Female operators as % of total employment*		
1975 National (all Mexico)	65,318	53,771	11,653	42,118	78·3	64·5		
1979 National	111,365	95,818	21,981	73,837	77·0	66·3	9,569	5,978
Border industries	100,537	86,879	20,343	66,536	76·6	66·2	8,613	5,045
1980 National	119,546	102,020	23,140	78,880	77·3	65·0	10,828	6,698
Border industries	106,576	91,308	21,455	69,583	76·2	65·3	9,626	5,639
1981 National	130,973	110,634	24,993	85,691	77·4	65·4	12,545	7,744
Border industries	116,540	98,931	23,047	75,884	76·7	65·1	11,033	6,486
1982 National	127,048	105,383	23,990	81,393	77·2	64·1	13,377	8,288
Border industries	113,227	94,455	22,254	72,201	76·4	63·7	1,956	6,816
1983 National	150,867	125,278	32,004	93,274	74·4	61·8	16,332	9,267
Border industries	134,915	112,531	29,862	82,669	73·5	61·3	14,747	7,437
1984 National	199,684	165,505	48,215	117,290	70·9	58·7	22,381	11,798
Border industries	176,909	146,944	45,338	101,606	69·1	57·4	20,184	9,781
1985 National	211,968	173,874	53,832	120,042	69·0	56·6	25,042	13,052
Border industries	186,000	152,819	50,195	102,624	67·2	55·2	22,313	10,868
1986 National	242,234	197,836	62,492	135,346	68·4	55·9	29,615	14,881
1987 National	290,579	236,088	78,940	157,090	66·6	54·1	35,138	19,403

Source: Calculated from Table 8, INEGI (Instituto Nacional de Estadística, Geografía e Informática), *Estadísticas de la Industria Maquiladora de Exportación*, Mexico, Secretaría de Programación y Presupuesto.

of women in the other sectors (that is, up to ninety per cent). In paper clothing, there was apparently a more even division between men and women in the labour force. Though sewing in Mexico is a traditionally female occupation, the employment of men in manufacturing paper clothing was explained by less need for accurate and reliable sewing skills on a product that is designed for a very short life (INET, 1975, p. 6).

The sectoral variation in the proportion of women and men in the labour force corresponded to the variation in the ratio of labour costs to total production costs. Those sectors which employed a predominantly female labour force were those in which labour costs were the largest component of total manufacturing cost, but at the same time, unit labour costs (that is the ratio of value of total output to labour costs) were the lowest. Labour costs, which include wages plus legally enforceable labour-related payments such as social security payments, comprised between fifty-eight and sixty-eight per cent of total value of the products in the electronics, clothing and food maquiladoras. In other sectors, notably transport and electrical machinery, where a higher proportion of male labour was employed, the importance of labour costs in total costs fell to below fifty per cent (*ibid*).

The reasons for the preference for women in labour processes which rely on manual dexterity performed under closely supervised and/or speed-regulated conditions have been discussed elsewhere (Elson and Pearson, 1981). In the Mexican situation, it is clear that the availability of a potential pool of female labour was a major inducement for North American firms locating in the region, in spite of the Mexican government's expectation that the BIP would provide jobs for unemployed men. A report by Arthur D. Little Inc. in 1968 recommended that the availability of women workers could be increased rapidly by increasing women's participation in the work-force, recruiting workers from the commercial and agricultural sectors, and attracting additional migrants from the interior of Mexico (cited in Carillo and Hernandez, 1985, p. 88).

Appraisal of the implications of the growth in female employment: the problem of male bias

Appraisal of the implications of this growth in female employment has centred on two issues – has it increased rather than diminished the problem of unemployment? Has it integrated women into development or led to their exploitation? Male bias can be seen in attempts to answer both questions.

The most crude form of male bias can be seen in the widely held view that maquiladoras have failed in their objective of employment creation because they have not provided enough jobs for male workers and may have actually deprived men of employment opportunities (Sklair, 1989, ch. 8). This argument is based on a number of gender-biased assumptions, the most common of which is that only male workers are considered to have an economic need to find employment. Yet Tiano's evidence (1987b), corroborated by the research carried out by Fernandez-Kelly (1983b), demonstrates that women's participation in the maquiladora industries is undertaken because of economic need, to support the households in which they are daughters, wives and/or mothers.

The second biased assumption is that before the establishment of the maquiladora factories women did not participate in Mexico's industrial labour force. In fact, it is well documented that since the initiation of industrialisation in Mexico in the 1950s, the participation of women has steadily grown (Noriega Verdugo, 1982). What has changed is the *visibility* of such employment; whilst women were employed in textile factories, food-processing factories and other traditional industries, they were part of a labour force that was not necessarily predominantly female, and were working in areas where men's industrial employment was very common, such as in the industrial areas around Mexico City, Monterey, Puebla and other centres of industrial growth. In the border regions, the situation is quite different. First, women are working in regions where no or few factories existed before; second, they are working in factories which employ a predominantly female labour force, so that they are a majority, not a minority, of the industrial labour force. And third, an enormous amount of government, academic and political attention has been focused on the maquiladora plants, which for some represented not only the opportunity to bring economic development to the Mexican border and increase its autonomy from the United States, but a new export-oriented development strategy that could have implications for the whole future of Mexico's development (see Sklair, 1988b).

However, there is a further question of whether the growth of the border industries has diminished the problem of *women's* unemployment. Some researchers argue that it has tended to increase the rate of female unemployment as conventionally measured. The logic of this position is that the demand for women in the maquiladora plants induced an increase in the level of women's labour force participation (that is, the proportion of women in any given age cohort who declare themselves in or seeking employment) in excess of the actual rate of employment creation, thus increasing women's unemployment rate (which is measured as the proportion of economically active women who are not in recognised employment). The findings of Tiano (1987b) that unemployment rates for women in the age groups from which the bulk of the maquiladora operatives are initially recruited are higher in the majority of the northern states than in Mexico as a whole, have been used to support this hypothesis, although statistically they are not conclusive.[7]

A UN-sponsored study suggests some reasons for the rising rate of measured unemployment. Konig (1975, p. 74) reports that 'much of the maquiladora manpower [*sic*], particularly at the operator level, is incorporated into the economically active population for the first time. In the case that the level of operations falls off, these people will not simply go back to their families, but rather join the ranks of those looking for work.' In addition, the numbers of unemployed are swelled by the many unsuccessful applicants for maquiladora jobs who prefer to wait for an opportunity for in-plant employment rather than take another job: '45 per cent of the total operators surveyed without previous work experience had not bothered to take up a job previously', and 'quite a few girls that had been suspended for some time in the past – three to eight months at a time because of the lack of work in maquiladoras . . . had not bothered to look for a job in the interim.' (*Ibid.*, p. 67).

However, the assumption that the women working in the maquiladora plants had become economically active for the first time is a further, more subtle, example of male bias. It is likely that women waiting for job opportunities in the maquiladora plants had not previously sought permanent, formal sector jobs, but had been involved in casual labour in the informal sector, though some may have been continuing their studies where economic circumstances permitted. This would be quite consistent with responses to a questionnaire, that earlier they had not been seeking or engaged in work, since, as is widely recognised, both interviewers and respondents to questions about work often adopt a conceptualisation of work which is restricted to formal sector employment, and excludes the range of other, informal, income-generating strategies which most women are constantly undertaking (see Beneria, 1981). Respondents were asked whether they had been in employment or had been seeking employment in the previous week. It is probable that the knowledge that formal sector factory work – 'employment' – now existed would have encouraged positive responses on 'seeking employment' from women who would previously have answered in the negative – either because they knew there were no possibilities of obtaining formal sector work, or to conceal informal sector casual work from the attention of the authorities. Konig's research techniques may thus have misidentified the reasons for an increase in measured unemployment.

There is a further argument that the labour supply has been increased because many of the maquiladora workers of non-local origin, who are successful in finding jobs, induce substantial migration of female relatives from elsewhere in Mexico to join them in order to seek similar employment. This would not only have the effect of increasing the available supply of appropriate labour for recruitment to the maquiladora plants, but also increase the economically active population by a larger amount than actual employment increases at any given time, thus again exerting an upward pressure on recorded rates of unemployment. Contrary to conventional assumptions, maquiladora workers were not necessarily recruited from the rural poor: Fernandez-Kelly's research indicates that, at least in the late 1970s , the majority of women workers in Cuidad Juarez's maquiladoras who were of migrant origin, came from smaller towns in the northern or neighbouring states – they were not the displaced rural migrants of the classical literature (Fernandez-Kelly, 1983a, p. 215).

Migration to the urban centres had been a continuing feature of the border regions for some years, and it is argued, would have continued even without the attraction of employment in the new manufacturing plants (Bustamente, 1983; Fernandez-Kelly, 1983b). What is new is the impact that the demand for female labour had on perceptions of women's labour force status. More women regarded themselves, and were regarded by labour force enumerators, as unemployed than would previously have been the case. Any discernible increase in measured unemployment rates is as likely to result from this change as from the migratory pull exercised by the growth of the maquiladora industry itself.

Another subtle form of male bias can be seen at work in the appraisal of whether women have been 'integrated' into national development by incorporating them into modern industry, or 'exploited' in the sense that maquiladora factories take advantage of and reinforce women's structural vulnerability within the labour market and the family (Sklair, 1989, ch. 8; Tiano, 1987a). The problem here is the treatment of women working in the border industries as an homogeneous category, so that 'women' are added on as a single category to a preconceived analytical framework. It is more helpful to use the concept of gender relations which permits a disaggregation of women by socio-economic class, age, education, marital status, etc., in order to understand the interaction between various sets of social relations within and between the labour market and the family (Pearson, 1986). This would modify Tiano's conclusion that the exploitation thesis cannot hold because the evidence indicates that 'companies do not appear to recruit their workers from the most vulnerable sections of the female labour force, as the exploitation thesis would predict' (Tiano, 1987b). However, evidence from Tiano's and others' research (Fernandez-Kelly, 1983a; Escamilla and Vigorito, 1977) indicates that different industrial sectors employ different women, and that conditions of employment and 'exploitation' also vary between sectors. In the electronics factories in Mexico, most of which are direct subsidiaries of MNCS, the work-force tends to be younger and better educated than those employed in the smaller garment factories, many of which are sub-contractors for US firms rather than direct subsidiaries. In the electronics factories, physical working conditions are superior and wages are more likely to comply with minimum wage legislation. Clearly, a greater disaggregation of both the maquiladora factories and the structure of the female labour force would modify the over-general conclusion cited above.

Whilst women's subordinate status in the abstract is often invoked as an explanation for the employment of women workers in labour-intensive assembly work, class, educational opportunities, age, marital status, domestic responsibilities and previous working experience all interact to determine the specific forms that women's employment takes. Moreover, different attributes are appropriate to different labour processes, and management uses a variety of strategies to try to ensure that the work-force recruited is optimal for the labour process in which it is being employed (see Pearson (1986) for an extended discussion on this point).

Characteristics of the female labour force in the border industries

In spite of the growth of other sectors within the border industries, clothing and electronics are still the largest, and comprise the sectors in which the bulk of women's employment continues to be concentrated. As demonstrated above, one of the consequences of the male bias in the discussion of employment in this, and other, export-oriented industrial locations is that an over-generalised analysis of the female labour force is produced. However, case study research reveals important differences between the characteristics of the women workers in each of these two sectors, differences which are related to the organisational structure of the industry, the technology of production, the organisation and control of labour in the production process, and the different contractual relationships between the maquiladora plants and their US partners.

The electronics plants in the Mexican northern border states tend to be larger (in terms of numbers of employees) than the clothing plants; are more often directly-owned subsidiaries of American companies; and are generally engaged in the production and assembly of components such as semiconductors or consumer products such as video recorders and colour television sets, which are re-exported and marketed in the US as the product of the parent company (Fernandez-Kelly, 1983a, pp. 102–7).

This association with the modern, American electronics industry is exploited by employers, who foster the impression that employment in electronics plants represents a superior option for the work-force. In part, this distinction reflects real factors, in that electronics workers are on average paid higher wage rates than those in clothing or comparable sectors. Moreover, the larger electronics plants have better and more modern working conditions. They are more likely to be located in specially constructed modern industrial parks, and to occupy newly built purpose-fitted factory buildings, which boast air-conditioning (to maintain the technical quality of the product rather than the comfort of the workers), piped music and company uniforms. Because of their more direct relationship with their US principals, and the larger scale of their investment, it is assumed – at least in normal (that is, non-recessionary) times – that these plants offer more stable employment, and that in general the wage level will approximate to the legal minimum wage, in addition to any fringe benefits such as health and social security insurance (Nurayama and Munoz, 1979, pp. 65–6).

In contrast, the clothing sector is characterised by smaller firms that generally operate under sub-contracting relationships with one or more US corporations, which are as likely to be marketing (retail or wholesale) companies (such as Sears Roebuck) as garment-production companies. These garment maquiladoras are very often owned, at least in name, by Mexican companies; and are distributed widely along the frontier region (and elsewhere) outside the special industrial parks. Partly because of their indirect relationship with their contracting partners in the United States, and also because of the volatility in the clothing market caused by fashion, the weather and intense competition, as well as fluctuations in consumers' disposable income, clothing maquiladoras have an unstable history. The composition of the garment sector fluctuates with continued closures of existing firms and establishment of new ones, or re-establishment of old firms with different legal identities (Escamilla and Vigorito, 1977).

The superiority of the electronics plants, at least up to the early 1980s, made them the preferred employment sector for women workers, and this allowed electronics employers to exercise a fair degree of control over whom they recruited. This is reflected in the disparity between the labour force in the electronics sector, compared to that in the clothing sector, over a wide range of characteristics. Fernandez-Kelly's study (1983a) in Ciudad Juarez confirms this view; of her sample, eighty-five per cent of women employed in the electronics plants were aged twenty-four or under, whilst seventy per cent were under twenty-one. On the other hand, only thirty-six per cent of those working for clothing maquiladoras were under twenty-four. At the youngest and oldest ends of the age range, the differences were even more extreme: only four per cent of workers in the clothing plants were under eighteen compared with thirty-two per cent in electronics – nearly a third of all electronics workers; but twenty-three per cent of clothing workers were over thirty-one, and a full sixty-four per cent were over twenty-five. None of the electronics workers surveyed was over thirty-one, and only fifteen per cent were between twenty-five and thirty. A later study confirmed this trend, showing that in 1978, 79·3 per cent of electronics workers were under twenty-four, whilst over thirty-eight per cent of clothing workers were over twenty-five.

There is a correlation between the different age profile of workers in these two sectors and their marital and maternal status. The electronics workers are more likely to conform to the 'young, single, childless' stereotype (see Pearson, 1986) than the older garment workers. Of Fernandez-Kelly's sample, sixty-one per cent were single, lower than what might have been expected from the literature, but higher than the fifty-four per cent of the garment-sector workers. While the younger age range of the electronics workers would tend to suggest a lower percentage of married women, there may be some discrepancy between the electronics firms' stated preference for single women and the actual situation.

The study by INET (1975, p. 12) reported that many women who were in fact married, declared themselves to be single because they knew that 'this increases their attraction to the firms'. Carrillo and Hernandez (1985, p. 115) reported that nearly ten per cent of all electronics workers were single parents; moreover, forty per cent of electronics workers were mothers, lower than the sixty per cent of clothing workers, but still a large deviation from the 'young, single, childless' stereotype. A study carried out by the authors in Cuidad Juarez in 1978 indicated that 57·5 per cent of electronics workers were single compared with thirty per cent of the clothing workers (*ibid*).

However, it was clear that the firms were concerned about whether the worker had children, responsibility for whom could detract from her productivity, availability for overtime and flexibility with regard to changing shift times and temporary shut-downs. Predictably, a higher proportion of the (older) women in the garment sector had children of their own, one in three of them being single parents. Electronics workers were more likely to live in households in which they were daughters, and to be one of two or more income providers in the household (sixty-eight per cent of total sample): whereas twenty-seven per cent of garment workers were the sole income earners in their households (Fernandez-Kelly, 1983a, pp. 54–7).

Comparison of educational qualifications also points up the differences between these two groups of workers. Women employed in the electronics factories had on average eight years' formal schooling compared to six in the clothing industry. It is interesting to note that nearly sixty per cent of electronics workers and thirty-three per cent of garment workers had over seven years' schooling compared to the average level for Mexican workers of just under four years. Many electronics managers demanded a high educational level from their workers, at least completion of primary school (six years' schooling); and many workers in the INET survey had commenced secondary school, whilst others had secondary school matriculation and even further educational experience in communal colleges, teacher training or even social work (INET, 1975, p. 27). This trend is confirmed by Carillo and Hernandez (1985, p. 120), who report that sixty per cent of women working in the electrical/electronics sector had some secondary education, and many had completed courses in commercial colleges or other professional training.

Male bias in selection procedures

The divergent characteristics of the women working in these two sectors and the superior status of the electronics sector indicate the freedom of the electronics sector management to target and recruit mainly those workers who meet their 'ideal' criteria. The higher educational qualifications demanded reflected not only employers' preference for a superior class background, which reinforced notions of the technological superiority of the sector, but also provided a guaranteed fluency in English, necessary not just for following the circuit diagrams and other working instructions from the American parent plant, but also the verbal commands and other communications from the predominantly US management and supervisory personnel employed at the plants.

Before the reported tightening of the labour market in the mid-1980s, the selection procedures of the electronics plants were extremely rigorous, and there was a low ratio of successful to total applicants. Konig (1975, p. 36) reported that the standard procedure 'usually involves a manual dexterity test, a check into vision and color perception (since deficient diet impairs color perception), a physical to check the applicant has no contagious diseases and is not pregnant, a check into hand-to-eye co-ordination and a general cultural test'.

However, the reasons given for rejection of unsuccessful applicants indicate the ability of management to use additional arbitrary and subjective criteria for the selection of what they consider a suitable labour force. Of 957 persons rejected, 241 had poor vision, 152 were physically incapable and lacked manual ability, 150 had too low an educational background and *130 lacked in appearance* (our emphasis) (*ibid.*). This was corroborated by two Mexican women researchers, who reported that women working in the smaller clothing plants believed that the large factories would not employ ugly workers (las feas). 'Since we considered it necessary to corroborate this view we interviewed all the owners of the larger plants who said, with no hesitation, that they preferred the prettier women, 'las bonitas', because the 'feas' caused a lot of problems and were always jealous. In order to double check we asked to be allowed to go into the plants and see for ourselves: in fact we could find no 'feas'.' (Escamilla and Vigorito, 1977, p. 24).

The selection of the ideal electronics worker, then, reflects a mixture of objective criteria (co-ordination and dexterity), social prejudice (against mothers, in spite of the existence of widespread evidence that women with children are more reliable workers because of both maturity and economic need), class prejudice (a preference for those with better schooling and a longer urban background) (Carrillo and Hernandez, 1985, p. 176), and sexist patriarchal fantasy (selection of only those considered good looking enough ('not lacking in appearance').

The rejection of older women with more obvious domestic responsibilities (children, husbands, etc.), who did not conform to the 'young, good looking' stereotype/fantasy of the managers, crowded such women into the lower-wage garment sector, where status, remuneration, benefits and security were inferior to those prevailing in the electronics sector (Fernandez-Kelly, 1983a).

Gender hierarchy in the maquiladora labour force

Whilst it is well documented that the majority of the workers at the maquiladora plants are women, little detailed research had been carried out regarding the sexual division of labour within the production process in the plants. The INET study contains an analysis of the production process, which indicates the manner in which male bias results in women being employed at the lowest levels of the hierarchy whilst supervisory positions are generally occupied by men (see fig.1). However, there is some contrast between the electronics and garment plants. Women are used in supervisory positions in garment plants where the dictates of the production process require that supervisors possess actual production skills. In contrast, where the supervisory functions are imbued with a technical mystique as in the electronics plants, women do not fill these positions.

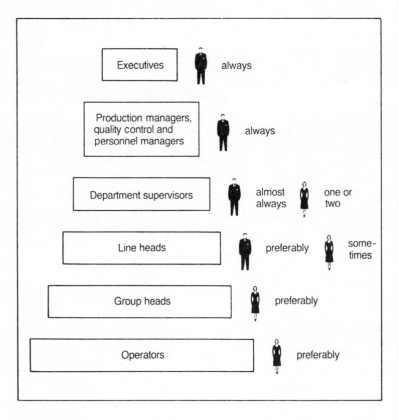

Fig.1　Schematic representation of the participation of women in the maquiladora workforce in Mexico.

Source: Translated and reproduced from INET, 1975, p.8.

The levels of work identified are operator, group head, line head, and supervisor (INET, 1975, p. 6). The high percentage of women in the maquiladora labour force as a whole reflects the concentration of women at operator level with the special exceptions described above. It is at this level that women's capacity to carry out boring and repetitive work is most appreciated by employers.

The next level in the hierarchy, the group head, refers to a person who is responsible for a group of five to ten operators. Her responsibility is to see that members of the group fulfil their work quotas, and to train new workers. Clearly, this job requires someone competent in the various tasks done by the workers in the group, and is consequently usually occupied by women recruited from the production line with the relevant work experience.

The line head occupies the next level in the hierarchy and undertakes a limited range of supervisory duties. Line heads have authority over five or ten groups (fifty to one hundred people). Their task is to distribute the materials amongst the different groups and to collect the processed articles and components, check that the required quality control norms have been met, and redistribute work for further processing. It is largely at this level that the differences between the sectors becomes most apparent. In the electronics sector line heads are always men, and it is reported that women are in fact reluctant to accept these jobs. There are two reasons for this: first, the production and quality control procedure is seen to be 'technical', in that the speed of production is controlled according to flow process procedures worked out by the management; and quality control is checked using machines rather than by the personal judgement of line heads. This creates the impression that the job is outside the capacity of women, who typically do not have technical qualifications. In addition, women are considered, and consider themselves, unsuitable for a position that demands authority and enforcement of discipline. The workers themselves identify these positions with management, causing the women who do occupy them to lose the solidarity and friendship of their work-mates. Since the companionship at work is one of the major reasons given by workers in electronics factories for job-satisfaction, women are reluctant to forego this, especially since the financial incentives are extremely small (*ibid.*, p. 7).

On the other hand, women are quite often found as line heads in the clothing factories where there is not such a distinction between groups and lines of production. In these plants, a production line will produce a complete garment. The person responsible for regulating the pace of the work and checking its quality must obviously be familiar with all the individual operations required. She must know how long it takes to insert a long zip rather than a short one, or to sew different kinds of sleeves or do different kinds of finishing or decorative operations, all of which vary with the type of garment produced and the efficiency of the sewing-machine being used. Quality control also rests on her judgement, which can only be reliable if she is fully experienced in all aspects of the production process. In this situation, line heads must obviously be recruited from experienced production workers, that is, from the female labour force.

The highest job amongst production workers is that of department supervisor, which is effectively a management position, demonstrated by the fact that no workers at this level are unionised. The department supervisor is responsible for the running of the whole production process. In the electronics sector, this job requires the ability to communicate the production targets and decisions of management to the workers in a manner which is both understood and acted upon; that is, it requires someone with both technical background and authority. Since women tend to lack technical education and, it is assumed, do not easily command obedience from other workers, whilst the reverse is true of men, companies usually appoint men to this position.

In fact, women do sometimes occupy supervisory positions in the clothing firms, especially the smaller firms which cannot afford to appoint a man, since he would not be able to work on the production line when necessary, as well as to supervise the operation. However, these women are both feared and reviled by the rest of the employees on the shop floor, which reduces women's willingness to accept this level of responsibility in a large plant.

The men employed on the factory floor who do not fall into the production and supervisory categories described above, carry out miscellaneous tasks peripheral to the main production process such as machine maintenance, materials handling and cleaning.

The gender hierarchy described here differs little from that prevailing in industry elsewhere in the world, where women form a major part of the unskilled labour force. Within this hierarchy, women are required to carry out jobs that are unskilled in the sense that the worker has no control over the pace of the work, or responsibility for the total production process. Male bias is only overcome when supervisory positions require more than the transmission of authority and discipline but actually rest on the production experience of the person appointed, as in the garment industry.

Changes in the gender composition of the maquiladora work-force

As employment in the maquiladora industries has grown throughout the 1980s, the proportion of women operators, in relation to total employment and to total manual workers, has declined quite significantly as Table 2 indicates, so that by 1987, women operators comprised only 66·6 per cent of total manual workers, and just over fifty-four per cent of total employment.

Three explanations have been put forward for the fall in women's share of employment in the maquiladora industries. First, there is a sectoral explanation: those sectors which have traditionally employed more male workers – metal products, furniture and wood products, and transport equipment – have steadily increased, so that employment opportunities have grown much faster than the overall growth in women's employment. (This explanation is discussed at length in Sklair (1989) ch. 8).

Table 3 reveals the extent to which male-intensive employment sectors have grown during the 1980s. Whilst employment in the main female-intensive industries, textiles and clothing, assembly of electronic apparatus, and electronic components, grew only 5·6 per cent, 36·4 per cent and 46 per cent respectively, in the male-intensive industries such as furniture, footwear and leather, and transport equipment, the rates of growth were significantly higher, with the latter showing a more than 400 per cent increase between 1980 and 1985.

Second, there is the suggestion that there has been a certain amount of change in the nature and organisation of the labour processes in the previously female labour-intensive industries in northern Mexico, which have led to an increase in the proportions of technical and administrative employees, and hence a fall in the proportion of women employed. Whilst much of the Mexican evidence is indirect (*ibid.*), this would be consistent with changes in these industries in Europe and in other parts of the Third World

(Pearson, 1986, 1989) where falls in the female intensity of the labour process can be partly attributed to changes in the technology and organisation of production leading to less reliance on manual production workers. Table 2 shows that in 1979 production workers accounted for eighty-six per cent of all maquiladora employment; by 1987, this had fallen to eighty-one per cent. On the other hand, the share of technical staff increased from 8·6 per cent to 12·1 per cent over the same period, while the share of salaried administrative and management employees rose from 5·4 per cent to 6·7 per cent.

The statistical evidence available indicates that the gender composition of employment *within* industries is changing as the proportion of operators falls. Table 3 indicates that women's manual employment as a percentage of total maquiladora employment fell from 65·5 per cent in 1980 to 55·2 per cent in 1985, and as a percentage of manual employment from 76·5 per cent to 67·2 per cent Since women are most heavily concentrated at the operator grade, it is instructive to look at the changes in the proportion of operator (manual) employment to total employment over this time period: overall, the proportion fell from 85·7 per cent to 82·2 per cent. However, in those sectors which are large employers of women, the decline is more significant; from 89·6 per cent to 85·0 per cent in textiles and clothing; from 84·0 per cent to 78·0 per cent in electronics assembly; and from 85·7 per cent to 79·5 per cent in the electronic components sector.

Since, as Sklair (1989, ch. 8) points out, 'it is safe to assume that most of the technicians are male, and that despite the growing numbers of women in administrative posts in the maquilas, men still had a clear majority of these posts', it would appear likely that the reduction in the proportion of operator labour in total employment is an important factor in leading to the declining proportion of women.

A third possible explanation is the direct substitution thesis: that as the pool of suitable female workers has dried up, managers are increasingly using men in tasks for which they would have preferred to recruit women. Certainly, there is evidence that the labour market in the northern states has tightened throughout the 1980s, and reports of labour shortages are frequent (*ibid.*). However, there is no clear evidence that this is because the maquiladora plants have already recruited all the available female labour; on the contrary, there is widespread evidence that women whom the firms would have liked to recruit are preferring other employment opportunities – in the service sector as informal undocumented workers in the south-west of the USA – because the level of real wages in the maquiladora plants has been held at a low level. Sklair suggests that this is the result of an employers' cartel to keep wages down, in the face of falling profits, preferring a high turnover of labour to the potential increases in labour costs which would result from open competition for suitable labour.

Whilst there is clearly statistical evidence for the increase in male employment at all levels of the occupational structure in the maquilas , there is as yet no unequivocal evidence that men have been employed in a large-scale way specifically to substitute for women production workers. Moreover, it is plausible to assume that far from there being an unusual tendency to substitute men for women throughout the maquiladora industries, there may well be discernible and contrasting tendencies between the different sectors. Table 3 indicates that, for the maquiladora industries in the northern states, women operators' share of total employment fell from 65·5 per cent to 55·2 per cent between 1980 and 1985, and this is paralleled by a decline in women's share of operator (manual) employment from 76·5 per cent to 67·2 per cent. In the industries which have had the highest percentage of women workers, and those which have employed the largest number of women – that is clothing and textiles, and electronics assembly and components – women operators' share of total employment and women's share of operator employment have also fallen substantially; whereas in other smaller sectors – furniture and wood, transport equipment, and other manufactures – women operators' share of total employment has risen, and so has women's share of operator employment.

In the case of garments and textiles, it is likely that the product mix and the structure of the sector have changed significantly; a higher proportion of paper (disposable) garments, a larger share of more mechanised large sub-contracting firms and a change in the labour process itself would lead management to rely less heavily on the skills of the women operators. In the electronics assembly and components sector it is widely documented elsewhere that changes in the technology of production, including increased automation and integrated fabrication, not only reduce the share of operator employment, but also lead to a redefinition of operator jobs, some

Table 3 *Gender composition of maquiladora labour force, northern states, 1980 – 85; by industrial sector*

Industrial sector	Total employment	Employment growth 1980–85 (%)	Total operator employment	Total operator employment as % of all employment	Female operator employment	Female operators as % of	
						Total operator employment	Total employment
All industries							
1980	106,576	74·5	91,308	85·7	69,853	76·5	65·5
1985	186,000		152,819	82·2	102,624	67·2	55·2
Food production							
1980	1,393	33·2	1,260	90·5	926	73·5	66·5
1985	1,855		1,600	86·3	1,201	75·1	64·7
Clothing & textiles							
1980	14,256	5·6	12,771	89·6	10,588	82·9	74·3
1985	15,098		12,839	85·0	9,854	76·8	65·3
Footwear & leather							
1980	1,531	182·7	1,355	88·5	650	50·0	42·5
1985	4,328		3,803	87·9	2,103	55·3	48·6
Furniture							
1980	3,163	106·2	2,779	87·9	354	12·7	11·2
1985	6,522		5,519	84·6	1,174	21·3	18·0
Chemical products							
1980	83		66	79·5	20	30·3	24·1
1985	[n.d.]		[n.d.]		[n.d.]		
Transport equipment							
1980	7,100	420·8	5,981	84·2	2,006	33·5	28·3
1985	36,978		31,055	84·0	14,746	47·5	39·9

Table 3 contd.

Machine tools (non-electric)							
1980	1,834	30·1	1,541	84·0	495	32·1	30·0
1985	2,386		2,010	84·2	679	33·8	28·5
Assembly of electronic & electrical apparatus							
1980	28,580	36·4	24,000	84·0	20,456	85·2	71·6
1985	38,994		30,430	78·1	23,089	75·9	59·2
Electrical and electronic components							
1980	33,530	46·0	28,393	85·7	22,568	79·5	67·3
1985	48,943		38,922	79·5	29,243	75·1	59·7
Toys and sports goods							
1980	2,803	157·7	2,517	89·8	2,170	86·2	77·4
1985	7,265		5,754	79·2	4,210	73·2	57·9
Other manufactures							
1980	7,483	66·7	6,250	83·2	3,810	61·0	50·9
1985	12,473		10,605	85·0	6,583	62·1	52·8
Services							
1980	4,420	152·6	4,395	91·2	3,841	87·4	79·7
1985	11,167		10,282	92·1	8,179	79·5	73·2

Source: Calculated from Table 8, INEGI, 1988.

being reconstituted as technical or skilled jobs which are then redefined as male jobs. (See Pearson (1989) and Goldstein (1989) for a discussion of these processes in the electronics industry in Britain; and Cockburn (1985) for a more general discussion.)

Indeed, all previous studies of gender divisions in work have indicated that the organisation of the production process is itself gendered, and that jobs are created typically male or female. Where the gender composition of the work-force has been reconstructed in the same industry in the same location, this has been simultaneous with substantial changes in the technology of production, and the design and control of the labour process (see Cockburn, 1985); or it has involved the reorganisation of job specifications, albeit using similar technology, to 'create new female or male jobs' (Humphrey, 1987).

Sklair (1988b) indicates that over many of the industrial sectors there has been an attempt to upgrade the level of professional and managerial employment for Mexican nationals, and to increase the quality of technology transfer. The growth of new plants over time, together with the shake-out of marginal plants that occurs when the industry is in recession, would also be conducive to a continuing upgrading of technology of production. More research is needed on technological change in the maquiladora plants in the 1980s, and its relation to the changing gender composition of the work-force.

Conclusion

In addition to the changes in the relative demand for women and men to work in Mexico's border industry, one of the interesting issues to emerge during the 1980s is the difficulty encountered in recent years in recruiting women workers. Employers seem to have assumed that women constitute an inexhaustible supply of cheap labour, not requiring a higher wage because they are secondary workers rather than bread-winners.

But the main reason women gave for their reluctance to accept maquila employment at the going rate in 1985 was their inability to survive on the wages paid, given their role in supporting children and/or contributing to the survival of households in which they were daughters or spouses (Sklair, 1989, ch. 8). The opportunity (legal or not) of working on the other side of the Rio Grande in the USA was a better-paid option. In addition, the novelty and glamour of the maquiladoras has become somewhat tarnished by the experience of some fifteen to twenty years when the employment they provide for women has remained intense and exhausting, insecure, risky in terms of personal health and safety, and offering no prospects for long-term employment, promotion, training or skills enhancement. Whilst the Mexicanisation of salaried employment has proceeded alongside the increase in the share of technical, managerial and administrative jobs in the maquiladora industries, these opportunities have not been made available to women, from the ranks of the production operators or elsewhere. Any assumption that the maquiladoras provide an avenue for the incorporation of women into the industrial labour force on anything more than a short-term, low-paid, risky basis has been shown to be false. The possibility exists for intervention – by both the Mexican authorities and the US companies – to enhance the prospects, conditions and rewards of the women employed in the maquila industries; there is as yet little evidence that any such policies are even under consideration.

Notes

1 'Maquiladora' is a term used solely in Mexico to describe manufacturing plants, both subsidiaries of MNCS or nationally owned, whose main activity is the assembly or processing of products to be exported primarily to the USA. It is believed to derive from the word 'maquilar' – to make up.

2 Export processing is the assembly or processing of goods from imported or other components for export markets.

3 A full discussion of the employment of women workers in export processing can be found in Elson and Pearson (1981).

4 This is only one organisational structure amongst a variety of ways in which the maquiladora plants are integrated into the USA economy. For a full guide to the literature on this and other issues see Sklair (1988a).

5 See Bettwy (1985) for an extensive discussion on the legal and administrative infrastructure of the maquiladora industry.

6 If it were possible to exclude shoe and leather products, which use a substantial proportion of male labour, the figure for female employment in the clothing sector would be higher.

7 To fully test the hypothesis it would be necessary to use longitutional time series data to establish the comparative unemployment rates before the inauguration of the maquiladora plants, and the extent to which these had changed since the mid-1960s.

References

Beneria, L. (1981), 'Conceptualizing the labour force: the underestimation of women's economic activities', *Signs*, vol. 7, no. 2.

Bettwy, S. (1985), 'Mexico's development: foreign trade zones and direct foreign investment', *Comparative Judicial Review*, no. 122, pp. 49–66.

Bustamente, J. (1983), 'Maquiladoras: a new face of international capitalism on Mexico's northern frontier', in J. Nash and M. P. Fernandez-Kelly (eds) (1983), *op. cit.*

Carillo, J., and Hernandez, A. (1985), *Mujeres fronterizas en la industria maquiladora*, SEP/CEFNOMEY, Coleccion Frontera, Mexico City.

Cockburn, C. (1985), *Machinery of Dominance: Women, Men and Technical Know How*, Pluto Press, London.

Elson, D., and Pearson, R. (1981), ' "Nimble fingers make cheap workers":
an analysis of women's employment in Third World export manufacturing', *Feminist Review*, spring, no. 7, pp. 87–107.

——(eds) (1989), *Women's Employment and Multinationals in Europe*, Macmillan, London.

Escamilla, N., and Vigorito, M. A. (1977), 'El trabajo feminino en las maquiladoras fronterizas', *Nueva Antropologia*, vol. 8, April.

Fernandez-Kelly, M. P. (1978), 'Mexican border industry: female labour force participation and migration', Paper presented at annual meeting of American Sociological Association, California.

——(1983a), *For We Are Sold, I and My people: Women and Industry in Mexico's Frontier*, SUNY Press, Albany.

——(1983b), 'Mexican border industrialisation, female labour force participation and migration', in J. Nash and M. P. Fernandez-Kelly (eds) (1983), *op. cit.*

Flores Cabellero, R. (1982), *Evolucion de de frontera norte*, Centro de Investigaciones Economicas, Monterrey.

Goldstein, N. (1989), 'Silicon Glen: women and semiconductor multinationals', in D. Elson and R. Pearson (eds) (1989), *op. cit.*

Humphrey, J. (1987), *Gender and Work in the Third World: Sexual Divisions in Brazilian Industry*, Tavistock, London.

INEGI (Instituto Nacional de Estadistica, Geografia e Informatica) (1988), *Estadisticas de la Industria Maquiladora de Exportacion*, Secretaria de Programacion y Presupuesto, Mexico City.

INET (Instituto Nacional de Estudios Sobre El Trabajo) (1975), *Incorporacion de la mano des obra Feminina a la industria maquiladora de Exportacion*, Informe Preliminar, Investigacion de Campo, Mexico City.

Konig, W. (1975), *Towards an Evaluation of International Sub-contracting Activities in Developing Countries: Report on 'Maquiladoras' in Mexico*, UNECLA, Mexico City.

NACLA (North American Congress on Latin America) (1975), 'Hit and run: US runaway shops on the Mexican border', *Latin America and Empire Report*, vol. 9, no. 5, July–August.

Nash, J., and Fernandez-Kelly, M. P. (eds) (1983), *Women, Men and the International Division of Labour*, SUNY Press, Albany.

Noriega Verdugo, S. (1982), *La Mujer trabajadora en Baja California: Una apreciacion estadistica*, Cuadernos de Ciencias Sociales Series, Universidad Autonoma de Baja California, Tijuana.

Nurayama, G., and Munoz, C. (1979), 'Empleo de la mano de obra feminina en la industria maquiladora de exportacion', *Cuadernos Agrarios*, ano 4, no. 9, September.

Pahl, R. (ed.) (1988), *On Work*, Blackwell, Oxford.

Pearson, R. (1986), 'Female workers in the First and Third Worlds: the greening of women's labour', in K. Purcell *et al.* (eds) (1986), *op. cit.*, Reprinted in R. Pahl (ed.) (1988), *op. cit.*

——(1989), 'Women's employment and multinationals in the UK: restructuring and flexibility', in D. Elson and R. Pearson (eds) (1989), *op. cit.*

Philip, G. (ed.) (1988), *The Mexican Economy*, Routledge, London.

Purcell, K. *et al.* (eds) (1986), *The Changing Experience of Employment*, Macmillan, London.

Ruiz, V., and Tiano, S. (eds) (1987), *Women on the US-Mexico Border: Responses to Change*, Allen & Unwin, Boston.

SIC (Secreteria de Industria y Comercio) (1974), *Zonas fronterizas de Mexico: perfil socio-economico*, Mexico City.

Sklair, L. (1988a), *Maquiladoras: Annotated Bibliography and Research Guide to Mexico's In Bond Industry 1980–88*, Monograph Series No. 24, Centre for US Mexican Studies, University of California, San Diego.

——(1988b), 'Mexico's maquiladora programme: a critical evaluation', in G. Philip (ed.) (1988), *op. cit.*

——(1989), *Assembling for Development: The Maquila Industry in Mexico and the USA*, Unwin Hyman, Boston.

Tiano, S (1987a), 'Women's work and unemployment in northern Mexico', in V. Ruiz and S. Tiano (eds) (1987), *op. cit.*

——(1987b), 'Maquiladoras in Mexicali: integration or exploitation', in *ibid.*

USITC (United States International Trade Commission) (1975), *US Imports for Consumption: Tariff Items 807·00 and 806·30*, Washington DC.

Male bias in macro-economics: the case of structural adjustment

Macro-economic problems, such as large balance of payments deficits, high inflation rates and very low growth rates, have devastated many countries in Asia, Africa, Latin America and the Caribbean in the 1980s. These problems have been caused by a mixture of internal and external factors. The governments in many of these countries have pursued inappropriate policies, and the external economic environment has sharply deteriorated. Higher oil prices, lower prices for primary products exported by less developed countries, and increases in the real rate of interest on international commercial loans have resulted in rising demand for, and falling supply of, foreign exchange. Many less developed countries (LDCs) have had no choice but to seek assistance from the International Monetary Fund (IMF) and the World Bank.

As a condition of this assistance, countries have to undertake programmes of economic stabilisation and structural adjustment. These programmes aim to reduce inflation; increase the rate of growth of output and exports; and increase productivity and efficiency. Typically they involve devaluation, a reduction in public expenditure, decontrol of prices and of the allocation of imports and foreign exchange, and attempts to improve incentives for the production of goods which are internationally tradable and to switch resources away from the production of goods which are not internationally tradable.

There is no doubt that policy changes are needed in many LDCs, but there is considerable controversy about the validity of the IMF and World Bank diagnosis and policy prescriptions (for example, Onimode (ed.), 1989). The need for complementary policy changes in developed countries has been urged by many critics (for example,

Cornia, Jolly and Stewart (eds), 1987) but, of course, the IMF and World Bank have no leverage over these countries. Here it will be argued that one serious deficiency of the IMF/World Bank approach is its disregard for gender, which leads to male bias.

Stabilisation and structural adjustment programmes are formulated on the basis of macro-economic concepts; that is, concepts that look at the economy as a whole rather than individual firms or households. Such concepts appear to be gender neutral. But a closer examination reveals them to be imbued with male bias. This male bias at the conceptual level predisposes such programmes to male bias in operation and outcome. Comprehensive evidence about the gender impact of stabilisation and structural adjustment programmes is not yet available, not least because of male bias in statistical information about the economy (Elson and Fleming, 1988). More evidence will be available in the near future from studies being undertaken by the Commonwealth Secretariat and the World Bank/UNDP research programme on the Social Dimensions of Adjustment in Sub-Saharan Africa. The incomplete and fragmented evidence currently available certainly suggests that there are substantial grounds for concern that such programmes tend to result in an unfair distribution of the burdens of stabilisation and structural adjustment as between women and men. This has short-term benefits for men in terms of preserving male privilege, but longer-term costs in so far as it hampers the achievement of sustainable and equitable adjustment for both men and women. Here it is argued that the effectiveness of the programmes in achieving such a goal is likely to be weakened by male bias. Male bias in macro-economics is not only bad for women, it is also bad for the prospects of setting in train a process of sustainable development.

The macro-economics of structural adjustment: from non-tradables to tradables

Macro-economic trends and macro-economic thinking are usually presented in a language which appears to be gender neutral. No specific mention is made of gender or of the sexual division of labour. The focus of attention is not on people at all but on monetary aggregates, such as the gross national product; tradables and non-tradables; imports and exports and the balance of payments; savings and consumption and investment; public expenditure and the budget deficit; or on impersonal concepts such as productivity and efficiency.

It may be argued that the absence of gender awareness in macro-economic analysis is immaterial and does nothing to disadvantage women, or to hamper the achievement of sustainable adjustment. Such analysis is concerned with fluctuations in the level of output and in rates of growth; and in changing the balance between different sectors of the economy: things, it may be argued, which have nothing to do with gender. However, this apparent gender neutrality masks a deeper gender bias. There is a hidden set of assumptions underlying macro-economic thinking which is deeply imbued with male bias. This hidden set of assumptions concerns human resources, their allocation to production, and their own reproduction and maintenance. It is assumed that human resources may be treated as if they were a non-produced factor of production, like natural resources; and as if they were costlessly transferable between different activities, in the way that a piece of land may be used for growing one crop one year and a different crop the next. These assumptions permit many macro-economic models to be constructed without any formal reference to human resources at all. But though there may be no variable in the equations labelled L for labour, and no axis on the diagram labelled L for labour, nevertheless drawing any policy conclusions from such models requires assumptions about human resources.

The usual macro-economic framework for analysing structural adjustment is constructed simply in terms of two categories of goods, tradables and non-tradables.[1] It is assumed that the primary resources of land and labour can either be used to produce goods and services which are internationally tradable; or to produce goods and services which are not internationally tradable and which are produced and consumed only within national boundaries. The prices of internationally tradable goods are assumed to be determined on international markets, and are assumed to be beyond the control of any one LDC, so that they can be taken as externally given. The prices of non-tradables are determined by supply and demand within the LDC economy. Examples of tradable goods are crops like rice and wheat; manufactures like clothing and machine tools; services like tourism and telecommunications. Tradables may be exports or efficient import substitutes: that is, goods that could be imported but which are produced within a country at costs which are internationally competitive. Many LDCs produce import substitutes at costs which are above the costs of imports because of policies to protect domestic industries. These high-cost import substitutes are non-tradables. Other examples of non-tradable goods are subsistence crops which are grown by farming households for their own consumption; construction, from housing to dams and roads and power stations; personal services and small-scale trading; and public services like health and education, and police and armed forces.

Using this framework, World Bank economists diagnose the problem as one of policy-induced price distortions leading to over-production of non-tradables and under-production of tradables.[2] This produces balance of payments deficits and a shortage of foreign exchange which hampers growth. Structural adjustment thus consists of switching resources from the production of non-tradables to the production of tradables. The model suggests that the way to do this is by changing the relative prices of the two categories of goods, making tradables relatively more expensive, so as to give an incentive to produce them rather than non-tradables; and to cut down on consuming them so as to save foreign exchange. A range of policies is recommended to achieve this, including devaluation, raising the prices paid to farmers, withdrawal of food subsidies, and cut-backs in public expenditure. This conclusion is reached on the basis of a type of reasoning that economists call comparative statics. That is, the pattern of output associated in a particular model with one set of relative prices is compared with the pattern of output associated with another set of relative prices, and it is inferred that by changing the relative prices, the output pattern can also be changed. The actual process of switching is not analysed. At the root of this neglect lie certain assumptions about the utilisation and reproduction of human resources.

It is assumed that there are no structural barriers to transferring labour from one sort of production to another. It may take time for households to realise that they can make more money producing tradables than non-tradables, but in the absence of government-imposed 'distortions', they will fairly quickly make the switch. It is also assumed that there is no need to take into account any costs of change. The conceptual framework explicitly assumes full employment in the sense that it assumes a given amount of labour and merely adjusts its allocation. There is no question of structural adjustment necessitating an increase in total labour input or a rise in unemployment, just a better utilisation of existing total labour time. Any transitional costs (considered solely in terms of consumption losses) will be compensated for by the end result. The possibility of social and personal disintegration during the transition is not considered – it is assumed that households and people will not fall apart under the stress of the decisions that adjustment requires.

These fundamental assumptions are open to a number of criticisms (for example, Bienefeld, 1988; Cornia, Jolly and Stewart (eds), 1987), the gravest of which is that if the transitional costs are great enough, some people will not survive in order to enjoy their compensation in the post-transition stage. Here we focus on the gender implications of these assumptions, contending that three kinds of male bias are at work: male bias concerning the sexual division of labour; male bias concerning the unpaid domestic work necessary for producing and maintaining human resources; and male bias concerning the social institution which is the source of supply of labour – the household.

The sexual division of labour

The model just considered ignores the barrier to labour reallocation which is presented by the sexual division of labour. By the sexual division of labour we mean not just the pattern of work allocation between women and men that can be empirically observed at any moment of time, but also the social practices that constitute some sorts of work as suitable for women but unsuitable for men, and other sorts of work as unsuitable for women but suitable for men. A change in the relative returns of different kinds of work will not be enough to reallocate labour if it requires men to do work which is constituted as 'women's work' or women to do work which is constituted as 'men's work'. This is not to claim that the sexual division of labour is unchanging and immutable, but that, in general, such change requires more than a shift in relative remuneration and tends to entail a redefinition of the work both technically and organisationally and culturally (Goldstein, 1989; Pearson, this volume).

One defence of the implicit treatment of labour as ungendered might be that gender has no practical significance for switching from non-tradables to tradables, but this is not true in the case of structural adjustment in LDCs. There are at least two areas of considerable practical significance: production of labour-intensive manufactures for export; and production of crops for export. The first is of more significance in Latin America, Asia and the Caribbean, while the second is of more significance in Africa. It is, of course, open to question whether the promotion of such exports will lead to *sustainable* development – it is a high-risk strategy vulnerable to fluctuations in the international market (Bienefeld, 1988; Elson, 1988; Elson and Fleming, 1988). But detailed consideration of this point is beyond the scope of this chapter.

The encouragement of the production of labour-intensive manufactures for export is an important component of the switch from non-tradables to tradables in many countries in Asia, Latin America and the Caribbean. Taking no account of gender leads to the belief, expressed by the Chief of the Trade and Adjustment Policy Division in the World Bank, that 'it is relatively easy to retrain and transfer labour originally working in, say, construction or commerce for emplyment in the export . . . of, say, radios or garments' (Selowsky, 1987). All the available studies of such production show that it is not just labour-intensive, it is female labour-intensive. This is not simply the result of women having a preference for such work, or men not considering the wages high enough. Many studies have shown that employers have a preference for employing women, particularly young and single women, for such work. A vivid example is given in a study of a Brazilian plant making electronic components (Hirata, 1989). Here the management had tried, and abandoned, employing men on the might shift to carry out jobs done by women in the day. The men were unable to match the productivity of the women. The reason, in management's view, was that the men lacked the patience and concentration of the women. Women were regarded as having greater endurance and the ability to carry out tasks which were 'painful for a man', as well as having a 'better sense of touch in their fingers'. Many firms are unwilling to make the experiment of employing men, even in the face of pressure from governments that see male unemployment as much more important than female unemployment, and are anxious for more jobs to be created for men (see Jackson and Barry (1989) for a discussion of this in the case of Ireland). The views of the management of the Brazilian plant seem to be the 'commonsense' of manufacturers around the world.

Underlying this 'commonsense' tends to be the view that women are 'naturally' suited to labour-intensive assembly operations. This view can be found in more sophisticated form in the literature on human capital in which it is assumed that labour is differentiated by different endowments of innate skills and aptitudes. If women have higher productivity than men in labour-intensive assembly jobs, then this is explained by women's greater endowment of relevant aptitudes (nimble fingers, perhaps?). Feminists reject this naturalistic approach, arguing instead that women have acquired the attributes that generate their higher productivity in their training both at home and at school for life as dutiful daughters, wives and mothers (Elson and Pearson, 1981; Kergoat, 1982).

Such gender differentiation means that while it is relatively easy to transfer women from construction and commerce to radios and garments, this is not the case for men. The only situation in which it seems at all plausible that the expansion of labour-intensive export manufacturing will increase the number of jobs for men is when technological changes lead to reorganisation of production and a demand for more technical skills, for which women are typically not given training (for an example of this in the electronics industry in Scotland, see Goldstein, 1989). Thus the assumption that changes in the relative returns of tradable and non-tradable activities will serve to reallocate labour to labour-intensive manufacturing for export depends for its validity on the assumption that there is plenty of female labour available for factory work, and that this labour can be mobilised simply by changes in relative wages. Studies of the integration of women into export industries show the process is more complex. Several other changes are also necessary to create a factory work-force of young women: social resistance to young unmarried women working outside the home may have to be overcome; suitable transport and accommodation may have to be provided; legislation may have to be changed to permit continuous night work for women (for a discussion of the complexities of constructing a female labour force, see Pearson, 1988). The evidence to date seems to suggest that meeting these conditions requires either of two contrasting situations. The first is when there is an absolute deterioration in the returns to alternative ways of getting a living so that they no longer offer enough to live on; for example, rural poverty pushing women into garment factories in

Bangladesh (Feldman, 1988). The second is when there is rapid accumulation and growth, and employers, especially multi-nationals, are so eager to expand that they will offer wages and conditions superior in absolute terms to anything else available to most young women, packaged as a new, modern, enticing life-style; for example, the expansion of the electronics industry in Malaysia and Singapore (Foo and Lim, 1989). It is, of course, the first case that is relevant in those LDCs with severe macro-economic problems. Both suggest it is not simply relative wages that matter, but absolute improvements or deteriorations in living standards: more important than relative wages is the overall state of accumulation. Case studies of both situations suggest that the incorporation of women into the factories is not accomplished through an impersonal labour market but through social networks, which, in the case of recruitment of young women in Asia, are frequently between employers and the parents of the prospective employees.

Granted that women can be pushed or pulled into the export factories, as barriers are swept aside under the pressure of necessity or the desire for social mobility, there is still a further question. Is an increase in the time that women spend in export factories the result of a substitution of this work for other work; or is it additional work, increasing women's total labour time? It could well be additional work, a second shift, undertaken in addition to unpaid domestic work as wives, daughters, mothers. Unlike many other kinds of work, such as handicrafts and farming, factory work cannot be undertaken at the same time as reproductive work. Children can be supervised while carpets are woven or crops picked, but not during work in a garment factory or on an electronics assembly line. Few of the studies of women in export factories have gathered much evidence on time spent on domestic tasks. One recent study in the Philippines which did concern itself with this issue found that domestic work still accounted for between twenty-seven and thirty-two hours a week for married women employees, which was fitted in through a reduction in leisure time (Miralao, 1984). In Singapore, there has been mounting concern at labour shortages caused by married women leaving factory work because they cannot cope with the burden of factory work combined with child care and housework (Heyzer (ed.), 1988b, ch. 13). Even if the woman factory worker is herself relieved of domestic work for others, as in the case of many daughters, the domestic work she formerly undertook is likely to fall on the shoulders of other women – her mother or younger sisters (Salaff, 1981). It is unlikely that much unpaid domestic work is reallocated to men dismissed from employment in work that is newly unprofitable: all the evidence tends to show that the sexual division of labour in the household is resistant to change. Taking care of children, and sick and old people, cooking, cleaning, shopping – all this is 'women's work' and a man taking responsibility for it is in danger of losing his dignity, of being 'unmanned', in many parts of the world. Enduring idleness while looking for a proper 'man's' job is the option men are steered towards.

Explicitly recognising the sexual division of labour means questioning the benign picture of structural adjustment presented in the model we have considered. Gender barriers to the reallocation of labour are likely to mean unemployment for men displaced from non-tradable activities, and extra work for women as factory work is added to unpaid domestic work (Heyzer (1988a) suggests that this has happened in the Philippines). This extra work is not recognised because unpaid domestic labour is not counted as work. However, it may be argued that, in return, women who work in export factories get an income of their own, and that this brings higher status, greater independence and more bargaining power within the household.

The precise benefits which women derive from earning an income of their own have been the subject of considerable debate, the details of which are beyond the scope of the present argument. In my view, the benefits, though they may be great, are incapable of fully emancipating women from gender subordination (Elson and Pearson, 1981); and the extent of the benefits depends very much on the context in which women enter into the labour market. In situations of economic crisis, women are often forced into 'distress sales', selling their labour on very disadvantageous terms in an overcrowded market, in which wages and conditions of work are worsening, in order to ensure survival for themselves and their children. Recent evidence from Latin America suggests that rising female participation rates in urban areas represent such distress sales rather than the opening up of new liberating opportunities for women (Joekes, 1987; Berger, 1988).

A different set of problems presents itself when we consider women's participation in smallholder export crop production in sub-Saharan Africa. Although as conventionally measured, female participation rates in economic activity are low there, we know that women make a major contribution to crop production, both as unpaid family workers and as own-account workers, farming in their own right (Elson and Fleming, 1988). Production is typically organised through a sexual division of labour that covers both tasks and crops. Certain tasks, such as land preparation are 'men's jobs', while other tasks such as transplanting and weeding are 'women's jobs', the tasks following in sequence in the crop cycle. Certain crops are 'men's crops' while other crops are 'women's crops', though the same crop may be a 'male crop' in one place and a 'female crop' in another place (Davison, 1988a, pp. 12–13). Cash crops, particularly those grown for export, tend to be men's crops, while subsistence food crops tend to be women's crops. However, there are exceptions: for example, cotton is largely in the hands of women in the Sahel; one-third of farmers producing cocoa in Ghana are women (Davison, 1988a; Elson and Fleming, 1988). The sexual division of labour in tasks cuts across the sexual division of responsibility for different crops: men clear the land for women's crops; women transplant, weed and help with harvesting of men's crops. But men control the proceeds from selling men's crops, while women control the use of women's crops, which are generally used to feed their families, though surpluses may be sold on local markets.

Thus women do not generally earn an income of their own from work they do on crops marketed by their husbands. The extent to which women benefit from such work depends on how their husbands spend the proceeds. There is evidence that many women lack confidence that the benefits of increased work on their husbands' cash crops will trickle down to them. Case studies show the reluctance of women to put more work into production of crops controlled by their husbands: in the case of rice in the Gambia (Dey, 1980), in Northern Cameroon (Jones, 1983) and in other rice-growing countries such as Madagascar, Senegal and Ivory Coast (Longhurst, 1987); tea production in Tanzania (Mbilinyi, 1988a and b) and Kenya (Davison, 1988b); and tobacco production in Nigeria (Babalola and Dennis, 1988). In the Communal Areas of Zimbabwe, a recent study found that 'Even in households in which there is a shortage of labour, women, if faced with loss of control over the product of their labour, will continue to withdraw it from household production in order to meet their needs and those of their children for cash income' (Pankhurst and Jacobs, 1988, p. 212).

The sexual division of labour in crop production could thus present a barrier to the reallocation of labour from non-tradable to tradable crops. Higher prices for producers of export cash crops give an incentive for greater production to the person controlling the proceeds from their sale, but not necessarily to all those whose labour is necessary for increased production. It may be argued that there is no need to consider this possibility because, however, reluctant wives may be, husbands have the power to compel them to supply the extra labour required. This is likely to be true in some cases. But we might note that reliance on this argument does compel recognition of male power over women and is incompatible with a model suggesting that labour reallocation is a matter of new choices in response to different incentives, rather than the extraction of additional work through unequal power relations. In other cases (similar to the Gambian rice case discussed by Dey, 1980), women have sufficient autonomy to resist demands for extra work on their husbands' crops, and the result will be a disappointing output response to increased crop prices. In some situations, women may through joint action secure a direct payment to them of part of the proceeds, as happened in the cases discussed by Mbilinyi (1988a) and Davison (1988b). In the latter case, the Kenyan Tea Development Authority already paid women directly for the amount of tea they picked, but a substantial yearly bonus related to the total amount of tea delivered by a household was paid only to the male owner of the tea land. Just before the award of the annual bonus in 1983, women began to organise a protest: 'A group of the most out-spoken women went to the local committee of the KDTA, angrily protesting that they rarely saw the annual bonuses because their husbands spent the cash on beer, meat and other items for their exclusive use. The women pointed out that they provided much of the labour for tea production, and demanded a share of the annual bonus. Their collective protest was successful' (Davison, 1988b, p.168). This problem could easily be avoided if marketing boards as a matter of course made payments directly to women for their contribution to production. This was suggested in Tanzania but was resisted by both local development planning agencies and international development agencies as too radical: as one official put it, 'Whatever happens, we do not want a revolution. If women have their own money, why will they marry?' (Mbilinyi, 1988a).

Ensuring that women would be direct recipients of higher crop prices would not solve all potential problems of adjustment. Women who farm on their own account and produce cash crops for export face other difficulties: lack of access to other inputs they need, such as fertilisers, credit and extension services; extra demands on their time for domestic tasks such as water collection and health care (to be discussed in the next section); and the danger of losing access to land as men take over more land, attracted by the new incentives – something which has already happened in a number of countries following the introduction of irrigation (Carney, 1988).

The examples we have considered show that the sexual division of labour will constrain the extent to which labour can be reallocated in the course of structural adjustment. Failure to give explicit consideration to the gender differentiation of labour may mean that structural adjustment policies, based on the kind of macro-economic framework discussed, fail to achieve their objectives. In so far as the gender barriers are overcome, this cannot be attributed simply to changes in the structure of incentives, but to women's relative lack of power which constrains them not simply to reallocate their time but to increase the total input of hours of female labour.

The reproduction and maintenance of human resources

The fact that adjustment implies an increase in female work time may be ignored because much of the time involved is unpaid time spent in the reproduction and maintenance of human resources. This time is not regularly accounted for in production statistics and thus remains 'invisible' in the national accounts that provide the statistical counterpart of macro-economic models (Elson and Fleming, 1988). Macro-economic models ignore this work, treating labour as if it were a non-produced natural resource.

When challenged, economists do not deny that human resources require inputs of caring and cooking, of nurturing and nursing; and do not deny that responsibility for providing these inputs lies chiefly with women. But macro-economic thinking assumes that it is perfectly correct to proceed as if such activities were not required because they would be undertaken regardless of changes in the level and composition of national income. This assumption may be based either on the idea that reproduction and maintenance of human resources is undertaken for love, not money, and is therefore not responsive to economic changes (Roston (1983) argues that Keynes's macro-economics is based on this assumption); or on the idea that changes in the level and composition of national income have no impact on the relative costs and benefits of maintaining and reproducing human resources. This assumption would be more consistent with neo-classical economics, which does assume that the reproduction and maintenance of human resources is responsive to economic signals (for example, Becker, 1976). Both the Keynesian and the neo-classical view are one-sided. Unpaid domestic labour is not carried out entirely for love, disregarding the economic costs and benefits; but neither is it simply another economic activity. The process of the reproduction and maintenance of human resources is different from any other kind of production because human resources are treated as having an intrinsic value, not merely an instrumental value. Women may to some extent weigh up the costs and benefits for themselves of the amount of services they provide without pay to other family members, but they do not regard their children as just another crop, to be tended if the benefits are high enough, and to be left to rot untended if the benefits become too low. Women may be forced through poverty to leave their children untended, but this is a source of intense anguish, not simply another rational economic decision.

The difference between human resources and other resources does not mean that macro-economic thinking can safely ignore unpaid domestic labour. This neglect would only be justified if there were no interdependence between unpaid domestic work and the paid work that economists do include in the gross national product; or if macro-economic changes had no implications for the amount of unpaid domestic work that has to be done. This is far from being the case. Paid and unpaid work compete for women's time; and in the conditions typical in countries attempting to stabilise and adjust their economies, there is pressure on many women to increase both their paid and unpaid labour input.

One of the main factors increasing the amount of time women must devote to the sustenance of human resources is the cut-back in the production of public-sector non-tradables such as health and education services, water and sanitation services, and rural transportation. Cut-backs in public expenditure are supposed to free labour for work in production of tradables and are a key feature of structural adjustment programmes. From this viewpoint, it is not undesirable that women teachers in the Philippines are leaving teaching, because of deteriorating conditions of work and pay, for employment overseas as maids (Heyzer, 1988a).

Declines in public expenditure per capita on health and education services during the 1980s have been documented for a considerable number of LDCs (Cornia, Jolly and Stewart (eds), 1987). Where there were not absolute declines, there tended to be marked deceleration in growth rates. There has been some debate about how far these cuts should be attributed to the conditions laid down by the World Bank and IMF, how far to mismanagement by LDC governments and how far to the recession of the early 1980s. Ultimately, this must remain a matter of judgement. The precise contribution of these three factors does not matter for the point being made here, which is that such cut-backs, whatever the cause, have implications for unpaid domestic labour that macro-economic analysis ignores. If fewer of the services required for the sustenance of human resources are provided by the public sector, then women have to make up some of the shortfall.

As yet there is little detailed documentation of this because statistics are not regularly collected on unpaid domestic labour. Recent work on Zambia indicates some of the potential effects (Evans and Young, 1988). In Zambia, real per capita expenditure on health fell by sixteen per cent between 1983 and 1985. For the majority of Zambian people, the only alternative to health services provided by the state are those that have been traditionally available in the community and household. The result of health expenditure cut-backs has been to shift more of the burden of health care to the community and household – which in practice means women. In the rural areas, the decline in health provision has had a direct effect on services which are particularly important to women and children, such as immunisation and mother-and-child health clinics. People now have to travel farther to get treatment and drugs, and wait longer in queues. Women interviewed for the study said they themselves could not afford to be ill because of the time it would take away from their work. They reported having to spend more time caring for other household members when they are sick. If husbands or children have to attend hospitals, shortages of equipment and personnel mean that women are expected to go with them to provide meals and care for the duration of the treatment.

One woman reported missing the entire planting season for this reason (Evans and Young, 1988), a perfect example of the interdependence between the labour that macro-economic models do include and that which they ignore.

The example just discussed highlights the ambiguity of terms like 'cost', 'productivity' and 'efficiency'. What is regarded by economists as increased efficiency may instead be a shifting of costs from the paid economy to the unpaid economy. It may appear that the cost per patient in hospital has been reduced and the efficiency of hospitals increased, when in reality there has been a transfer of the costs of care for the sick from the paid economy to the unpaid economy of the household. The financial costs fall but the unpaid work of women in the household rises. This is not a genuine increase in efficiency: it is simply a transfer of the costs from the hospital to the home.

Such a transfer of costs has been explicitly advocated under the banner of promotion of self-help practices by exponents of 'Adjustment with a Human Face': 'there is scope for decentralising many activities in health, nutrition, child care, sanitation, etc., to the family (or community) level . . . while such an approach may increase time costs for women, it will place extremely modest monetary costs on the household; and will lead to substantial savings in the public sector . . . ' (Cornia, 1987, p. 174). The implication is that increased time-costs for women do not matter, a result perhaps of the belief that women have lots of spare time.[3] This has been criticised by feminists, who point to the enormous pressure on the time of most women, especially poor women (Antrobus, 1988; Elson, 1988).

Another time-pressure comes from rises in the price of food. Such rises are the result of a combination of withdrawal of food subsidies, devaluation and increases in the prices paid to farmers, all typically components of structural adjustment programmes. The aim is to provide more incentives for farmers to produce tradables and to reduce government budget deficits. An underlying assumption is that households that buy food will adjust their expenditure patterns, spending less on other things in order to buy food and switching from dearer foods to cheaper foods.[4] But cheaper foods require more input of women's unpaid labour: coarse grains and root crops take a longer time to prepare than wheat products; home-baking takes more time than buying bread.

Research on Sri Lankan food consumption patterns has found that time-saving has been a significant factor in the switch from rice consumption to bread consumption in urban areas (Senauer, Sahn and Alderman, 1986). Shopping also takes longer when prices rise, as women have to shop around to find the cheapest source, and buy smaller quantities more often.

Ignoring the implications of macro-economic changes for unpaid domestic labour inputs is tantamount to assuming that women's capacity to undertake extra work is infinitely elastic – able to stretch so as to make up for any shortfall in incomes and resources required for the production and maintenance of human resources. However, women's capacity for work is not infinitely elastic and breaking-point may be reached. There may simply not be enough female labour time available to maintain the quality and quantity of human resources at its existing level. This may not have an immediate impact on the level and composition of gross national output, but in the longer run a deterioration in health, nutrition and education will have an adverse impact on output levels. The assumption of a given quantity and quality of labour, which is invariant as switching from non-tradables to tradables proceeds, will be revealed as untenable.

Data assembled by UNICEF provide evidence that women's unpaid labour has not been able to absorb all the costs of switching (Cornia, Jolly and Stewart (eds), 1987). Special studies of ten countries (Botswana, Ghana, Zimbabwe, the Philippines, South Korea, Sri Lanka, Brazil, Chile, Jamaica and Peru) show that the nutritional status of children has deteriorated in all but two, while infant and/or child mortality statistics have ceased to improve at previous rates, and have shown a deterioration in three of the ten.

There has been very little research at the micro-level into exactly how women are juggling with the competing demands on their time in the context of structural adjustment. Heyzer (1988a) reports the findings of one small-scale village study in East Java, Indonesia, which investigated the implications for poor women of the Indonesian devaluation of 1986, and associated policy changes. Rising prices placed heavy burdens on poor women: longer hours of field work for those with some land; the necessity for those without land to offer themselves as hired workers at low wages in whatever job was available; as well as the continuing daily grind of collecting fuel and water, cooking, looking after children, etc. The overall result was a longer and harder working day for women. Male out-migration had risen rapidly, and most of the women did not know exactly where their husbands were. All the women interviewed spoke of worry, tiredness and stress as they struggled to make ends meet.

A study of an urban low-income community in Guayaquil, Ecuador (Moser, 1989), found that women had been forced to allocate more time to income-earning activities and to unpaid participation in the provision of community services, such as housing improvements and health care, as the economy had undergone structural adjustment and stabilisation programmes in a deteriorating international economic environment. Their working day (paid and unpaid) continued to be between twelve and eighteen hours, but they had been forced to reduce the time allocated to looking after their families. An increasing burden was falling on the shoulders of their elder daughters, who had less time for school work. The sexual division of labour which designates reproduction and maintenance of human resources as female tasks had not changed. Total input of female labour time had increased, though since adult women already worked very long hours, much of the extra input was coming from school-age daughters. In about thirty per cent of the 141 households surveyed, women were managing to cope; in about fifty-five per cent, women were just hanging on, mortgaging the futures of their sons, and especially daughters, in order to survive; in about fifteen per cent, women were exhausted, their families disintegrating, their children dropping out of school and roaming the streets, becoming involved in street gangs and exposed to drugs. As Moser concludes, 'Not all women can cope under crisis and it is necessary to stop romanticising their infinite capacity to do so'.

What Moser's valuable study graphically shows is that the process of reallocating labour from non-tradables to tradables may place severe stress upon, and even lead to the disintegration of, the process of human resource production and maintenance that macro-models assume can safely be taken for granted. Complacency about human resource production and maintenance is fostered by the models of the household that form the micro-level underpinning of most macro-economic models.

Gender divisions and household expenditure

Conventional economic analysis assumes that the household may be treated as a unity. The macro-economy is an aggregation of household units, firms and the public sector. Labour and goods are supplied by households, which also buy goods and hire labour. The unity of the household may be theorised in one of three different ways. In an illuminating critique of such theories, Sen has labelled them the glued-together family, the despotic family and the super-trader family (Sen, 1983).

The first two assume that the household can be treated as if it were an individual with a single set of objectives – this is known as the assumption of a joint utility function or unified family welfare function (Evans, 1989). The difference between them is that the theory of the glued-together family does not allow for differences between individuals and, in effect, treats all household members as identical, whereas the theory of the family ruled by a despot does allow for variation within the household. In the latter case, individual family members do have differing objectives, but a despotic head of household takes decisions for them, and they just fall into line. Much of the analysis by economists of households in developing countries makes use of the despot assumption,[5] but with the added twist that the despot is benevolent, and altruistically takes decisions that will maximise the welfare of all family members, not just his own. (It is usually assumed that the benevolent despot is male – indeed, Evans has found one author who explicitly claims that the household decision-maker will 'feel the disutility of labour, say of his wife, as much as that of his own' (*ibid.*).)

The super-trader model allows for a multiplicity of decision-makers within the household, each pursuing his/her individual objectives, and makes household unity the outcome of these individual decisions (Becker, 1981). In effect, the household is treated as if it were a market with household members buying and selling from each other. The division of labour and distribution of income between different household members is treated as resulting from individual choices freely exercised – there is no room for notions of inequality of power. Such a model is unable properly to take account of children, since they are born into households and cannot in any sense be regarded as choosing to join them.

Despite the variation between them, the outcome of all three approaches is a vision of the household as a unity. The result is also generally an uncritical approach to the household as an institution which maximises the welfare of all its members, either through the altruism of the benevolent dictator, or through the freely exercised choices of its members to exchange goods and services with one another. The household is celebrated as a pooling and sharing institution which strengthens its members in their interconnections with the rest of society. Such a vision supports a view of the household as capable of absorbing any transitional costs of adjustment, and as an institution that can safely be taken for granted by designers of structural adjustment programmes.

However, there is now available a wealth of theorising (Sen, 1983; Folbre, 1986a and b) and evidence (Beneria and Roldan, 1987; Blumberg, 1988; Dwyer and Bruce (eds), 1988) which undermines this complacency. The household is a site of conflict as well as of co-operation; of inequality as well as of mutuality; and conflict and inequality are structured along gender lines.

This does not mean that women are passive victims within the household and play no decision-making role. Rather, it means that women do not enjoy the same decision-making power as men: their bargaining power is weaker. The fundamental reason for this is that their fall-back position is weaker. If no bargain can be struck and the household disintegrates, women are generally in a worse position than men, both economically and socially. Female-headed households are usually among the poorest households. Women on their own, without a male 'protector', in the shape of husband, brother or father, frequently face social denigration and physical violence.

Evidence from a large variety of case studies suggests that women play an active role in decision-making about the reproduction and maintenance of human resources, and typically bear the responsibility for managing household income and expenditure to secure the day-to-day welfare of household members. The problem is that they do not control access to all the resources they require to discharge these responsibilities. They are dependent on men's goodwill. A recent case study of low-income households in Mexico City vividly depicts the stress and anxiety frequently attendant upon women's role as manager of household resources. As Dona Soledad put it:

'He gives me the gasto [housekeeping allowance] all right, but I must see that everything is fine, that nothing is lacking, good food for him, yes, the best pieces are for him . . . He usually wants beer . . . He says: '... bring me some beer. I'll pay you later!' He never does. On Thursday I am without a cent and I have to ask my comadrita to complete the week [borrow from a woman friend]. He collects his money on Saturday and that day I get the gasto, and start returning what I owe. You know, to manage the allowance is a difficult job, prices are going up and we must buy food, no matter what. And if something goes wrong, or he gets angry at me, he may even cut off the allowance of that week!' (Beneria and Roldan, 1987, p. 121)

African women's lack of confidence that income accruing to men will trickle down to them and their children has already been discussed above. When adjustment is necessary to changing external circumstances, it is women who must manage the adjustment so as to minimise damage to household members. But in doing so, women are generally in a situation of responsibility without power. This is particularly acute with respect to the determination of household expenditure.

When the household is viewed as a unity, it is assumed that income of household members is pooled and is spent in such a way as to maximise their joint welfare. However, the wealth of evidence assembled by Dwyer and Bruce (eds) (1988) and Blumberg (1988) from case studies in all major regions of the Third World, makes clear that such procedures are far from being the norm: not all income is pooled, some is kept for personal discretionary spending, and men and women actively strive over the use of pooled income and have differing expenditure priorities. This is not just a feature of Third World countries but is just as true of richer countries, as work by sociologists makes clear (Whitehead, 1984; Pahl, 1980). A general finding is that women's income is almost exclusively used to meet collective household needs, whereas men tend to retain a considerable portion of their income for personal spending. A key source of male bargaining power within the household is determining what proportion of their income to pass on to other household members. Family interaction over the use of income is fraught with friction, and family members are frequently ignorant of the magnitude of each other's earnings.

There are a wide variety of systems of organisation of household expenditure, but in understanding their dynamics, the crucial distinction is between discretion over how much of one's income to allocate to household as opposed to personal needs, and discretion over exactly what to buy for dinner tonight, or whether to give priority to a son's need for new shoes or a daughter's need for a new dress. Typically, the first type of discretion is enjoyed by men, while the second type of discretion is endured by women. This is true whether the household expenditure system is organised through a male earner making a housekeeping allowance to a non-earning wife (as in the Mexican example above); or through a common fund to which both husbands and wives contribute earnings to finance all household expenditure; or through a system of separate budgets and responsibilities, as occurs in much of rural sub-Saharan Africa, where women are typically responsible for providing food, while men are responsible for paying for items like clothing, medical and educational expenses and taxes. It is important to stress that personal spending money for male adults cannot be assumed to be residual, determined by what is available when household needs have been satisfied. In some cases discussed in Dwyer and Bruce (eds) (1988), it appears to be a priority, and the amount allocated to household expenditure is residually determined by the difference between male income and personal spending. The good husband is one who strictly limits his personal spending, but his prerogative to enjoy such spending remains.

The process of adjusting expenditure to rising prices of food and other basic items is thus constrained by gender divisions within the household. It may not be easy to maintain decent standards of health and nutrition and clothing and schooling by switching expenditure from non-basic items like alcohol, tobacco and entertainment when these items are part of male personal spending. As yet, little research has been done on the adjustment of household expenditure in the context of structural adjustment, but the forebodings expressed here are confirmed by Moser's study of low-income households in Guayaquil, which found that expenditure adjustment was embedded in domestic conflict and violence. The system in most households was a daily housekeeping allowance. While the allowance had tended to rise, the amount had not kept pace with inflation. Moreover, forty-eight per cent of the women interviewed said that there had been an increase in domestic violence, claiming that it always occurred when they had to ask for more money. Some women specifically linked this with the desire of men to maintain their own personal expenditure on alcohol and other women. With younger men, there was a growing problem of drug addiction; during the field work period, a young man addicted to cocaine killed himself after a row with his wife about his spending most of his income on drugs (Moser, 1989).

Economic stress and unemployment is particularly conducive to male use of hard drugs, and tobacco and alcohol; and addiction is one reason why men may resist a reduction in their personal expenditure. Another reason is ignorance: Dwyer and Bruce (eds) (1988) cite case studies suggesting that men simply do not know the level of prices or appreciate the level of needs of other members of the household, because they do not do the shopping and spend little time at home. A further reason is disagreement about what level of provision is required, particularly for children: a study of poor families in Mexico City found that husbands and wives disagreed about what is the minimum acceptable standard of children's clothing and schooling, and about what is urgently required and what can be deferred (Beneria and Roldan, 1987). A more subtle point is made by Sen (1985), who suggests that women tend not to have as strong a sense of self and self-worth as men, and tend to identify with the needs of their children.

An examination of the process of adjusting expenditure within the household to cope with an economy-wide switch in resource allocation highlights the neglected issue of the stress and anxiety of adjustment. This does not only affect women, but it affects women with peculiar force because of their responsibility for provisioning the household, unmatched by control over the allocation of household income. Besides the costs in time, discussed in the previous section, there are costs in terms of sleepless nights, deteriorating health and deteriorating human relationships.

The examples considered here show that there are gender barriers to the reallocation of expenditure within the household that constrain the extent to which the costs of adjustment can be absorbed without a deterioration in the quality of human resources. It is not simply a matter of income foregone during the switching process, or even of extra work having to be done; it is a matter of the disintegration of people's lives.

Conclusions

Models of structural adjustment which depict the problem as something that can be solved by changing relative prices so as to switch resources from non-tradables to tradables in fact rely on an increase in the provision of a non-tradable that is not explicitly included: an increase in women's time and effort in the reproduction and maintenance of human resources. The process of switching, which is regarded as sufficiently unproblematic as to require no detailed analysis, is only unproblematic in so far as women are willing and able to act as the 'shock absorbers' of the system. Failure to specifically address the role of this important non-tradable is a form of male bias, compounded by a failure to perceive how unequal gender relations may themselves prevent adjustment from working in the way envisaged, by limiting women's willingness and ability to absorb the shocks.

Any worthwhile form of structural adjustment must be equitable and sustainable. It must not deplete and degrade resources, particularly human resources.[6] This requires a view of macro-economics that includes the reproduction and maintenance of human resources alongside conventionally included goods and services. It requires a national accounting system that accounts for unpaid labour as well as paid labour. It requires a diagnosis of the structural problems of development that includes gender barriers, as well as price distortions. It requires a strategy for tackling gender barriers as well as for improving the functioning of prices and markets. A full elaboration of this will not be undertaken here, but it is clear that the core of the strategy would be to channel more resources to women and to enhance women's organisational capacity.

Equitable and sustainable adjustment cannot be achieved simply by getting the prices right so as to switch resources from non-tradables to tradables. It requires increased investment.[7] There is growing evidence that investment channelled to women may have a higher rate of return and do more to increase productivity, to improve children's welfare and to improve the use of natural resources, than investment channelled to men (Herz, 1988; Dwyer and Bruce (eds), 1988). There is also growing evidence that women's ability to make the best use of resources is enhanced by participation in extra-familial organisations. Such participation improves women's bargaining power within the household and within the public sphere from which women have been so often excluded, and transforms their consciousness of their rights and abilities (*ibid.*). Outstanding and well-known examples are the Self-Employed Women's Association in India, and the Grameen Bank in Bangladesh. But effective action can also be taken on a very small-scale, localised and spontaneous basis, as is shown by the example, discussed earlier, of a group of Kenyan women mobilising to demand their rightful share of the proceeds of tea production.

The issue now is to what extent are those with economic and political power prepared to channel resources directly to women, rather than hope for resources channelled to men to trickle down to women and children? To what extent are those with economic and political power prepared to restructure gender relations, as well as other social institutions such as markets and bureaucracies? For how long will equitable and sustainable adjustment continue to be constrained by male bias, vividly expressed in the fear that 'whatever happens, we do not want a revolution. If women have their own money, why will they marry'?

Notes

1   This framework was originally produced to analyse how to deal with the balance of payments problems of the Australian economy (see Salter, 1959). It was subsequently adapted for analysing IMF stabilisation policies and World Bank structural adjustment policies (see Lal, 1984).

2   This diagnosis offers an unduly restrictive view of the nature of the structural problems of LDCs, which many social scientists would see as more fundamentally determined by the social relations of production, both national and international. The distinction between tradables and non-tradables is itself open to question, and is likely to vary geographically within a country, owing to variations in transport costs to the border. The concept of price distortion is equally problematic. However, further discussion of these important issues is beyond the scope of this chapter.

3   This belief is fostered by models of the household which conflate leisure time and time spent on unpaid domestic labour. Such models are frequently used in neo-classical economic analysis.

4   There are gender constraints on such expenditure switching, which are discussed later in the chapter. Here we focus on the time implications.

5   The assumption of a despotic male household head may also be attractive to feminists – but the weakness of such an assumption is that it leaves to women only the role of passive acquiescence, and fails to take account of women's active role in household decision-making, and their strategies of resistance to male power.

6   The idea of sustainable development has been popularised with particular reference to the depletion of natural resources and environmental degradation. These concerns are also linked to gender awareness (see Agarwal, 1986), but to discuss them is beyond the scope of this chapter.

7   The evidence for this is now emerging from studies of the impact of World Bank structural adjustment programmes. Those countries that have been claimed as 'success stories', like Turkey and Ghana, have enjoyed massive inflows of foreign aid, which have enabled them to increase their investment. Many World Bank economists now agree that ability to switch

resources and increase production of tradables depends not just on incentives but also on investment.

References

Agarwal, B. (1986), *Cold Hearths and Barren Slopes: The Woodfuel Crisis in the Third World*, Riverdale, California.

Antrobus, P. (1988), 'Consequences and responses to social and economic deterioration: the experience of the English-speaking Caribbean', Workshop on Economic Crisis, Household Strategies and Women's Work, Cornell University.

Babalola, S. O., and Dennis, C. (1988), 'Returns to women's labour in cash crop production: tobacco in Igboho, Oyo State, Nigeria', in J. Davison (ed.) (1988), *op. cit.*

Becker, G. (1976), *The Economic Approach to Human Behaviour*, University of Chicago Press, Chicago.

——(1981), *A Treatise on the Family*, Harvard University Press, Cambridge, Mass.

Beneria, L., and Roldan, M. (1987), *The Crossroads of Class and Gender*, University of Chicago Press, Chicago.

Berger, M. (1988), 'Women's responses to recession in Latin America and the Caribbean: a focus on urban labor markets', Workshop on Economic Crisis, Household Strategies and Women's Work, Cornell University.

Bienefeld, M. (1988), 'Structural adjustment and its impact on women in developing countries', Discussion Paper submitted to CIDA, RC/ Project 839/11109.

Blumberg, R. L. (1988), 'Income under female vs. male control', *Journal of Family Issues*, vol. 9, no. 1.

Carney, J. (1988), 'Struggles over land and crops in an irrigated rice scheme: The Gambia', in J. Davison (ed.) (1988), *op. cit.*

Cornia, G. (1987), 'Social policymaking: restructuring, targeting, efficiency', in G. Cornia, R. Jolly, and F. Stewart (eds) (1987), *op. cit.*

Cornia, G., Jolly, R., and Stewart, F. (eds) (1987), *Adjustment with a Human Face*, Clarendon Press, Oxford.

Davison, J. (ed.) (1988), *Agriculture, Women and Land*, Westview Press, Boulder and London.

——(1988a), 'Land and women's agricultural production: the context', in *ibid.*

——(1988b), 'Who owns what? Land registration and tensions in gender relations of production in Kenya', in *ibid.*

Dey, J. (1980), 'Gambian women: unequal partners in rice development', *Journal of Development Studies*, vol. 17, no. 3.

Dwyer, D., and Bruce, J. (eds) (1988), *A Home Divided: Women and Income in the Third World*, Stanford University Press, Stanford.

Elson, D. (1988), 'Gender aware policymaking for structural adjustment', unpublished report for the Commonwealth Secretariat.

Elson, D., and Flemming, S. (1989), 'Women's contribution to the economy and structural adjustment', unpublished report for the Commonwealth Secretariat.

Elson, D., and Pearson, R. (1981), '"Nimble fingers make cheap workers": an analysis of women's employment in Third World export manufacturing', *Feminist Review*, no. 7.

——(eds) (1989), *Women's Employment and Multinationals in Europe*, Macmillan, London.

Evans, A. (1989), 'Gender issues in rural household economics', Institute of Development Economics, Discussion Paper No. 254.

Evans, A., and Young, K. (1988), 'Gender issues in household labour allocation: the case of Northern Province, Zambia', ODA ESCOR Research Report.

Feldman, S. (1988), 'Crisis, Islam and gender in Bangladesh: the social construction of a female labor force', Workshop on Economic Crisis, Household Strategies and Women's Work, Cornell University.

Folbre, N. (1986a), 'Hearts and spades: paradigms of household economics', *World Development*, vol. 14, no. 2.

——(1986b), 'Cleaning house: new perspectives on households and economic development', *Journal of Development Economics*, vol.22.

Foo, G., and Lim, L. (1989), 'Poverty, ideology and women export factory workers in Asia', in H. Afshar and B. Agarwal (eds), *Women, Poverty and Ideology*, Macmillan, London.

Goldstein, N. (1989), 'Silicon Glen: women and semiconductor multinationals', in D. Elson and R. Pearson (eds) (1989), *op. cit.*

Herz, B. (1988), 'Briefing on women and development', World Bank/IMF Annual Meeting, Berlin.

Heyzer, N. (1988a), 'Economic crisis, household strategies, and women's work in South East Asia', Workshop on Economic Crisis, Household Strategies and Women's Work, Cornell University.

——(ed.) (1988b), *Daughters in Industry*, Asian and Pacific Development Centre, Kuala Lumpur.

Hirata, H. (1989), 'Production relocation: an electronics multinational in France and Brazil', in D. Elson and R. Pearson (eds) (1989), *op. cit.*

Jackson, P., and Barry, U. (1989), 'Women's employment and multinationals in the Republic of Ireland: the creation of a new female labour force', in *ibid.*

Joekes, S. (1987), *Women in the World Economy: An INSTRAW Study*, Oxford University Press, New York.

Jones, C. (1983), 'The mobilisation of women's labour for cash crop production: a game theoretic approach', *American Journal of Agricultural Economics*, vol. 65, no. 5.

Kergoat, D. (1982), *Les Ouvrières*, Editions Le Sycomore, Paris.

Lal, D. (1984), 'The real effects of stabilisation and structural adjustment policies', World Bank Staff Working Papers No. 636, Washington DC.

Longhurst, R. (1987), 'Policy approaches towards small farmers', in G. Cornia, R. Jolly, and F. Stewart (eds) (1987), *op. cit.*

Mbilinyi, M. (1988a), 'The invention of female farming systems in Africa: structural adjustment in Tanzania', Workshop on Economic Crisis,

Household Strategies and Women's Work, Cornell University.
—(1988b), 'Agribusiness and women peasants in Tanzania', *Development and Change*, vol. 19, pp. 549–83.
Miralao, V. A. (1984), 'The impact of female employment on household management', i G. W. Jones (ed.), *Women in the Urban and Industrial Workforce: Southeast and East Asia*, Australian National University, Canberra.
Moser, C. (1989), 'The impact of recession and structural adjustment policies at the micro-level: low income women and their households in Guayquil, Ecuador', *Invisible Adjustment*, vol. 2, UNICEF.
Onimode, B. (ed.) (1989), *The IMF, the World Bank and the African Debt*, Zed Books, London.
Pahl, J. (1980), 'Patterns of money management within marriage', *Journal of Social Policy*, vol. 9, no. 3.
Pankhurst, D., and Jacobs, S. (1988), 'Land tenure, gender relations, and agriculturl production: the case of Zimbabwe's peasantry', in J. Davison (ed.) (1988), *op. cit.*
Pearson, R. (1988), 'Female workers in the First and Third Worlds: the greening of women's labour', in R. E. Pahl (ed.), *On Work*, Blackwell, Oxford.
Roston, M. (1983), 'Early neoclassical economics and the economic role of women', Social Science Working Paper, Open University, Milton Keynes.
Salaff, J. (1981), *Working Daughters of Hong Kong*, Cambridge University Press, Cambridge.
Salter, W. (1959), 'Internal and external balance: the role of price and expenditure effects', *Economic Record*, August.
Selowsky, M. (1987), 'Adjustment in the 1980s: an overview of issues', *Finance and Development*, vol. 24, no. 2, pp. 11–14.
Sen, A. K. (1983), *Resources, Values and Development*, ch. 16: 'Economics and the family', Blackwell, Oxford.
——(1985), 'Women, technology, and sexual divisions', UNCTAD and INSTRAW, Geneva.
Senauer, B., Sahn, D., and Alderman, H. (1986), 'The effect of time on food consumption patterns in developing countries: evidence from Sri Lanka', *American Journal of Agricultural Economics*, vol.68, no.4.
Whitehead, A. (1984), ' "I'm hungry mum": the politics of domestic budgeting', in K. Young, C. Wolkowitz, and R. McCullagh (eds), *Of Marriage and the Market*, Routledge & Kegan Paul, London.

Overcoming male bias

Male bias is transformed in the course of development, but as the cases discussed in earlier chapters show, we cannot rely on the development process to overcome male bias automatically. Development may weaken or decompose existing forms of male bias; but it may also intensify existing forms, or recompose new forms (Elson and Pearson, 1981, p. 99). It does not abolish the underlying supports of male bias. For though the modes of integration of getting a living and raising children do change during the course of development, there is no sign that the changes serve to give women the kind of independent entitlement they need. Conscious action is needed if male bias is to be permanently weakened and if progress is to be made towards undermining its ultimate foundations: 'Few who have studied women's position would conclude that fundamental change for women . . . can be based solely on increasing their individual earning power. Feminist theorists have identified collective action as a primary step for women in achieving personal power and status in the public domain.' (Bruce, 1989, p. 987).

This chapter discusses strategies for overcoming male bias in everyday attitudes and practices, in theoretical reasoning, and in public policy. It explores the possibility of weakening the underlying supports of male bias through extra-familial ways of integrating getting a living and raising children, involving some measure of collective, public responsibility for children, and changes in the way that paid employment is structured. It discusses how far progress in overcoming male bias can be made within the context of existing forms of development and the question of whether alternative development strategies are required. No magic recipes guaranteeing instant success are available: overcoming male bias is a long, slow process which has not yet been completed anywhere in the world. But step by step the entitlements and capabilities of women may be enlarged.

The first step towards overcoming male bias in everyday attitudes and practices is enabling women to develop a better sense of their own worth and their own contribution to the family and to the wider society. Following this, women need to be able to develop a sense of their own identity, an identity which is not submerged in their roles as wives, mothers and daughters. On this basis, they can develop a voice of their own, both individually within the family and collectively within the community, and begin to act with other women to weaken the forces constraining them. To achieve all this, women's organisations are essential, but there is a wide range of different types of women's organisations, and by no means all of them have the goal of empowering women and enabling them to challenge male bias.

One influential classification of women's organisations in the Third World, proposed by Gita Sen and Caren Grown, distinguishes six different categories (DAWN, 1985). They are: major, traditional service-oriented organisations concerned with women's health, education and welfare; women's organisations affiliated to political parties; worker-based organisations such as trade unions and organisations of self-employed women; donor-sponsored organisations promoted as part of the UN decade for women, such as handicraft co-operatives; grass-roots organisations, often with a specific focus such as women's health or violence against women; research organisations.

This is a rather *ad hoc* descriptive categorisation, which has been criticised for not employing any analytical criteria, such as the groups' goals or methods of working; and for leaving out some important types of women's groups, such as women's centres (of which there are 120 in Latin America alone) and international solidarity groups working on issues like sex tourism and rights of women workers (Yu, 1989, p. 16). It is also not clear where what Moser (1989) calls women's community managing work (such as self-help groups for provision of neighbourhood infrastructure) fits in.

In analysing the potential of such organisations in combating male bias we may ask to what extent they have a transformative perspective that includes the empowerment of women; and to what extent they are concerned more with enabling women to cope with the status quo and to perform their traditional roles better. We need to beware of making too sharp a distinction between empowerment and coping. Empowerment is not something that can be fought for in the abstract. Women's organisations must always have some immediate goals that are related to women's immediately-felt concerns – what have been called women's practical gender interests (Molyneux, 1985); and women's organisations have to work within society as it currently is. But to challenge male bias, women's organisations must be able to connect women's practical gender interests with what have been called women's strategic gender interests (*ibid.*) – that is, women's interests in autonomy and an end to subordination. Women thus have to act simultaneously within and against the societies in which they live (Kessler-Harris, 1987, p. 59). So it is not a matter of wanting organisations that empower women as opposed to enabling them to cope, but of wanting organisations that seek to empower women as well as enabling them to cope – organisations that have the goal of transforming gender relations through practical action (Bhat, 1989).

We may also ask to what extent organisations seek to mobilise women in support of goals determined by others; and to what extent they place stress on the self-determination of the women in the organisation. It is often suggested that women's wings of political parties have been more concerned with mobilising women to support male-determined party goals than with giving women a voice within parties, or making parties responsive to women's interests. Similarly, trade unions have often been criticised for being dominated by men. Major traditional women's organisations concerned with women's welfare, health and education have frequently been criticised for being run by well-off women who take a patronising attitude to the poor women whose lives they see themselves as trying to improve. Research organisations have been criticised for failing to use participatory research methods and for treating women simply as sources of data which could be used to further the researcher's careers. Grass-roots organisations have frequently been seen in a more favourable light, but care must be taken not to romanticise them. Moser (1989) offers a more realistic appraisal. She argues that women frequently take primary responsibility for the formation, organisation and success of local-level protest groups, putting pressure on local authorities for provision of services to the community. But they often tend to do this as an extension of their domestic role, implicitly accepting the sexual division of labour and the subordination of women. Often women's grass-roots groups are self-help groups mobilising women's unpaid labour to provide items of collective consumption. Men's role in grass-roots organisations is different. Moser's survey of a wide variety of Third World community-level organisations found that men tend to take leadership roles that involve political organising within a wider sphere than the immediate neighbourhood; whereas women take more 'rank and file' localised roles (Moser, 1987).

Other studies have revealed considerable differences in the degree of democracy in grass-roots organisations; in the extent to which leaders hand down decisions and determine objectives rather than facilitate the self-organisation of the members. (For an interesting case study of women workers' organisations in Sri Lanka, see Rosa, 1989.) There is a difficult issue here which should not be glossed over. In so far as an organisation has the objective of transforming the perceptions of its members and enabling them to see how their practical gender interests connect with strategic gender interests that they may not yet have articulated, then leadership is needed. The problem is how to prevent leadership from degenerating into dominance. Considerable thought needs to be given to building up democratic structures and to enlarging the skills of members of the organisation – as appears to have been done in the case of the Self-Employed Women's Association in Ahmedabad, India (Bhat, 1989).

Women's organisations that focus on empowerment do seem to be flourishing in many parts of the Third World (Kishwar and Vanita (eds) 1984; DAWN, 1985; Antrobus, 1988; Kumar, 1989; Moser, 1989; Yu, 1989). Dwyer and Bruce, summarising evidence for India and Bangladesh, suggest that in these two countries women's organisations have been successful in changing women's perceptions, increasing their bargaining ability within the family, enabling them to mobilise community resources, such as literacy classes, and to gain a voice in local government (Dwyer and Bruce (eds), 1988, p. 9). Some women's organisations have used innovative and imaginative methods of linking women's practical and strategic gender interests in such a way as to change women's perceptions and enhance their capacities. For instance, in the Philippines, GABRIELA (an alliance of local and national women's organisations) ran a project combining the traditional female task of sewing tapestry with a discussion of women's rights. A nation-wide tapestry-making drive facilitated the discussion of women's rights in communities, factories and schools, and produced a 'Tapestry of Women's Rights' (Gomez, 1986). In the Caribbean, Sistren Theatre Collective reaches working-class women through involving them in the writing and performing of plays, such as 'Downpression Get a Blow' about women in a garment factory (Yu, 1989). In Sri Lanka, an independent women's collective produces a newspaper with and for women workers in the Free Trade Zone, encouraging them to find a voice by writing about their experiences (Rosa, 1989).

A common thread running through such initiatives is a concern that women should become more self-reliant in the sense of being more capable of making their own choices and gaining greater control over the resources needed to implement those choices. But there are structural limits to what can be achieved on their own by Third World women's organisations which do consciously have the goal of empowering women and enabling them to challenge male bias. An important limit is imposed by the lack of resources, both for the organisations themselves and for the wider societies of which they are part. Most of these organisations remain grievously short of resources and under pressure, many leading a hand-to-mouth existence. The women whom they support live in societies that are relatively poor and occupy subordinate positions in the world economy and world political system. The DAWN network, in particular, has argued that liberating Third World women is intrinsically linked to liberating their countries from domination by the industrialised capitalist countries. This is not necessarily to claim that a lessening of such domination would be a sufficient, or even a necessary, condition for lessening male dominance in the Third World, but rather to emphasis that it is much easier to increase the capabilities and entitlements of women in the Third World if the capabilities and entitlements of the societies in which they live are increasing. Diminishing male bias against Third World women is in that way linked to diminishing bias against Third World countries in the international economic and political system.

This is not a simple issue of more aid. More aid may create more difficulties. For instance, an Indian feminist argues that divisions within the women's movement in India were exacerbated 'by a problem which is common to many developing countries, of aid for 'developmental activities' being poured into social movements, creating competition, schisms and bitterness.' (Kumar, 1989, p. 27).

Another important limit is imposed by existing structures of state power. Ela Bhatt, the founder of the Self-Employed Women's Association (SEWA) in India, recounts some of the obstacles faced by grass-roots women's organisations in the informal sector: 'The labor department, for example is meant to protect the workers, but it has become corrupt and tries to avoid the labor laws. Municipal governments treat poor vendors as criminals. The courts take years to render final judgements . . . . When cities and towns are planned, no space is set aside for vending: as a result, vendors remain 'illegal'.' (Bhatt, 1989, p. 1062). Initially, SEWA was refused permission to register as a trade union and enjoy the legal rights that trade unions have; and to register its co-operative bank. In many countries, including India, women's groups have faced much more than corruption and bureaucratic obstacles, suffering the full weight of violent repression by police and troops (Kishwar and Vanita (eds) 1984; Committee of Asian Women, *Newsletter*, various issues).

A further limit is the particular form of the development process. Different types of development process concentrate resources in different hands and prioritise different needs. For instance, a development process which is spearheaded by large corporations producing for the world market may generate new employment opportunities for women but leave women vulnerable to fluctuations in the world market and the power of such corporations to relocate their activities (Heyzer, 1989). Women may gain control of a wage packet, but control over the means of production is concentrated in a few, male, hands; and as the analysis of chapter 6 shows, that control is exercised in ways that confine women to low-paid jobs with few promotion prospects.

To push back such structural limits, organisations concerned with the empowerment of women have to move beyond challenging male bias at the level of everyday attitudes and practices to challenge the systemic factors that underpin these everyday attitudes and practices. This requires a challenge to male bias, both in the theoretical understandings of social systems generated in educational and research institutions, and in the public policy and political processes that seek to uphold or modify social systems. Self-reliance should not be understood as separatism or a refusal to engage with existing social structures. Rather, it means the ability to set one's own priorities and to make one's own choices on how to engage with those structures.

Engaging with the structures through which dominant meanings are generated and through which entitlements are determined is undoubtedly hazardous. Grass-roots feminist organisations are rightly worried about their urgency and anger being dissipated in bland academic discourse; about losing touch with their constituency; about the appropriation of their struggle by researchers concerned mainly with their own careers. They are worried about being co-opted if they start to engage with the policy process. They fear that accepting resources from the state will jeopardise their autonomy. There are real dangers here (for a discussion of them in the Canadian context, see Weir, 1987), which are particularly acute for activist women's groups in Third World countries because theoretical interpretations are so often monopolised by researchers from First World countries, and the sources of funding are so often foreign aid agencies. But there are also dangers in holding aloof from the policy process and from contesting theoretical understandings that underpin public policy. For autonomous and self-reliant women's organisations which have a critical stance can nevertheless in some circumstances help to stabilise and prop up the system of gender they with to contest. The provision of refuges for women who have been subjected to domestic violence; the provision of non-traditional training and education for women; the provision of well-women centres concerned to offer women medical care free of male bias; all these might be welcome to governments, especially those concerned to reduce public expenditure. The voluntary labour of women activists may be seen as a saving to the public purse regardless of whether the aim of such labour is the empowerment of women or more traditional welfare concerns (Moser, 1989). These different hazards cannot be wished away, but explicit recognition of them may help to prevent the project of empowering women from being wrecked on them: 'It is only by understanding the contradictions inherent in women's location within various structures that effective political action and challenges can be devised.' (Mohanty, 1988, p. 74).

Effective challenges to male bias in theoretical reasoning need to demonstrate how supposedly gender-neutral theories are in fact imbued with male bias, to show how to overcome this bias, and how introducing gender awareness improves the theory. The last stage is particularly important for overcoming the marginalisation of gender in the largely male world of theoretical reasoning. Those theorists, and there are many, who are not especially concerned with the empowerment of women, are more likely to take notice of the argument that lack of gender awareness disables their theories, than the argument that lack of gender awareness disables women. To recognise this is not to capitulate to patriarchal attitudes but rather to improve one's chances of having some impact.

The starting-point is making gender differences visible to theory by insisting on the need to disaggregate all the categories of analysis by gender. No one should be allowed merely to say 'farmer' without specifying whether male farmer or female farmer is meant. No one should be allowed merely to say 'informal sector' without specifying whether the male or the female sub-sector of that sector is implied; and so on. There is still an enormous amount of work to be done here despite the fact that women analysts have been making this point for the last fifteen years. To give just one recent example, the Report of the Commonwealth Expert Group on Women and Structural Adjustment notes several times how the inadequacy of gender-disaggregated data has constrained its work (Commonwealth Secretariat, 1989, pp. 1, 45, 59, and 104). There seems to be a particular resistance to disaggregating household surveys so as to look within households at the distribution of resources between household members and at gender differentiation in decision-making processes (Elson and Fleming, 1988). Thus it appears that the major new data-gathering initiative for sub-Saharan Africa being sponsored by the UNDP and World Bank under their Social Dimensions of Adjustment Programme will content itself with dividing households into male-headed and female-headed, but will not investigate gender asymmetries within the households. It is essential that household surveys be redesigned and that questions be put to *all* adult members of the households, in confidence, if possible by enumerators of the same sex as the respondent. It is well-established that male enumerators asking questions of male household members will come up with a very different picture of women's roles than will female enumerators asking questions of female household members (Beneria, 1981).

Besides making gender differences visible by disaggregating categories of analysis, the unpaid labour of reproduction and maintenance of human resources must be made visible. Women analysts have been campaigning for some time to have such unpaid labour counted and included in the gross national product, so far without much success. It is perhaps more strategically important to contest notions of efficiency and productivity that ignore such unpaid labour, and to point out that the work of caring for the labour force and nurturing the future generation of workers has benefits to society at large (positive externalities, in the jargon of economics) that justify the provision of public facilities for such work.

We have to move beyond this starting-point and show how theories make implicit assumptions about gender even though they may have no explicit reference to it. This requires deconstructing theories, not just adding on 'women' as an area of concern. Demonstrating male bias in a theory means showing how its implicit assumptions about gender work to women's disadvantage; and how they prevent the theory from providing an adequate understanding of the social processes it addresses, and hence from providing an adequate basis for development policies. The work of Nancy Folbre (1986; 1988) deconstructing the new household economics is an exemplary case. It also illustrates two other points. The first is the importance of more gender-aware critiques of economic theory. Economic theory has greater salience in public policy for development than any other branch of social science, but it is the branch with fewest women practitioners and least gender awareness. Those of us concerned to overcome male bias have to increase our expertise in economics. At the moment, most of the research on gender and development is carried out under the auspices of anthropology, sociology and social policy analysis. Such research has contributed an enormous amount, but it needs to be complemented by a feminist economics capable of deconstructing cost-benefit analysis, IMF stabilisation programmes, arguments about the relative benefits of export oriented and import-substitution oriented strategies, and much more. As Jamaican economist and activist, Marjorie Williams (1988), has written, 'Women need economic literacy'.

The second point illustrated by the work of Folbre is that though careful logic and critical argument can have a considerable impact in shifting the terms of intellectual debate, it will not altogether vanquish male-biased theory. The leading practitioners of the new household economics continue to defend their position, resorting to the argument that their theory is correct so long as it is compatible with observed outcomes; no matter that their theory gives an inadequate account of the process leading to the outcome, and that gender-aware theories are also compatible with observed outcomes. This should not lead us to the conclusion that it is no use trying to contest male bias in theoretical reasoning. A gender-aware critical theory is crucial for showing that there is an alternative. The social sciences are marked by the continued clash of different theoretical schools. Theory that defends the status quo on class, and national, asymmetries has remained alongside critical theory that seeks the end of class exploitation and of the hegemony of the industrialised capitalist countries over the rest of the world. It is utopian to expect that critical theory will win acceptance by everyone, but it is a vital resource for those struggling for change.

When it can be clearly shown that there are gender barriers that prevent the achievement of an outcome predicted by a gender-blind theory, then analysis may well be modified. Thus the argument put forward in chapter 7 – about gender barriers in smallholder farming in sub-Saharan Africa preventing an adequate supply response when crop prices are raised – is beginning to be accepted by economists working on structural adjustment. The importance of providing sufficient incentives directly to women themselves for their work in agriculture, rather than relying on male farmers pooling and sharing their income with other household members, is recognised in some of the recent documents produced by the Social Dimensions of Adjustment Programme. Recognition is perhaps helped by the fact that the problem can be described in terms of a theory thoroughly familiar to mainstream economists – that of the 'principal agent'. Of course, more than one solution to this problem may exist. The solution preferred by women farmers may be that marketing boards make direct payments to them as well as to their husbands, as in some of the cases discussed in chapter 7. The solution preferred by designers of structural adjustment programmes may be to transform peasants into workers so that women are directly paid for their work, but as agricultural labourers, as Mbilinyi (1988) argues is happening in Tanzania.

What are the best organisational strategies for contesting male bias in development theory? Is it a good idea to have separate gender and development research units and courses? Or will this lead to female ghettos which have little impact on mainstream (some would say, malestream) theory? The dilemma is somewhat similar to the dilemma about whether to have separate women's projects. Separate projects ensure that at least some resources are devoted to women, but research on women's projects shows that they tend to be marginalised and that gender-sensitive mainstream projects are the most effective way of improving women's situation (Carloni, 1987). There appears to be no comparable research on the effectiveness of separate gender and development (or women in development) research units and courses. Personal experience suggests that separate units and courses are a necessary first stage, but that it is now important to consider how to promote gender awareness in all research units and courses dealing with development issues, among male as well as female researchers and teachers. Gender-aware curricula need to be devised for all those courses that are not typically seen as women's issues. Gender-aware research training needs to be provided alongside training on statistical techniques and the use of computers. More men must teach and research on gender – something which will not be without costs, such as attempts to theorise gender with unsuitable conceptual tools, and tendencies to divert resources away from women teachers and researchers, most of whom occupy more marginal positions in the academic hierarchy. But this may be the cost of dispelling the prejudice that male bias is only an issue for women; and only thus can more progress be made in overcoming male bias in theoretical reasoning.

Attempts to dispel male bias in development theory will not have much practical impact unless parallel attempts take place to dispel male bias in policy and the operations of the state. Dixon puts the point forcefully:

The reluctance to 'see' women farmers comes not from their invisibility, but from a reluctance to share scarce resources with them . . . . Including women in labor force statistics in proportion to the amount of work they actually do is an essential first step in making female farmers visible to planners and policy makers. But it is only a first step, necessary but not sufficient. The challenge of the future is to see that women as food producers receive their fair share of recognition not only in the full panoply of economic and demographic statistics intended to count workers and value their labor, but in the institutional/political systems that provide access to resources that will raise agricultural productivity and the returns of women's work.' (Dixon, 1985, pp. 32–3).

During the UN Decade for Women, many governments set up ministries for women's affairs, women's bureaux, commissions on the status of women, etc. But such offices have rarely managed to have much impact on male bias in the policy process. They have lacked the resources and expertise, and in many cases, the will to contest male bias and promote gender awareness in the design and implementation of the full range of policies. They have rarely been fully committed to the empowerment of women and have more usually focused on traditional welfare issues (Gordon, 1984; Commonwealth Secretariat, 1987). Undoubtedly, they could achieve more with better resources and training and stronger links with women's organisations: a detailed strategy for improvement is provided by Kate Young in Commonwealth Secretariat (1987). But it would be unwise for a strategy for overcoming male bias in the policy process to confine itself to improving the performance of women's bureaux.

Two broader goals need to inform any such strategy: developing and implementing techniques for gender-based planning and programming throughout the apparatus of government; and democratising state structures so that groups concerned with the empowerment of women can have more power. This second goal extends concern beyond questions of machinery of government to the wider political process.

The first goal is increasingly being highlighted (Elson, 1988a; Moser, 1989; Chen, 1989; Commonwealth Secretariat, 1989) and some progress is being made. For instance, Uganda now has a woman as Minister for Agriculture and she has instituted a 'women's desk' within the Ministry and is organising training of women as agricultural extension officers (Boyd, 1989). The government of Zimbabwe has undertaken to try to integrate women's concerns into the formulation and design of macro-economic policies through the establishment of focal points in the relevant ministries, and through gender sensitisation training programmes for personnel in finance and economic planning ministries (Commonwealth Secretariat, 1989).

But there is one danger in pursuing the goal of gender-aware planning and programming that needs some discussion. Much the easiest way to persuade policy-makers to consider gender-based

planning and programming is to present women as an overlooked
and underutilised resource which can be mobilised to make
implementation of existing policy easier, and approach which
Moser (1989) labels the 'efficiency' approach. However, the problem
for all but small numbers of well-off women, is not that they are an
underutilised resource but that they are an overutilised resource
(Elson, 1988a). All available time budget studies confirm that
women have longer working hours on average than men, when their
unpaid as well as their paid labour is counted. To ensure that
women, as well planners, benefit, then the emphasis must be on
redirecting resources towards women. Evidence can be deployed to
show that redirecting investment resources to women increases
productivity more than if the same quantity of resources were
directed towards men (Palmer, 1988; Herz, 1988). Gender
asymmetries can be presented as barriers to the rational allocation of
resources.

However, it would be utopian to put all one's faith in rational
argument as the means of overcoming male bias in the policy
process. Policy-makers have other goals besides policy
implementation – and preserving male privilege may well be among
the more important. This brings us to the second broad goal of
democratising the state to bring it under popular control. This is
partly an issue of decentralisation and accountability of the state
apparatus, and partly an issue of the nature of the political process
and the ability of the people to control their representatives. These
are complex issues which cannot be fully explored here.
Improvements in decentralisation and accountability at local level
can be achieved in the context of a one-party state (Mackintosh and
Wuyts, 1988); a liberal democratic political process with competing
parties and regular elections all too frequently leaves the state in the
hands of the rich and provides no genuine accountability to the
people. But the absence of a liberal democratic political process
forecloses most of the space required for the development of
autonomous popular organisations, which must flourish if there is to
any firm and long-lasting basis for the popular control of the state.
Many activists and writers in Third World countries which have
suffered under authoritarian one-party and military states now see
the struggle for liberal democratic rights as crucial for widening the
democratic space within which autonomous popular organisations
can develop and can organise for genuine popular control of the

state (Beckman, 1989). Alongside this needs to go a struggle for transforming the state apparatus to make it the servant, not the master, of the public in its day-to-day operations. State employees must become more responsive to the needs of those who use its services; this is not a matter of managerially defined efficiency but of popular participation in planning public services.

The issue of democratising the state is particularly important for women because the underlying supports of male bias cannot be weakened without public intervention in the way in which getting a living is integrated with raising children. Although public intervention can take place through community organisations as well as through state agencies, the power of the latter in mobilising resources and conferring rights makes them indispensable given the scale of intervention that is needed.

A basic income entitlement provided through the state for all members of society, children and adults, irrespective of the work they do, would do much to topple the underlying supports of male bias, as it would free those caring for children from dependence on other family members or on charity. A strong case has been made for the feasibility of such an entitlement in those Western industrialised countries with a relatively egalitarian income distribution (Purdy, 1990). However, there are fears that it would not do enough to change the prevailing distribution of housework and child care between women and men (Barrett, 1980, p. 244). It would need to be supplemented by other measures to enable and encourage men to take more responsibility for housework and child care (*ibid.*, p. 226; Molyneux, 1981, pp. 197–200).

Such measures would include a redesign of paid employment so as to take account of domestic responsibilities. This would need to include not just shorter and more flexible working hours, and parental leave, but also positive recognition of child care experience in pay and promotion. Time away from paid work for child care and other domestic responsibilities would have to become a qualification for higher pay and promotion to a better job, rather than a disqualification, as it universally is at present. To argue for this is not to reject considerations of efficiency; rather, it is to argue for a more comprehensive definition of efficiency. The responsibility for looking after children does develop a range of skills in management of resources and people which are transferable but go largely unrecognised because of male bias in the world of paid work.

Time away from paid work should not be seen as merely de-skilling. Moreover, employers need people to raise the next generation of workers; and not all aspects of child care can be transferred to paid workers in crèches and nurseries. Unpaid child care has positive externalities to employers in the sense of generating benefits for them that they have not paid for. This will tend to result in an underinvestment of resources in looking after children. A good way to prevent such underinvestment is to design jobs with the requirement that all employees, regardless of sex, will take some time away from paid work to help raise children, either their own or those of other members of their community. Failure to fulfil this requirement would then be a bar to advancement. Thus male-biased norms of working life would be overturned, and men would have a positive incentive to change the division of unpaid labour.

In the current conditions of Third World countries, such comprehensive strategies are not on the agenda. The precise form of desirable and feasible changes in the way that getting a living is integrated with raising children will depend on particular circumstances, but some general issues can be distinguished. If women are to become less dependent on men for the resources they need while raising children, then there must be public provision of many of the necessary inputs, from clean water on tap in each home to electricity, to transport, to health care. There must be public action to enlarge women's independent entitlements to land, to credit, to training. But public action must not stop at trying to equip women both to earn their own living and to raise children; if it does, the result may simply be an addition to women's burdens and a further withdrawal of men's responsibility to their children. In addition, there must be public action to begin to reshape the conditions of employment of both men and women to take account of child care responsibilities, and to reshape the legal rights and duties of parents towards their children and towards each other so as to create a framework for egalitarian rather than male-biased family structures. One step forward would be to require all development projects to make some collective provision for child care and housework facilities so as to ease the time constraints on women. Another would be to devote more public sector resources to combating the widespread domestic violence perpetrated by men against women.

Of course, it must be recognised that the state plays a major role in perpetuating social, economic and ideological processes that subordinate women. But this does not mean that women have a simple interest in reducing the role of the state in resource allocation and in structuring family forms (Barratt, 1980, p. 246). Rather, women have an interest in restructuring both the state apparatus and the political process to make them more accountable to women. 'There is a constant struggle at various levels to make laws and policies responsive to the needs of poor self-employed women, to reinterpret laws and policies, to defend our existence against policies that destroy our livelihoods, to make new laws and policies.' (Bhatt, 1989, p. 1062). Not all women share this interest to the same extent; women's class interests as well as their gender interests are a determining factor in the precise way they have an interest in restructuring the state. Any specific struggle for contesting male bias will always be from the point of view of a particular group of women. The struggle with the most comprehensive implications will be that from the point of view of the women with least entitlements and least capabilities.

The final issue for discussion is the question of the relation between overcoming male bias and the form of development. Here, there is considerable debate. Some analysts who stress the need for gender awareness suggest that there is no need for any re-orientation to alternative forms of development. Gender awareness and a reduction in male bias can, in their view, be incorporated into existing forms of development and will lead to more effective implementation of existing strategies. This is the point of view of Barbara Herz, Chief of the World Bank Women in Development Division, who writes of the need to bring women into the economic mainstream. With respect to structural adjustment programmes, she argues:

In this area, the fundamental task is to switch labour and resources from less productive to more productive lines of work. The Bank's women-in-development strategy emphasizes the types of investments (education, health/family planning, credit, extension) that can help women make this switch faster and more effectively. In the meantime, special efforts may be needed to tide over the poorest women until they can produce or earn more. (Herz, 1989, p. 25)

There is no doubt that male bias does hamper the effective implementation of structural adjustment programmes and that the diminution of some forms of male bias would lead to more effective implementation of such programmes. An example is the removal of gender barriers to incentives for women farmers, which was mentioned earlier in this chapter and discussed at some length in chapter 7. A further example is targeting poverty alleviation measures on women, given the gender divisions in the determination of household expenditure (Elson, 1988a). But structural adjustment programmes work primarily through market forces and thus give only paid labour explicit recognition. For their effectiveness they in fact rely on an increase in male bias in the burdens of unpaid labour, as explained in chapter 7. As a forthcoming major study of gender issues in structural adjustment concludes: 'It may simply amount to a shifting of the costs from the paid to the unpaid economy, through further exploitation of women's reproductive work. It is precisely this point which casts doubt on the relevance of structural adjustment to the empowerment of female human resource to participate in new opportunities . . . .' (Palmer, 1990). Palmer's solution is to bring more reproductive work into market exchange, with paid workers providing child care, tap water, fuel, etc., so that such labour become properly costed and explicitly recognised.

Other voices are more sceptical about the benefits of marketisation for women, emphasising the risks, as well as opportunities, that markets bring (Elson, 1988a; Mackintosh, 1990). This does not imply that a non-market form of development would be possible and preferable, but that markets have to be socially managed to reduce risks and support social goals (Mackintosh and Wuyts, 1988; Elson, 1988b). The DAWN network – DAWN stands for Development Alternatives with Women for a New Era – has particularly emphasised the risks of the international market and advocated alternatives based around expanding and improving subsistence production and moving away from production for export markets. It is certainly true that better market incentives for women farmers to produce export crops can have only a limited impact on their living standards so long as the international prices of tropical produce continue to decline. Nevertheless, foreign exchange earnings are vital for development. This point raises the issue, emphasised by the DAWN network, of a link between overcoming the asymmetries of gender and overcoming the asymmetries of the international economic and political system. Much more work needs to be done on constructing alternative theoretical frameworks and alternative development policies that address both issues. A start is being made with the Women's Alternative Economic Summit on Beyond the Debt Crisis: Structural Transformations, in New York, 1990. Further work will need to consider two questions emphasised by Mackintosh and Wutys (1988). First, the social location of accumulation – in whose hands is control of the means of production being placed? In the food sector, is it in the hands of women farmers or multinational agribusiness? In the garment sector, is it in the hands of women's co-operatives or sub-contractors for large corporations? In the provision of credit, is it in the hands of organisations like SEWA, or international banks? The second question concerns the integration of strategies for producing social services and social infrastructure with strategies for producing marketed goods, so as to improve the productivity of both paid and unpaid labour. Alternatives that focus on these questions, backed up by the mobilisation of women's organisations that link practical and strategic gender interests, offer the most promising way forward for overcoming male bias in the development process.

References

Antrobus, P. (1988), 'Consequences and responses to social and economic deterioration: the experience of the English-speaking Caribbean', Workshop on Economic Crisis, Household Strategies, and Women's Work, Cornell University.

Barrett, M. (1980), *Women's Oppression Today*, Verso, London.

Beckman, B. (1989), 'Whose democracy? Bourgeois vs popular democracy', *Review of African Political Economy*, no. 45/46.

Beneria, L. (1981), 'Conceptualising the labour force: the underestimation of women's economic activities', *Journal of Development Studies*, vol. 17, no. 3.

Bhat, P. (1989), 'Women's organisations: issues and debates', MA Dissertation, University of Sussex.

Bhatt, E. (1989), 'Toward empowerment', *World Development*, vol. 17, no. 7.

Boyd, R. (1989), 'Empowerment of women in Uganda', *Review of African Political Economy*, no. 45/46.

Bruce, J. (1989), 'Homes divided', *World Development*, vol. 17. no. 7.

Carloni, A. (1987), *Women in Development: A.I.D.'s Experience, 1973 – 1985*, Program Evaluation Report No. 18, USAID, Washington DC.

Chen, M. (1989), 'A sectoral approach to promoting women's work: lessons from India', *World Development*, vol. 17, no. 7.

Committee of Asian Women, *Newsletter* various issues, Hong Kong.

Commonwealth Secretariat (1987), 'The policy process: integrating women and development initiatives', Paper 2 WAMM 87/IV/(i), Second Meeting of Commonwealth Ministers Responsible for Women's Affairs, London.

——(1989), *Engendering Adjustment for the 1990s*, Report of a Commonwealth Expert Group, London.

DAWN (1985), *Development, Crisis, and Alternative Visions: Third World Women's Perspectives*, DAWN, Delhi.

Dixon, R. (1985), 'Seeing the invisible women farmers in Africa: improving research and data collection methods', in J. Monson and M. Kalb (eds), *Women as Food Producers in Developing Countries*, UCLA African Studies Center and African Studies Association.

Dwyer, D., and Bruce, J. (eds) (1988), *A Home Divided: Women and Income in the Third World*, Stanford University Press, Stanford.

Elson, D., and Pearson, R. (1981), ' "Nimble fingers make cheap workers": an analysis of women's employment in Third World export manufacturing', *Feminist Review*, no. 7.

Elson, D., and Fleming, S. (1988), 'Women's contribution to the economy and structural adjustment', unpublished report for Commonwealth Secretariat.

Elson, D. (1988a), 'Gender aware policy making for structural adjustment', unpublished report for Commonwealth Secretariat.

——(1988b), 'Market socialism or socialisation of the market?', *New Left Review*, no. 172.

Folbre, N. (1986), 'Hearts and spades: paradigms of household economics', *World Development*, vol. 14, no. 2.

——(1988), 'The black four of hearts: toward a new paradigm of household economics', in D. Dwyer and J. Bruce (eds), *op. cit.*

Gomez, M. (1986), 'Development of women's organisations in the Philippines', *ISIS International Women's Journal*, no. 6.

Gordon, S. (1984), *Ladies in Limbo: The Fate of Women's Bureaux*, Commonwealth Secretariat, London.

Herz, B. (1988), 'Briefing on women in development', World Bank/IMF Annual meetings, Berlin.

——(1989), 'Bringing women into the economic mainstream', *Finance and Development*, vol. 26, no. 4.

Heyzer, N. (1989), 'Asian women wage-earners: their situation and possibilities for donor intervention', *World Development*, vol. 17, no. 7.

Kessler-Harris, A. (1987), 'Equal Opportunity Commission *v.* Sears, Roebuck & Company: a personal account', *Feminist Review*, no. 25.

Kishwar, M., and Vanita, R. (eds) (1984), *In Search of Answers: Indian Women's Voices From Manushi*, Zed Books, London.

Kumar, R. (1989), 'Contemporary Indian feminism', *Feminist Review*, no. 33.

Mackintosh, M. (1990), 'Abstract markets and real needs', in H. Bernstein *et.al.* (eds), *The Food Question: Profits Versus People?*, Earthscan, London and Monthly Review Press, New York.

Mackintosh M., and Wuyts, M. (1988), 'Accumulation, social services and socialist transition in the Third World: reflections on decentralised planning based on Mozambican experience', in E. V. K. Fitzgerald and M. Wuyts (eds), *Markets Within Planning*, Frank Cass, London.

Mbilinyi, M. (1988), 'Agribusiness and women peasants in Tanzania', *Development and Change*, vol. 19.

Mohanty, M. (1988), 'Under Western eyes: feminist scholarship and colonial discourses', *Feminist Review*, no. 30.

Molyneux, M. (1981), 'Women in socialist societies: problems of theory and practice', in K. Young, C. Wolkowitz, and R. McCullagh (eds), *Of Marriage and the Market*, CSE Books, London.

——(1985), 'Mobilisation without emancipation? Women's interests, state and revolution in Nicaragua', *Feminist Studies*, vol. 11, no. 2.

Moser, C. O. N. (1987), 'Are there few women leaders or is it that the majority are invisible?', paper presented to Conference on Local Leaders and Community Development and Participation, University of Cambridge.

——(1989), 'Gender planning in the Third World: meeting practical and strategic gender needs', *World Development*, vol. 17, no. 11.

Palmer, I. (1988), 'Gender issues in structural adjustment of sub-Saharan African agriculture and some demographic implications', World Employment Programme Research, Working Paper, International Labour Organisation, Geneva.

——(1990), *Gender Issues in Structural Change in African Economies and Some Demographic Implications*, International Labour Organisation, Geneva.

Purdy, D. (1990), 'Citizenship, basic income and democracy', *Basic Income Research Group Bulletin*, no. 10.

Rosa, K. (1989), 'Women workers' strategies of organising and resistance in the Sri Lankan Free Trade Zone', Discussion Paper No. 266, Institute of Development Studies, University of Sussex.

Weir, L. (1987), 'Women and the state: a conference for feminist activists', *Feminist Review*, no. 26.

Williams, M. (1988), 'The global economic crisis and the fate of women', in World Council of Churches, *Women, Poverty and the Economy*, Geneva.

Yu, J. (1989), 'Facing industrialisation: women's actions', MA Dissertation, University of Sussex.

Index

Africa
  household expenditure patterns, 184
  Social Dimensions of Adjustment Programme, 198
  women's labour force participation, 85
  women's role in farming, 9, 24
agriculture
  feminisation of, in Zimbabwe, 51, 55–6
  in China, 16, 29–49
  in Nigeria, 90
  in Zimbabwe, 51–76
  sexual division of labour in, 31, 37, 52, 56, 66, 173
aid, foreign, 196, 197
Asia
  production of labour-intensive manufactures for export, 169

Bangladesh, 171, 194
birth control
  policy in China, 16, 35–6, 45–7
  women's wish for in Zimbabwe, 74
Botswana, 9, 179
Brazil, 169, 179

Cameroon, 9, 173
Caribbean
  production of labour-intensive manufactures for export, 169
  women's organisations, 195

cash crops
  and women farmers, 173–5
  in Nigeria, 90
  in resettlement areas, Zimbabwe, 69, 72
children
  access to resources required for raising, 13, 19
  and overcoming male bias, 205
  and underlying supports of male bias, 13–15
  burden on daughters, 180
  son preference, 16, 30, 45–6, 48
Chile, 179
China, 16, 29–49 passim
class
  and gender in Zimbabwe, 61–4
  and male bias, 6, 206
  and women's careers in Nigeria, 19, 87
  in Lima, Peru, 110
clothing industry
  in Mexico, 140, 148, 152–5, 157
consciousness
  acquiescence in inequality, 5, 8
  consciousness raising, 7–8, 192
  formation of preferences, 4
  male bias in everyday attitudes, 7
  perceptions of interests, 6
co-operative conflicts
  and lack of entitlements, 14
  defined, 6
  evidence of, 11